STARTING
ECONOMICS

Also by G. F. Stanlake:
Introductory Economics
Introductory Economics Workbook
Macroeconomics: an introduction
A Macroeconomics Workbook
Objective Tests in Economics

STARTING
ECONOMICS
G F Stanlake MA BSc (Econ)

Longman

Longman Group UK Limited
*Longman House, Burnt Mill, Harlow, Essex CM20 2JE, England
and Associated Companies throughout the world.*

First published 1988
Fourth impression 1992

ISBN 0 582 02189 8

Set in 10/12 point Plantin Roman

*Produced by Longman Singapore Publishers Pte Ltd
Printed in Singapore*

*The Publisher's policy is to use paper
manufactured from sustainable forests.*

Contents

Preface

This book provides a comprehensive coverage of the core content for a GCSE course in Economics. The selection of, and the treatment of, the subject matter have been designed to meet both the general and the specific aims set out in the *National Criteria for GCSE Economics*. Close attention has been paid to the requirements of the syllabuses issued by the examination boards and to the needs indicated by the specimen questions set by these boards.

Elementary economic concepts and theories are fully explained in simple terms and these explanations are supported by abundant illustrations of their relevance to the real world. Data is provided in numerical, diagrammatic, pictorial and graphical forms in order to assist the student's understanding of terminology, concepts and theories.

Each chapter contains a summary of the main points and a varied selection of questions. It finishes with a data response question which is relevant to the particular chapter and which, in many cases, could provide stimulus material for coursework. The final chapter provides guidance on the ways of tackling a project for coursework, together with an exemplar that shows how the general guidelines might be applied to a particular project.

Answers to numerical questions and to those of a 'multiple choice' nature are provided at the end of the book.

I must acknowledge with gratitude the valuable advice I have received from Gordon Springall in the preparation of this book.

G. F. S.

Acknowledgements

We are grateful to the following for permission to reproduce copyright material:

Philip Allan Ltd for extracts from article 'Unions and Pay' by D. Metcalf in *Economic Review* Vol 2, No 1 pp 24–7; The Daily Telegraph plc for extracts from article 'Unemployment Blackspots' in *Sunday Telegraph* 21.12.86 p 23; Economist Publications Ltd for articles in *The Economist* 16.3.85, 4.5.85, 30.8.86, 25.10.86; Financial Times Ltd for adapted article from *The Financial Times* 24.10.86 p 1; Her Majesty's Stationery Office for adapted extracts from *Economic Progress Report* March/April 1986 pp 4 & 5; International Monetary Fund for an adapted extract from *Finance and Development* Vol 20, No 1, pp 30–3; World Bank for extract from speech by B. B. Conable (President of the World Bank) to *Annual Meeting of IMF and World Bank*, 1986.

We are grateful to the following for permission to reproduce photographs:

Aramco World, page 192 *above*; John Birdsall, page 124 *below*; Birds Eye Wall's, page 85; British Shoe Corporation, pages 46 *above*, 93, 98 *below*; Camera Press, pages 30 *below centre* (Patrick Zachmann), 36 (Freddie Mansfield), 61 (Jacques Haillot), 71 (Glen Brent), 89 *right* (Peter Francis), 94 (Ray Hamilton), 133 (Jon Blau), 166 *above right* (Lionel Cherruault), 166 *below*, 239 *left* (R Taylor), 239 *right* (Sven Simon); J Allan Cash, pages 19, 30 *above left*, *below left* and *below right*, 44, 79, 84, 89 *left*, 190, 242; Chris Fairclough, page 239 *centre*; Ford Motor Company, page 70; John R Freeman & Co, page 45 *left*; Stanley Gibbons, page 219; Sally & Richard Greenhill, pages 32, 41, 46 *below*, 59 *below left*; InterCity, page 69 *centre right*; International Institute for Cotton, page 45 *right*; London Features International, page 76 (R Wolfson); Longman Photographic Unit, pages 59 *above*, 69 *centre*, *below left* and *below right*, 106 *below*, 124 *above centre*, 192 *below*; Massey–Ferguson, page 13 *below*; National Express, page 69 *above right*; Network, pages 30 *above right* (Mike Abrahams), 166 *above left* (Katalin Arkell), 224 (John Sturrock); Panasonic UK, page 69 *below centre*; Panos Pictures, pages 249 (Wendy Wallace), 253 (Paul Harrison); Popperfoto, page 30 *above centre*; Smith & Nephew plc, page 98 centre; Stock Photobank, pages 59 *below right*, 98 *above*, 132 *right*; Don McCullin *Sunday Times* London, page 248; Texaco, page 52; Thorn EMI Major Gas Appliances, page 69 *centre left*; Tricity, page 69 *above left*; University of Reading, Institute of Agricultural History and Museum of English Rural Life, page 13 *above*.

Cover: Rice planting, North Vietnam – Network (Mike Goldwater); Lloyds Building, London – Network (John Sturrock).

CHAPTER 1

An introduction to economics

1.1 Economics – what is it about?
1.2 The meaning of scarcity
1.3 Choice and opportunity cost
1.4 Production, consumption and exchange
1.5 Wealth and income

1.1
Economics – what is it about?

Many of the words used by economists are very familiar to us. We know that they talk and write about such topics as money, prices, wages, employment, taxes, exports and imports, earning, and spending. Every day some economic problem or other is mentioned in the newspapers, on the radio and on the television. Economics is part of our everyday lives, for

– we live in an economic system,
– every day we take part in economic activities, and
– we are familiar with the words used by economists.

This does not mean, however, that we understand how the economic system works. For example, could we provide sensible answers to the following questions?

1. What is the most important form of money used in the UK, and how is it created?
2. Why can farmers sometimes earn a higher income from a poor harvest than from a good harvest?
3. Do high wages always mean high labour costs?
4. Why is water (which is necessary for survival) so cheap, when diamonds (which are by no means a necessity) are so expensive?
5. Why is a book with 100 pages often more expensive than one with 200 pages?

These are the kinds of question which economics tries to answer.

Economising

Economics is about economising, that is, 'making the most of what we have'. For the individual, this means using one's abilities and spending one's income in the way that gives the most satisfaction or benefit. For the community as a whole, it means using the people's skills and energies, the land, the buildings, the machinery and the other economic resources so as to obtain the highest possible standards of living.

1.2
The meaning of scarcity

One of the great benefits of television is that it enables us to see how people in the rest of the world live. We see that in some parts of the world, such as Western Europe and North America, people are generally well off. Pictures from other parts of the world, such as Africa and Asia, show millions of people living in poverty.

It seems very strange, therefore, that economists say that scarcity is a world-wide problem, that it is a feature of all societies.

This puzzle is explained by looking at the way the word 'scarcity' is used in economics. When economists say that something is scarce, they do not mean that it is rare or that only a very small quantity is available. They simply mean that there is not enough of it to completely satisfy everyone's wants.

When the word is used in this way, it is true to say that scarcity exists in all countries, both rich and poor. In all of them people want more goods and services than they can obtain. It is because their wants are not fully satisfied that people everywhere work for and demand higher and higher living standards.

Unlimited wants

Why is it that so many wants remain unsatisfied, in spite of the enormous increases in the output of goods and services in modern times?

An important reason is that our wants are not limited. They are always growing and changing. How often do we hear the comments, 'You are never satisfied' and 'The more you have, the more you want'?

Technical progress has an important influence. It continues to produce a seemingly-endless stream of more interesting and more attractive ways of satisfying our wants. Motor cars, washing machines, refrigerators, domestic telephones and television sets are now regarded as necessities by many families in Britain. Yet only a hundred years ago, these things either did not exist, or were regarded as great luxuries, available only to the privileged few.

Economic goods are scarce goods

There seems to be no limit to people's wants and no limit to new ideas for satisfying them. At any moment in time, however, there is a limit to the amount of goods and services which can be produced. The economic resources – land, labour, materials, fuel, factories, machinery, etc. – which are needed to produce goods and services are limited in supply.

It is true that, as time goes by, technical progress enables us to produce more of the things people want. The problem is that our wants seem to grow as fast as, or even faster than, our ability to produce goods and services.

The basic problem of economics, therefore, is that economic resources are limited in supply but people's wants seem to be unlimited.

1.3
Choice and opportunity cost

Since we cannot have everything we want, we are forced to make choices. With our limited income

we cannot buy all the things we would like to have. When we make a choice, we select from the things we can afford those which give us the most satisfaction or pleasure.

When we make a choice, something has to be given up or forgone. The thing we decide to give up is the sacrifice we have to make in order to obtain the thing we have chosen.

What we give up is described as the *opportunity cost* of obtaining the thing we have chosen. For example, suppose a motorist has enough money to buy some petrol *or* a meal in a restaurant. She chooses to buy the petrol. The opportunity cost of the petrol is the meal that she has to forgo.

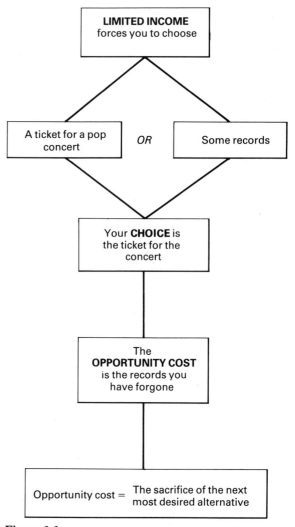

Figure 1.1

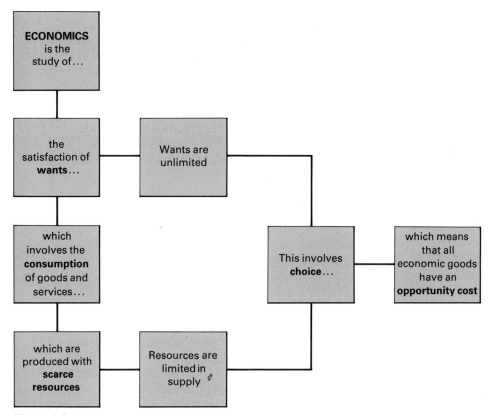

Figure 1.2

When we buy something, we normally hand over money in exchange for it. What we are really giving up, however, is the next most desirable thing we could have bought with that same amount of money. A firm may have sufficient funds to purchase a new computer *or* to redecorate and refurnish its offices. If it chooses to buy the computer, the true cost of the equipment will be the lost opportunity to improve its offices.

The community as a whole, just like the individual and the firm, must also make choices. If economic resources are used to build houses, the *money cost* will be the payments made for land, materials and labour. The *opportunity cost* will be the hospital, school, library or office block which might have been built with the same resources.

Free goods

If there were an unlimited supply of economic resources, and unlimited amounts of every commodity could be produced, human wants could be fully satisfied. Scarcity would not exist. There would be no need to economise. The problem of choice would disappear. We would not have to go without one thing in order to obtain another. All goods would be *free goods* – there would be no opportunity cost. Producing more of one thing would not mean producing less of another.

There are relatively few free goods. The most obvious example is air. Other examples might include ice at the North Pole. In a hot country, of course, ice is not a free good. Sand in the Sahara Desert is a free good, but sand in Britain is not.

In Britain, several things are described as 'free' because we can obtain them without paying a price. For example, we have 'free' education, 'free' health services and 'free' libraries. In these cases, however, a zero price does not mean a zero cost. All these services are produced with scarce resources – land, labour, fuel, materials, etc. They all have an opportunity cost and are, therefore, not free goods.

1.4
Production, consumption and exchange

Every day we can see people carrying out economic activities. They are taking place in houses, shops, offices, factories and banks, on farms, on building sites, and so on. The study of this great variety of activities is made much easier by classifying them into three main types of activity – production, consumption and exchange.

Production

The word *production* is usually taken to mean the making of some physical object, such as a motor car, a piece of furniture or a pair of shoes, or the growing of some particular crop, such as wheat or potatoes.

In economics, however, the word 'production' has a much wider meaning. Production takes place so that people's wants can be satisfied. Any kind of work which helps to satisfy people's wants, and for which they are prepared to pay a price, is productive work.

Production, therefore, includes the output of *services* as well as goods. If people are prepared to pay a price for a service, it must be satisfying a want in the same way as a physical object.

The people who work in service industries (such as wholesaling, retailing, banking, insurance, accountancy, transport, the law, education and health) are productive in the same way as car workers and farmers. It is clear that, in a modern economy, factories, mines, power stations, farms, etc. would find it impossible to operate without such services.

Consumption

Consumption describes the 'using up' of goods and services in order to satisfy our wants.

Durable consumer goods

These are consumer goods which have a fairly long life – many of them last for several years. They include such items as household furniture, domestic appliances and the family car. We consume the services such things give us rather than the goods themselves.

Non-durable consumer goods

These are commodities which are used up immediately (i.e. in a single use) or in a relatively short period of time. Food, drinks, soap and toothpaste are obvious examples of non-durable consumer goods.

Services

In a modern economy, a large part of total consumption consists of services. In Britain, for example, we are all very dependent on the transport, telephone, legal, education and health services. Entertainment is another important service industry.

Exchange

In all but the most primitive societies, some kind of exchange must take place before people can satisfy their wants. Very few, if any, of us can produce for ourselves all the things we need to maintain our present standard of living.

The great majority of workers *specialise*. Some spend their day producing some small part of a product (e.g. workers on an assembly line). Others specialise in supplying some particular service (e.g. accountants, teachers and shop assistants). Specialist workers can survive and enjoy a high standard of living because there is a system which enables them to exchange what they produce for the goods and services produced by other specialists.

This system of exchange depends upon the use of money. What happens is that we sell our services for money (wages and salaries), and then use this money to buy the things which others have produced. It is a remarkable system, which enables a miner in Durham and a car worker in Coventry to exchange what they produce for goods and services produced not only in Britain but in countries all over the world.

What the economist calls the modern system of exchange involves transport services by land, sea and air, banking services, insurance services, advertising, wholesaling, retailing, and many other services. All these services are required so that a person can sell what he or she produces and buy what others have produced.

1.5
Wealth and income

Wealth

Wealth consists of a stock of goods which have a money value. It includes such assets as land, houses, factories, shops, machines, and many kinds of personal possessions.

Private wealth

This describes the possessions of individuals. It will obviously include land, houses, works of art, jewellery, motor cars and so on. Private wealth also includes financial assets such as notes and coin, bank deposits, building society deposits and company shares.

Social wealth

This consists of those assets owned by the community as a whole (i.e. by central and local government). It includes such things as roads, hospitals, schools, parks and libraries.

National wealth

This is the sum of all the wealth possessed by the citizens of a country, whether it is privately owned or publicly owned.

Income

Whereas wealth is a *stock* of assets which have a money value, income is a *flow* of money.

Income refers to the amount of money earned or received during a given period of time – usually one year. An individual may receive income in various forms, such as wages, salaries, interest on savings, rent from the ownership of property, profits on shares, or social security payments.

The basic difference between income and wealth is that
- income is a flow of money received during a given period of time, while
- wealth is a stock of assets owned at some moment in time.

Figure 1.3
How people hold their wealth, UK, 1986

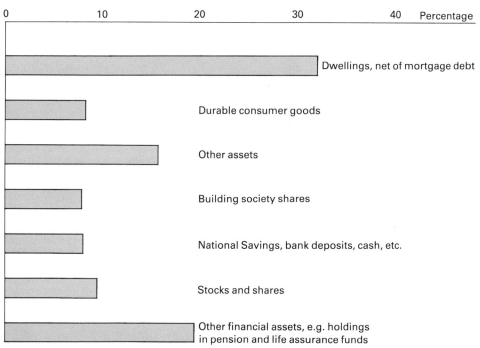

Source: *Social Trends*, HMSO, 1988

The Main Points

- Human wants appear to be unlimited. Rising standards of living seem to encourage demands for even higher standards.

- The economic resources available at any time cannot supply enough goods and services to fully satisfy human wants.

- Scarcity and choice are features of all societies, rich and poor alike.

- Opportunity cost refers to the fact that whenever a choice is made, something has to be given up. The thing we have to give up is the true cost of the thing we have chosen.

- Free goods are those which can be obtained without sacrificing something else. The production of these goods does not use up scarce resources.

- Production includes the outputs of services as well as physical goods.

- In a modern economy, we are, as individuals, incapable of producing for ourselves all the things we need for survival. We are all dependent upon a system of exchange.

Test Your Understanding

1. Use the following words to complete the sentence below:

   want   choices   resources

   In every society, ... have to be made because there are insufficient .... to produce all the things which people ....

2. What are the missing words in the following passage? 'Mary spent her pocket money on some books. This meant that she could not afford the scarf which she also wanted. The .... of the books, therefore, was the scarf which she had to forgo.'

3. Explain why, from an economist's point of view, the tea set in Figure 1.4 cannot be described as a free good.

Figure 1.4

4. People cannot obtain all the things they would like to have. Would this economic problem be solved if everyone had a lot more money to spend? Explain your answer.

5. A worker devoted many hours to making an article, but then found that no one was prepared to buy it at any price. Would an economist describe this work as 'production'? Explain your answer.

6. Say whether the following statements are true or false:
   (a) Air has no opportunity cost.
   (b) In economics, the word 'scarcity' is applied mainly to things like gold, precious stones and Rolls Royce cars.
   (c) 'Free' education is not really free.
   (d) Clerks, lawyers and teachers do not make anything – they are, therefore, non-productive workers.

BOX 1
Choice and opportunity cost

Mary has two favourite forms of entertainment – the cinema and dancing. She has £24 per month which she can spend on these entertainments. She usually spends £3 on a visit to the cinema and £1.50 on a visit to the disco.

Number of visits she can make in one month

Cinema		Disco
8	and	0
....	and	....
....	and	....
....	and	....
....	and	....
....	and	....
....	and	....
....	and	....
0	and	16

Questions
1. Copy and complete the table to show all the different combinations of visits to the cinema and to the disco which Mary can make in one month.
2. Plot all these combinations on a sheet of graph paper. Use one axis to show visits to the cinema and the other axis to show visits to the disco.
3. Assume that Mary has been in the habit of going to the cinema four times each month. She now decides to visit the cinema six times each month. What will be the opportunity cost of the two additional visits to the cinema?

CHAPTER 2
Economic resources

2.1 The factors of production
2.2 Land
2.3 Labour
2.4 Capital
2.5 The entrepreneur

2.1
The factors of production

Economic resources comprise human beings and all the things they use to produce the goods and services which people want. In economics, these resources are described as *factors of production*. They are usually classified into three main groups:

1 Natural resources

These are the resources provided by nature and not by human beings. The word *land* is used to describe the gifts of nature.

Figure 2.1
Factors of production

2 Human resources

These consist of the energies, skills and knowledge of the working population. These resources are described as *labour*.

3 Manufactured resources

The word *capital* is used to describe manufactured resources. They consist of such things as factories, machines, railways, roads, power stations, docks and so on.

Many economists include a fourth factor of production – the *entrepreneur*. This is the person (or persons) who organises land, labour and capital into units of production. These units of production are described as *firms*.

| LAND (natural resources) | LABOUR (human resources) | CAPITAL (manufactured resources) |

Brought together and organised by

THE ENTREPRENEUR

2.2
Land

The word 'land' is taken to mean all those gifts of nature which are available to us for the satisfaction of our wants. It includes, therefore,
- the natural fertility of the soil,
- the minerals in the earth's surface, and
- forests, rivers, and the riches in the sea.

A surprisingly small part of the earth's surface is suitable for habitation by human beings. 72 per cent of the earth's surface is occupied by oceans, which leaves only 28 per cent as land. But much of this land is not suitable for human settlement either, because it is covered by ice or consists of desert, tropical jungle or towering mountain ranges.

The fact that land, unlike labour and capital, is limited in supply led some early economists to make some pessimistic predictions. In the late nineteenth century, Thomas Malthus saw little prospect of any permanent improvement in living standards. He believed that population has a natural tendency to grow faster than the output of food from a fixed amount of land. Events subsequently proved him wrong – vast new food-producing areas were developed in the New World, and higher living standards led to a fall in the birth rate. However, the present high rates of population growth in parts of Africa and Asia are leading to fears that Malthus's predictions may yet prove correct.

Most of the problems in economics, however, are not about the total supply of land, but about the supply of land for some particular use. This can be changed, since the same piece of land can often be put to different uses. The supply of land for grazing can be increased by reducing the amount of arable land. The supply of land for building can be increased by reducing the supply of agricultural land.

There are some cases, however, where the supply of land for a particular use is fixed. An obvious example is the number of sites for shops, offices, banks, cafes, etc. in the high street. Nothing can be done to increase the supply of these sites.

It is also true that there is a strictly limited supply of minerals in the earth's surface. This point has been brought home to us by the present worries about the future supply of oil. Minerals are *non-replaceable resources*.

2.3
Labour

The word 'labour' means human effort of all types – manual and non-manual, skilled and unskilled.

The supply of labour

How much can be produced depends to a large extent on the number of workers available and upon the number of hours, on average, which each worker is prepared to work. Any change in the length of the working week or in the length of annual holidays will obviously affect the supply of labour. A country's supply of labour, therefore, depends upon
- the size of the total population,
- the proportion of the total population which is available for work and is willing to work, and
- the average number of hours (per week or per year) worked by members of the working population.

The efficiency of labour

Although the total supply of labour is very important in determining a country's output of goods and services, the quality or efficiency of labour is also very important.

The efficiency of labour is generally taken to mean its *productivity* and this is usually measured in terms of output per worker-hour (see page 29). Many different things can affect the productivity of labour. Some of the more important influences are:

1 Education and training facilities

The standard of general education and the variety and quality of the training facilities available to the population are probably the most important influences on the efficiency of labour in modern economies.

2 Working conditions

Damp, cold, badly-lit, badly-ventilated and generally depressing places of work will not encourage the people working in them to give of their best.

3 Management and equipment

Workers in firms which are well organised, well managed and which use up-to-date equipment will generally be more efficient than those employed in firms which are poorly equipped and badly managed.

2.4
Capital

Goods which are wanted for their own sake, because they provide immediate satisfaction, are described as *consumer goods*. The list of such things is almost endless but it obviously includes food, clothing, household furniture, TV sets, videos, washing machines and so on.

Capital goods are not wanted for their own sake, but because they help firms to increase their outputs of consumer goods. Some examples of capital goods were given at the beginning of this chapter.

Whether a good is classed as a consumer good or a capital good sometimes depends upon the use to which it is put. A sewing machine used only in the home, for making and repairing clothes and other items for the family, is a consumer good. A sewing machine used in a clothing factory, however, is a capital good.

Perhaps the most striking feature of modern manufacturing industry is the very large amount of capital which each worker needs to do his job. In industries such as those producing motor cars, oil, chemicals and steel, this amounts to many thousands of pounds worth of capital for each worker employed.

Types of capital

Businesses usually describe their capital as either fixed capital or working capital.

Fixed capital

As the name suggests, this is long lasting and consists of things which do not change their form in the process of production. A manufacturing firm would describe its factory buildings and machinery as fixed capital. For a farmer, fixed capital would comprise assets such as barns, cowsheds, milking machines and tractors.

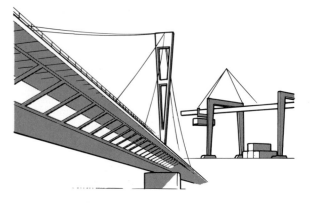

Figure 2.2
Fixed capital

Working capital

This includes those things which are 'used up' in the process of production; that is, they are changed into some other form. A farmer's seeds and fertilisers, a shoe manufacturer's stocks of leather, and a furniture maker's supplies of timber are good examples of working capital. Firms also include in their working capital the stocks of money they hold for 'running' expenses (e.g. buying materials and paying wages).

The supply of capital

The factors of production which are used to make capital goods might have been employed in making consumer goods. The production of capital goods, therefore, reduces the possible output of consumer goods. The opportunity cost of using resources to build factories, roads and bridges, and to manufacture machinery and other capital goods, is the sacrifice of the consumer goods which these resources might have produced.

Why is a community prepared to make this sacrifice? The answer is that the use of capital greatly increases the productivity of an industry. This is clearly demonstrated in the motor car industry. At the Rover Group's Longbridge works, for example, the robot assembly line welds and assembles a complete car body in 42 seconds.

We are prepared to accept some reductions in our living standards *now* (by producing capital goods) because these capital goods will make it possible to achieve a much greater *future* output of consumer goods.

The supply of capital, therefore, depends on the extent to which people are prepared to forgo consumer goods *now*. In modern societies, forgoing consumption takes the form of saving. If we do not spend all our income, we are going without some consumer goods which we might have bought. Later in this book we shall see how some of these savings help to pay for the production of capital goods.

Investment

In economics, the word 'investment' does not mean buying shares on the Stock Exchange or putting money into a savings account. The word is used to describe the production of real capital goods. Investment takes place when capital goods are produced. *Gross investment* is the total output of capital goods during a given period of time, usually one year.

But capital goods are always wearing out or becoming out of date. Some part of the total output of capital goods, therefore, will be required to replace the worn-out and outdated equipment. *Depreciation* describes the extent to which a stock of capital loses its value owing to wear and tear and obsolescence. (A machine is suffering from obsolescence when it can be replaced by a far more efficient machine.)

Net investment is the annual increase in the total stock of capital. This will obviously be less than gross investment, because some of the new capital will be required to replace the outdated and worn-out capital. Therefore

Gross investment − Depreciation = Net investment

The rate of net investment in a country is a very important item. It tells us the rate at which that country's stock of capital is increasing. *Future* productivity depends very much on the *present* rate of net investment.

2.5
The entrepreneur

Land, labour and capital are required if production is to take place. If left to themselves, however, these factors of production will not produce anything. They have to be brought together and organised into a unit of production. Someone must take the decisions on what to produce, and on how and where to produce it. In addition, the services provided by the land, labour and capital have to be paid for.

The person (or persons) who undertakes the responsibilities and risks of employing land, labour and capital, and who decides how these resources are to be used, is described as an *entrepreneur*.

Entrepreneurs, then, are decision-takers and risk-bearers. They must take risks because they purchase and employ the services of the factors of production without any guarantee that the money they will obtain from selling their outputs will cover their costs. They can have no certainty that they will make a profit. It is the *expectation* of profit which persuades them to accept the risks of setting up and carrying on a business.

Entrepreneurs as risk-bearers, organisers and managers are recognised as a fourth factor of production. In the one-person business it is easy to recognise the entrepreneur, because one person takes all the risks and all the important decisions. In a large company, however, the risks are borne by the people who put their money into the business (the shareholders), while management decisions are taken by the directors. The different tasks of the entrepreneur are carried out by different groups of people.

The Main Points

- The total supply of land is fixed, but the supply for any one use can usually be increased or decreased. In the case of sites with special features, however, the supply may be fixed. Some important economic resources are non-replaceable.

- The supply of labour refers to the number of hours of labour supplied in a given period of time. It will depend upon
  - the size of the total population,
  - the percentage of those in the working age groups who offer themselves for work, and
  - the average number of hours worked by members of the labour force.

- The efficiency of labour or the productivity of labour depends upon
  - the education and training facilities,
  - the quality of management and capital equipment, and
  - the working conditions.

- The production of capital helps to increase productivity in the future. The opportunity cost of capital is the consumer goods which might have been produced with the resources used to make capital goods.

- The entrepreneur bears the risk of failure and takes the decisions which affect the management and organisation of a firm.

Test Your Understanding

1. The main reason why people are worried about the future supply of oil is the fact that it is a .... resource. What is the missing word?

2. Some goods are produced because they are 'wanted for their own sake', while other goods are produced because they help to produce those goods which are wanted for their own sake. What names are given to these two types of goods?

3. Which THREE of the following are capital goods?

   A a professional photographer's camera
   B a diesel locomotive
   C a builder's supply of bricks
   D a domestic refrigerator
   E a household's books of reference (e.g. dictionaries and atlases)

4. Many people have a great desire 'to be their own boss'. An economist would say that they wish to be .... What is the missing word?

5. In what way does the supply of land differ from the supply of the other factors of production?

6. What would happen to the country's supply of labour if
   (a) the school-leaving age were raised?
   (b) there were a fall in the percentage of school-leavers entering full-time further education?

7. (a) What is meant by the depreciation of capital?
   (b) At the beginning of a particular year, a firm's stock of capital was valued at £10 million. Depreciation takes place at a rate of 5 per cent per annum. Towards the end of the year the firm bought new machinery for £1 million. What was the firm's net investment for this year?

BOX 2
Land, labour and capital

1900

1988

The photographs show a remarkable change, during the course of this century, in the methods used to produce cereal crops.

Questions
1. What has happened to the way in which the factors of production are used? In other words, what changes have taken place in the *proportions* in which the factors are combined?
2. How do you think *these particular changes* have affected
   (a) employment in agriculture?
   (b) employment in engineering?
   (c) the average size of farms?

CHAPTER 3

Economic systems – how economic resources are allocated

3.1 The meaning of resource allocation
3.2 The questions every society must answer
3.3 Types of economic system
3.4 Why governments exercise control over the economy

3.1
The meaning of resource allocation

All communities have to deal with the same basic economic problem – they have limited amounts of land, labour and capital which cannot produce enough goods and services to satisfy all the people's wants, and they have to decide how these limited resources are to be used. Economists describe this as a problem of *resource allocation*, because decisions have to be made on the way in which the resources are to be distributed (i.e. allocated) to different industries and occupations. The following questions illustrate the kind of problems to which solutions have to be found:

1. Should more resources be devoted to agriculture and fewer to manufacturing?
2. Should more resources be devoted to modernising railways and fewer to building motorways?
3. Should more of the factors of production be used to make consumer goods and fewer of them be used to make capital goods?
4. Should more resources be allocated to the nuclear power industry and fewer to the coal industry?

3.2
The questions every society must answer

All societies, from the most remote Indian village to the large industrialised country, must find ways of answering the following questions.

1 What goods and services should be produced, and in what quantities?

A country can only produce some of the goods and services its people want. It must, therefore, find some method of choosing which particular goods and services to produce. If the aim is to produce those things which best satisfy the people's wants, then it has to find a way of discovering what people really want.

2 How should the goods and services be produced?

Many commodities can be produced by using different methods of production. Some manufactured goods can be produced either by small firms using a lot of skilled labour or by mass-production methods, in which a lot of capital equipment is used. The photographs in Box 2 (page 13) show two very different methods of producing cereal crops. All economies, therefore, have to make choices between different methods of production.

3 For whom should the goods and services be produced?

Questions 1 and 2 are problems of *production*. But even if the problems of production are solved, there is still the problem of *distribution* – how should the things which have been produced be shared out among the members of the community? In a modern economy, goods and services have money prices. This means that people with larger incomes can claim larger shares of the national output of goods and services; they will have higher *real* incomes (see page 22). The basic problem is to decide how the total real income should be shared out. Once again, we can pose some questions to illustrate the difficulties in finding satisfactory solutions to this problem:

1. Should there be equal shares for all?
2. Should those who produce more have larger shares than those who produce less?
3. Should skilled workers receive more than unskilled workers?
4. Should each person's share be based on his or her needs? (And who should decide what a person needs?)

There are other important questions that affect the way in which a society uses its economic resources. Two examples are given below.

The present versus the future

We have seen that the production of capital goods makes possible a greater future output of consumer goods. But the production of capital goods also means that the *present* output of consumer goods is less than it might have been.

To what extent are people prepared to go without some consumer goods today so that they can have an increased supply of consumer goods in the future? The answer to this question will decide how resources should be allocated between the production of consumer goods and the production of capital goods.

There is another important problem concerning the choice between the present and the future. Many of the resources we are using today are non-replaceable. Modern civilisation is very dependent upon non-replaceable minerals such as oil, copper, zinc, tin, lead and so on. Should we make the maximum use of these resources *now*, or should we restrict the use we make of them so that supplies will be available for future generations?

Full employment

It is quite obvious that a country is not getting the most out of its economic resources if some of them are lying idle. In the mid-1980s, many workers and large amounts of capital were unemployed in most developed countries. The *actual* outputs of goods and services in these countries were much less than the *possible* outputs. All countries would like to make the fullest use of their economic resources, but many of them have found it difficult to achieve this objective.

Types of economic system

The economic systems which have been adopted to deal with these economic problems differ from country to country; each has its own particular features. Nevertheless, some of the systems are very similar to one another, and they can be classified into three or four groups.

Traditional economies

These are communities with relatively low living standards, where the way of life has remained virtually unchanged for centuries. Isolated villages in Africa and Asia, and the nomadic Bedouin tribes, provide examples of traditional economies.

In this type of economy, people live according to age-old customs – doing things the way they have always been done. What is to be produced, and how it is to be produced and shared out, are not seen as economic problems, because these things have all been decided long ago. These economies are often described as *subsistence economies* because what is produced, in most cases, amounts to little more than the minimum necessary for survival.

Market economies

Any arrangement which enables buyers to do business with sellers is described as a market. A market economy is one in which there is considerable freedom for people to buy what they want and sell what they produce. Prices are determined by the strength of people's demand for goods and services, and the quantities which suppliers are prepared to offer for sale, that is, by the *market forces* of demand and supply. Some of the main features of a market economy are set out over the page.

1 Private property

Individuals have the right to own, control and dispose of land, buildings, machinery and other natural and manufactured factors of production. It is this feature of market economies which causes them to be described as *capitalist* economies.

2 Freedom of choice

Individuals are free to set up in business for themselves, firms are free to decide what and how they should produce, workers are free to enter and leave occupations, and consumers are free to spend their incomes as they wish.

3 Self-interest

The system encourages people to do what is best for themselves. Firms will try to maximise profits, workers will try to maximise their incomes, and consumers will try to maximise their satisfactions.

4 The price mechanism (competition)

In a market economy, changes in the demand for goods and services, or changes in the supply of goods and services, or both, cause changes in prices. It is these changes in prices which lead to changes in the way in which economic resources are used.

For example, if the demand for a commodity increases, the commodity will become more scarce and its price will increase. This increase in price will make it more profitable to produce. Firms producing this commodity, therefore, will increase their outputs and other firms will be tempted to enter this industry. An increase in demand, therefore, will cause more resources to be used in the production of this commodity.

If the demand for a commodity falls, its price will tend to fall. It will become less profitable to produce, and this will lead to a fall in output. Fewer resources will be used in this industry.

A fall in the costs of producing a commodity will lower its price. Consumers will tend to buy more at lower prices, and production of the commodity will increase.

In a market economy, changes in prices act as a kind of signalling device to producers and consumers, and cause them to change their plans. This is more fully explained in Chapter 8.

5 A very limited role for government

A market economy is often described as a *free enterprise* economy, where the word 'free' means 'free from government controls'. A government has very few economic functions in a market economy. Early economists who were very much in favour of the market economy thought that the main business of government was to secure the defence of the country and to maintain law and order.

Command economies

These economies are so named because the government has the power to *command* the nation's economic resources. It has complete control over the way these resources are used. It is the government which decides how land, labour and capital shall be employed. It has the powers to decide *what* shall be produced, *how* it shall be produced and *for whom* it shall be produced. These economies are generally described as *centrally-planned* economies. Some of the main features of this type of economy are set out below.

1 Public ownership

A most important feature of command economies is the public ownership of 'the means of production'. The land and all types of capital are owned by the state. Private ownership is usually limited to personal possessions, although small businesses are sometimes privately owned, and farm workers are often allowed to own small plots of land and sell their produce in local markets.

2 Planned production

Production is carried out according to a national plan which sets production targets for the different industries. Resources are allocated to industries by government directives. In this type of economy, resources are *directed* to different uses by the government. In the market economy, they go to the highest bidders – the successful firms are able to offer higher prices for the services of land, labour and capital.

A national plan consists of thousands of very complicated relationships. The planned outputs of the various enterprises (mines, factories, farms, power stations, steelworks, etc.) must all be fitted together. For example, the planned output of a large steelworks becomes the planned inputs of many other industries that use steel. A large number of officials are required to prepare and operate a national economic plan.

3 Prices

In a centrally-planned economy, prices are not free to change in response to changes in supply and demand; they are fixed by the government. In a market economy, a shortage of a commodity will cause its price to rise. In a command economy, however, a shortage will often mean that some form of physical rationing has to be used.

4 Profits

In a market economy, the main incentive for firms to supply goods and services is the prospect of making a profit. This is not the case in a command economy. Enterprises are not privately owned and there are no shareholders. They do not produce for profit; they produce what the government thinks will be in the best interest of the people.

Mixed economies

In the real world, there are no completely planned economies. In the centrally-planned economies such as those of the USSR and the countries of Eastern Europe, we find some features of the market economy, and some use is made of the price mechanism. For example, if there is a shortage of workers in particular industries or regions, workers are not normally *directed* to where the shortages exist. Workers are often attracted to where they are most needed by being offered higher wages.

Similarly, there is no example of a completely free market economy. In all of the so-called market economies in the real world, we find a great deal of state control of economic activity.

It would be true to say, therefore, that, to some extent, most real-world economies are mixed economies. They have both a public and a private sector; some enterprises are owned by the state, while some are privately owned. But there are very important differences.

Communist countries lean very strongly towards the fully planned economy – there is relatively little private ownership, and the market system plays little part in the way the economy is run. In the non-communist countries, far more reliance is placed on private ownership, the price mechanism and free markets.

The term 'mixed economy' is commonly used to describe the economies found in North America, Western Europe, Japan and other developed countries in the non-communist world. In the UK, which is a typical mixed economy, about 26 per cent of the labour force is employed in the public sector and about 74 per cent in the private sector (see Figure 3.1).

Figure 3.1
Percentages of the UK labour force employed in different sectors, mid-1987

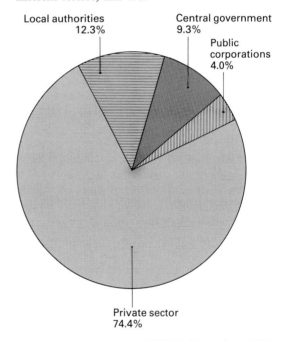

Source: *Economic Trends*, HMSO, December 1987

3.4
Why governments exercise control over the economy

Many people believe that the market economy has several advantages over other types of economic system. Some of these 'advantages' are:

1. There is more freedom of choice for producers and consumers.
2. The system encourages competition between firms. This compels firms to strive for greater efficiency, because less efficient firms are driven out of business.
3. The more successful firms can earn higher profits. This gives firms an incentive to search for new products and for new and better techniques of production.
4. Large numbers of civil servants are not required to run the system.
5. The system gives great power to consumers. Only those firms which supply what the consumer is prepared to buy will survive.

Over the years, however, certain features of the market economy have led to increasing dissatisfaction. This has led to demands for governments to take actions to eliminate or reduce what are widely regarded as disadvantages of a market economy. Some of the major criticisms of the system, which governments have attempted to deal with, are set out below. The policies adopted by governments are discussed in Chapter 20.

Inequalities

Private ownership of land and capital enables those who are more successful in the world of business to accumulate large amounts of wealth. Private ownership also enables people to acquire wealth by inheritance rather than by effort.

Instability

The history of the economies of Western Europe and North America shows that, if left to itself, a market economy is subject to booms and slumps. Most people find this state of affairs unacceptable because it creates uncertainty about employment.

Dominant firms

Competition allows the more successful firms to drive out the less successful ones. This could well mean that, eventually, a very small number of large firms could come to dominate a whole industry. Such firms will have great market power which they could use to charge prices well above the costs of production. This is most likely, of course, where an industry is dominated by a single firm, that is, where there is a monopoly.

Welfare

The market system rewards those who are successful or more fortunate. It make no provision for the unsuccessful or less fortunate. For example, firms which suffer a serious fall in the demands for their products will fail. Workers will lose their jobs and shareholders will lose the money they have put into the businesses. Only the state can provide adequate help for those who fall by the wayside.

Social costs and benefits

The costs incurred by a firm producing goods and services are described as *private costs*. In a market economy, these are the only costs which influence a firm's decision to produce. Sometimes, however, the production of a commodity imposes costs on society as a whole; these costs are not borne by the producer.

For example, the price of a good produced by a firm which pollutes the atmosphere with smoke from chimneys or with unpleasant smells does not include the 'costs' of the nuisance and dangers suffered by the people in that neighbourhood. Firms in a market economy can ignore the social effects of their activities.

The benefits gained by a person who buys a good or service are described as *private benefits*. There are cases, however, where the market price of a product does not give a true indication of the total benefits provided by that product. For example, the price paid by an electricity authority for the removal of unsightly pylons and overhead lines and their replacement by underground cables would not be a good measure of the total benefits from this work. The community as a whole would place a high value on the improvement of the countryside when these ugly structures were removed. The value of this benefit would not be included in the price paid for the work done.

In planning projects such as airports, motorways and underground transport systems, governments now try to take into account *all* the costs incurred – these are described as *social costs*. They also try to estimate the value of *all* the benefits derived – these are described as *social benefits*.

Figure 3.2
Pollution – a cost which is borne by society, but not by the firm

Merit goods and services

Merit goods are those which the government thinks everyone ought to have. The best examples are education and health services. It is believed that in a market economy, at market prices, people would buy fewer merit goods than they ought to have. This would be either because they could not afford to pay the price or because they would not act in their own best interest. Many people, when it was too late, would wish that they had spent more on such things as health and education.

Many governments, therefore, reject the free market as a way of supplying merit goods; they supply services such as health and education to everyone, regardless of their level of income.

It is also argued that the value of the social benefits of public spending on health and education is much greater than the costs of providing these services. The opportunities for a better life are much greater in a society where there is a high standard of public health and the people are well educated.

Other examples of merit goods are public libraries, personal social services and the road network.

Public goods and services

This term refers to goods and services which would not be supplied in a market economy because it is not possible to charge a person for the amounts he or she consumes. Typical examples are the services provided by the police force, street lighting and the barrages which prevent flooding. Payments for such services could not be made on a voluntary basis, because those who refused to pay could not be denied the benefit of such services. They must, therefore, be financed from taxation and provided by the state.

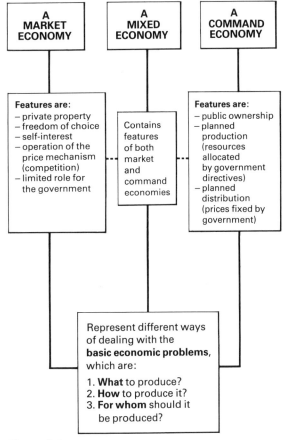

Figure 3.3
Economic systems

The Main Points

- Because there are many different ways of using their limited resources, all societies have a problem of resource allocation.

- Different economic systems use different methods of dealing with the following problems:
  - What goods and services should be produced?
  - How should these goods and services be produced?
  - For whom should the goods and services be produced?

- In command (or centrally-planned) economies, the state owns and controls the economic resources, which are allocated according to a national plan.

- In market economies, resources are privately owned, markets are free from government controls, and market prices have a great influence on the ways in which economic resources are used.

- In the economic systems of the real world, we find both state ownership and control, and free markets, but there are great differences between the systems operated in different countries.

- The economic systems in the communist countries contain most of the features of a command economy, and free markets are relatively unimportant.

- The economies of most non-communist countries are described as mixed economies. A large proportion of the economic resources are privately owned, and most prices are determined by market forces. Several important industries, however, are publicly owned and governments have considerable powers to regulate the economy.

Test Your Understanding

1. Which THREE of the following economic resources are non-replaceable?
   A timber
   B highly skilled labour
   C natural gas
   D copper
   E coal

2. Which TWO of the following are features of a centrally-planned economy?
   A The prices of most goods are fixed by the state.
   B Firms are owned by shareholders.
   C A firm's success is measured by its profits.
   D Most of the land and capital is publicly owned.

3. Which ONE of the following statements is *not* true in a mixed economy?
   A Most people work for privately-owned firms.
   B The government normally provides education and health services.
   C There is no public ownership of land and capital.
   D The prices of most goods and services are free to change according to movements in supply and demand.

4. Say whether these statements are true or false:
   (a) In a market economy, there are often great inequalities in the ownership of wealth.
   (b) In a capitalist economy, most of the land and capital is owned by the state.
   (c) Lighthouses are examples of public goods.
   (d) In a command economy, firms produce only those goods and services which are profitable to produce.

5. Explain how the price mechanism would bring about a re-allocation of resources in the following situations:
   (a) A world shortage of oil causes a very steep rise in its price, and there seems little prospect of this situation changing.
   (b) A new invention greatly reduces the costs of producing nylon and terylene.

BOX 3

Economic systems

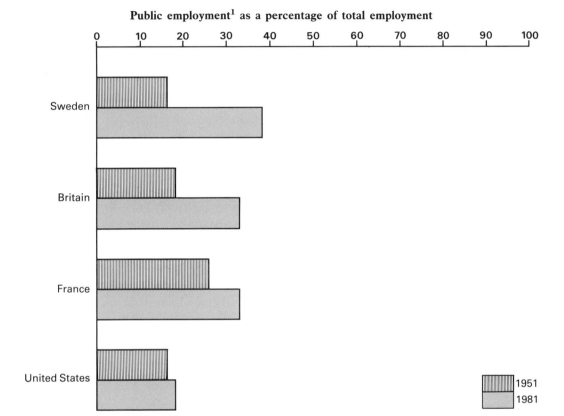

Public employment[1] as a percentage of total employment

¹ Including employees of central government, local
government and nationalised industries
Source: Adapted from *The Economist*, 16 November 1985

Questions

1. Does the information in the diagram enable us to say which country had the largest *number* of workers in the public sector in 1981? Explain your answer.
2. Measured as a percentage of total employment, which country had the largest private sector in 1981?
3. Into which of the following categories would you place these economies?
   A centrally-planned economies
   B market economies
   C mixed economies
4. Among the possible reasons for the increase in the size of the public sectors from 1951 to 1981 are the nationalisation of certain industries, and an increased provision of merit goods and services. Give some examples of the types of public employment which are likely to increase when a government increases the supply of merit goods and services.

CHAPTER 4

Consumers' spending and saving

4.1 Types of personal income
4.2 Income and consumers' spending
4.3 Other influences on consumers' spending
4.4 Changes in household expenditure
4.5 Saving

In Chapter 1, consumption was defined as the 'using up' of goods and services in order to satisfy our wants. The things we consume were classified as durable consumer goods, non-durable consumer goods, and services.

Strictly speaking, we do not 'use up' many of the things we buy. Durable goods, for example, have a long life, and we often discard them long before they are worn out. We consume goods because they provide us with satisfaction, pleasure or benefit. Early economists used the word *utility* to describe these satisfactions. When we speak of consuming a good, therefore, we are describing the using-up of the utility the good provides rather than of the good itself. We consume the pleasures provided by a television set, not the set itself. Durable consumer goods are capable of yielding utility over a long period of time.

Consumption spending is often described as household spending, because many decisions to spend are taken by families rather than by individuals. The amount which households spend on consumer goods and services is clearly influenced by the amount of income they receive. Most people would spend more than they do now if they had the opportunity. Their spending is limited by their income.

savings, private pensions and various social security benefits (e.g. state pensions and unemployment benefit).

There are several ways of measuring personal income:

1 Gross personal income

This is the total personal income from all sources.

2 Disposable personal income

This is the amount which remains after income taxes and national insurance contributions have been deducted from gross personal income, i.e.

Gross personal income
    − Income tax and NI contributions
  = Disposable personal income

3 Real disposable income

This refers to the quantity of goods and services which disposable income can buy. It is the purchasing power of the money income. Money income and real income can move in opposite directions. For example, if money income increases by 8 per cent, but prices increase by 10 per cent over the same period of time, real income will fall.

4.1
Types of personal income

Personal income is obtained from several different sources: wages and salaries, rent from the ownership of property, dividends on shares, interest on

4.2
Income and consumers' spending

Personal disposable income can be either spent or saved. As one would expect, an increase in total disposable income leads to an increase in total

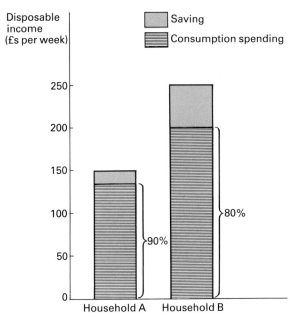

Figure 4.1
Spending and saving

consumer spending. As people become better off, they tend to buy more goods and services, and better-quality goods and services. When incomes increase in developed countries, much of the extra spending goes on durable consumer goods (e.g. cars, microwave cookers, videos, etc.) and on a variety of services (e.g. holidays abroad).

But consumer spending does not usually increase as fast as income increases. Although people spend more as their income increases, they also tend to save a larger percentage of their income. When incomes are very low, there will be no saving – the whole of disposable income will be required to buy the basic necessities of life. As incomes increase, however, and the most urgent needs can easily be satisfied, it becomes possible to spend more and save more.

Figure 4.1 helps to explain the way in which consumption and saving change as income increases. It shows that Household B, with the much higher income, still consumes more than Household A, with the lower income, even though it spends a smaller percentage of its income. This diagram compares two households, but it helps to explain the way in which total consumer spending in a country changes as income changes. As

people's incomes increase, we find that both consumer spending *and* saving increase.

4.3

Other influences on consumers' spending

Although the amount of money spent on consumer goods and services depends mainly on the level of disposable income, it is also influenced by other factors.

Wealth

The income households receive is not their only source of money for spending. The ability to spend depends upon the amount of wealth held as well as on the amount of income received. Money for spending can be obtained by withdrawals from savings accounts and from the sale of other forms of personal wealth, such as shares, property, jewellery, land, etc.

Borrowing

Schemes which allow people to borrow, such as hire-purchase facilities and bank loans, make it possible for households to spend more than their current income. This is only possible over a fairly short period, because the loans have to be repaid.

The cost of borrowing is the rate of interest which has to be paid on the loan. Changes in the rate of interest, therefore, will affect the ability and willingness to borrow. If it became easier and cheaper to obtain goods on credit (i.e. by borrowing), there would tend to be a significant increase in consumer spending on durable consumer goods.

Changes in the rate of income tax

The ability to spend depends mainly on the level of people's *disposable* income. Any changes in the rate of income tax or national insurance contributions, therefore, will change the amount available for spending. A fall in the rate of income tax will tend to increase consumer spending. An increase in the rate of income tax will probably reduce consumer spending, although, in this case, many people might decide to reduce their saving instead.

Changes in the distribution of income

We have seen that lower-income households spend a greater proportion of their income than households with larger incomes do. This means that a policy which transfers income from the better off to the less well off will tend to increase total consumer spending. For example, suppose one pound is taken, in the form of taxation, from a high-income household and transferred, in the form of a social security benefit, to a much poorer household. The high-income household might have spent 60p of the pound and saved 40p; the poorer household is more likely to spend the whole of the pound.

4.4
Changes in household expenditure

Statistics of households' expenditure show how the pattern of spending changes as living standards improve. These changes are due mainly to the increase in real incomes, but changes in taste and fashions, and the introduction of new consumer goods, have also been important.

Table 4.1
UK household expenditure, 1953–86

	Percentage of total expenditure	
	1953–54	1986
Housing	8.8	16.4
Fuel, light and power	5.2	5.6
Food	33.3	19.3
Alcoholic drink	3.4	4.5
Tobacco	6.6	2.5
Clothing and footwear	11.8	7.8
Durable household goods	6.8	7.9
Other goods	7.0	7.8
Transport and vehicles	7.0	14.9
Services	9.5	12.9
Miscellaneous	0.6	0.4
	100.0	100.0

Source: *Family Expenditure Survey*, HMSO, 1986

Table 4.1 shows the changes which have taken place in the distribution of household expenditure in the UK in the period 1953–86. Note that it does not show the *amount* of money spent on each item: it shows the *proportion* of total household spending devoted to it.

Food

One feature of Table 4.1 which clearly indicates a rise in the standard of living is the substantial fall in the share of total spending accounted for by food. As real incomes rise, people tend to buy a greater variety of better-quality foodstuffs. But spending on food does not rise as fast as incomes, so the *share* of income spent on food tends to fall.

Transport and vehicles

A further indication of the rise in real incomes is the increased share of household spending accounted for by transport and vehicles. This is due mainly to the growth of private transport (the motor car), at the expense of public transport.

Housing

Housing took a very much larger share of total household expenditure in 1986 than it did in 1953–54. Large increases in local authority rates are part of the explanation for this change, but the main reason is the growth in home ownership. In the early 1950s, only about 30 per cent of households were buying their houses or owned them outright. In the mid-1980s, about 60 per cent of householders either owned their homes or were buying them.

Durable household goods

As real incomes have risen, there has been a steady growth in the percentage of total spending devoted to durable consumer goods. The result is that the UK has one of the highest living standards in the world in terms of the percentages of households that possess durable household goods (see Figure 4.2).

Services

This has been another growth area. Spending on holidays, air travel, catering services and communications all increased substantially between

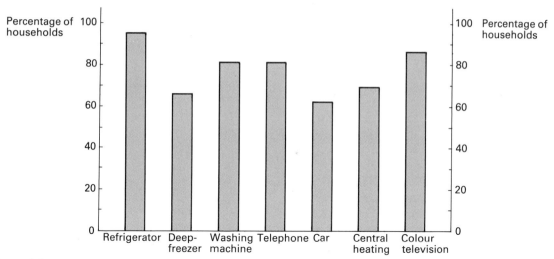

Figure 4.2
Availability of durable goods, UK, 1985
Source: *Social Trends*, HMSO, 1987

1963 and 1986 (80 per cent of UK households now have a telephone, for example).

4.5
Saving

That part of personal disposable income which is not spent is saved. Table 4.2 lists some of the major institutions which collect personal savings. There are many others. The attractions of various savings schemes are widely advertised in the newspapers, on television and in the windows of banks and other financial institutions in the main streets of our towns.

Table 4.2
Some major UK savings institutions

The commercial banks (e.g. Lloyds, Midland, Barclays, National Westminster)	
The Trustee Savings Banks	
The National Girobank	
The National Savings Bank	operated through the Post Office
National Savings Certificates	
Premium Savings Bonds	
Building societies	
Insurance companies	
Pension funds	

Why and how people save

The amounts which households save depend mainly on the following factors.

Income

The main influence on personal saving is the level of disposable income, because this determines the ability to save. (Saving cannot take place until income has risen above the level which is needed to buy the basic necessities.)

The social attitudes towards saving

In some societies, saving is regarded as a 'good' social habit, and is thought to be a sensible and correct way of dealing with part of one's income. In other societies, this is not the case. Income is seen as something which should be spent and enjoyed when it is received, and a person who saves may be regarded as mean. Saving will obviously tend to be higher where people regard it as a good habit.

The desire to provide for future needs

Many people save because we live in a world of uncertainty. They wish to build up a reserve of money which will help them cope with any misfortune which may befall them in the future (e.g. illness or redundancy). People also save to make their years of retirement more comfortable. These reasons explain why a major part of personal saving takes the form of contributions to pension funds and insurance funds.

Saving for a particular objective

Some saving is carried out in order to accumulate a sum of money to pay for a particularly expensive item, such as for the deposit on a house, the purchase of a motor car, or a holiday abroad.

Another objective, particularly for older people, is to build up a fund of savings which they can leave to their sons and daughters or, perhaps, their grandchildren.

The number and variety of savings schemes

The availability of a large number of attractive and convenient savings schemes will tend to encourage people to save. In the UK, as mentioned earlier, there is a very large number of such schemes.

The rate of interest

For some people, it is likely that the amount of interest they receive on their savings will have some effect on the amounts they save. One would expect that higher rates of interest would attract more savings than lower rates.

In fact, evidence seems to show that changes in the rate of interest do have some effect on the amounts saved, but that the influence is not very strong. This is probably because a large part of personal saving is *contractual*. This means that people have made agreements to save a given amount of money every week or every month with organisations such as insurance companies and pension funds. They have committed themselves to saving these amounts whatever happens to the rate of interest.

This account of savings has dealt with *personal* saving. This is not the only form of saving. Companies save by keeping some of their profits in the business, rather than paying out the whole of their profits to shareholders. Governments too can save. They can do this by arranging things so that revenue from taxation is greater than government spending.

The Main Points

- Personal income is derived from many sources, such as wages and salaries, rent, dividends, interest, private pensions and social security benefits.

- Disposable personal income
  = Gross personal income
      − Income tax and NI contributions

- Total consumer spending depends upon the level of income, the rates of income tax and NI contributions, the holdings of personal wealth, the ability to obtain loans and the cost of these loans, and any changes in the distribution of income.

- At very low levels of income, households will be obliged to spend all their income. As income increases, consumption spending also increases, but at a slower rate than income.

- Total personal saving is influenced by the level of income, the social attitudes towards saving, people's views about the future, the availability of attractive savings schemes and, to some extent, by the rate of interest.

Test Your Understanding

1. To which of the categories below do the following items belong:
   (a) a holiday abroad,   (b) a home computer,
   (c) a vacuum cleaner,   (d) toothpaste,
   (e) a journey by train?

   A durable consumer goods
   B non-durable consumer goods
   C services

2. Family A has a weekly income of £150, and Family B has a weekly income of £300.
   (a) Which family is likely to spend more money than the other on items such as food, clothing, lighting and heating?
   (b) Which family is likely to spend a greater percentage of its income on these items?

3. Which ONE of the following developments is likely to lead to a decrease in consumer spending?

   A Consumers expect a large increase in prices in the near future.
   B The Chancellor of the Exchequer reduces the rate of VAT.
   C Hire-purchase companies and banks raise the rate of interest on loans.
   D The rate of income tax is reduced.

4. The following details refer to the income of a particular household:

Wages	£250	Income tax	£30
Interest on building society deposit	£10	National insurance contributions	£18
Child benefit	£15	Saving	£20

   (All the amounts of money shown are received or paid weekly.)
   (a) What is this household's disposable weekly income?
   (b) What is this household's total weekly expenditure?

5. In a particular country, prices are rising at the rate of 15 per cent per annum, on average. The average rate of interest paid on savings accounts is 10 per cent per annum.
   (a) What is happening to the *money* value of savings?
   (b) What is happening to the *real* value of savings?
   (c) During a period of high inflation, would you expect people to increase their rate of saving or to reduce it? Explain your answer.

BOX 4
Personal income and expenditure in the UK

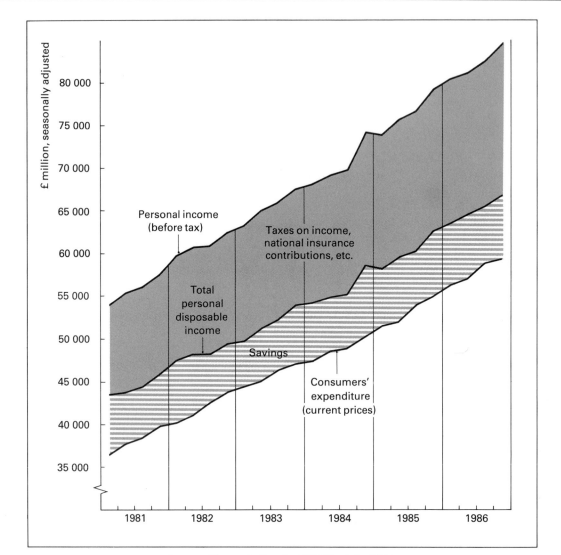

Source: *Economic Trends*, HMSO, July 1987

Questions
1. What different kinds of income are included in personal income?
2. Does this graph support the idea that consumers' spending is determined mainly by the level of disposable income? Explain your answer.
3. Over the period covered by the graph, total consumer expenditure increased by nearly 60 per cent. Does this mean that living standards increased by nearly 60 per cent over this period of time? Explain your answer.

CHAPTER 5

Production and productivity

5.1 The meanings of production and productivity
5.2 The main divisions of production
5.3 The division of labour (specialisation)

5.1

The meanings of production and productivity

Production

Chapter 1 explained that the main purpose of production is to produce goods and services which satisfy people's wants. Production includes, therefore, the output of all those goods and services for which people are prepared to pay a price.

One aspect of production which is of the greatest importance is how much is produced per hour or per day by each unit of land, labour or capital. For example, in several major industries we find that one hour's labour will produce a much greater output in Japan than in the UK. On the other hand, one acre of farmland in Britain yields nearly three times as much wheat as an acre of land in the USA.

Measuring the output of a factor of production against time is one method of estimating the *productivity* of that factor.

Productivity

Productivity is a measure of the efficiency with which goods and services are produced. A simple example will make this clear.

Suppose two workers, A and B, are making identical articles, both of them using exactly the same equipment.

In a 40-hour week, Worker A produces 400 articles.

In a 40-hour week, Worker B produces 600 articles.

$$\text{Worker A's productivity} = \frac{400 \text{ articles}}{40 \text{ hours}}$$
$$= 10 \text{ articles per hour.}$$

$$\text{Worker B's productivity} = \frac{600 \text{ articles}}{40 \text{ hours}}$$
$$= 15 \text{ articles per hour.}$$

This simple example shows that productivity takes account of two quantities:
- the *output* (in this case, the number of articles produced), and
- the *input* (in this case, the number of hours worked).

Very simply, therefore,

$$\text{Productivity} = \frac{\text{Output}}{\text{Input}}$$

The productivity of labour is usually measured in terms of output per worker-hour.

The difference between production and productivity

It is important to be perfectly clear on the difference in the meanings of the words 'production' and 'productivity'.

Suppose two firms are making very similar footwear and have the following weekly outputs:

	Pairs of shoes
Firm X	10 000
Firm Y	5 000

We can say that Firm X's production is twice as great as that of Firm Y. But this statement tells us nothing about the efficiency of the two firms. If Firm X is using more than twice as much labour and capital as Firm Y, for example, then its productivity is less than that of Firm Y.

5.2
The main divisions of production

The many different industries producing goods and services are divided into three broad groups.

1 Primary industries

These industries are described as 'primary' because they carry out the first stage in the process of production. They produce raw materials, either by extracting them from the ground or by growing

them. Examples include agriculture, mining, quarrying, forestry and fishing.

2 Secondary industries

These are the processing and manufacturing industries, which carry out the second stage in the process of production. They change the raw materials into finished or semi-finished products. Examples include the industries producing steel, chemicals, furniture, clothing, footwear, motor cars and so on.

3 Tertiary industries

Firms in these industries provide *services* of all kinds to firms in the primary and secondary sectors. They also supply services directly to consumers. In a modern society, the firms in the primary and secondary sectors would find it impossible to function without the services

Figure 5.1

Primary industries
– extracting the gifts of nature

Secondary industries
– manufacturing and processing

Tertiary industries
– supplying services

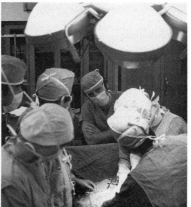

supplied by banks, insurance companies, transport undertakings, communications (e.g. the postal services and telephone network), wholesalers and retailers. Services supplied directly to consumers as well as to firms include the education and health services, catering services, tourism and entertainment.

The importance of the different sectors

The proportions of the labour force employed in the different sectors of the economy vary according to the level of economic development. In the developing countries, a large percentage of the working population is employed in the primary sector (mainly agriculture). For example, in some developing countries such as India, Pakistan, Vietnam and Burma, about 70 per cent of the labour force work in agriculture. In developed countries such as the USA, Japan and West Germany, only about 7 per cent work in agriculture.

In the UK, the proportion of the working population employed in primary production has been falling for a long time. In recent years there has also been a steady decline in the numbers employed in manufacturing (see Figure 5.2).

A drop in the percentages of the population working in the primary and secondary industries does not *necessarily* mean that outputs in these sectors are falling. The changes in employment are often due to technical changes which have greatly increased the productivity of labour. British agriculture is a good example of an industry where falling employment has been accompanied by increased output.

The percentages of the labour force in the primary, secondary and tertiary industries change as an economy becomes more developed. In the earlier stages of development there is a movement of workers from agriculture to manufacturing industries. As real incomes continue to rise, there is an increasing demand for services of all kinds. Improvements in productivity in the manufacturing industries lead to a movement of workers to the service industries. In the UK, more than half the working population is employed in service industries (see Figure 5.2).

Figure 5.2
Employment in the UK

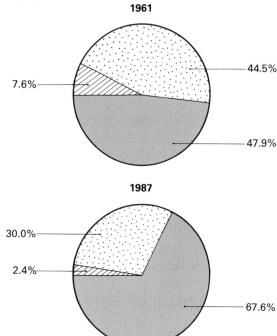

Primary (e.g. agriculture, mining, quarrying, forestry, fishing)

Secondary (e.g. manufacturing, construction, gas, electricity, water)

Tertiary (e.g. transport, communications, health, education, banking, and other services)

Sources: *Economic Trends*, HMSO, November 1979; *Department of Employment Gazette*, August 1987

5.3
The division of labour (specialisation)

Perhaps the most remarkable feature of modern production methods is the way in which work is specialised. The production of a good or service is broken down into a large number of separate and simple operations. Each worker is responsible for, and spends the whole of his or her time carrying out, one of these operations. Thus, in many industries, the finished product is the result of the combined efforts of many hundreds of specialised workers.

This technique of breaking down production into a large number of specialised tasks is described as the *division of labour*. The most striking examples are found in industries making such goods as motor cars, television sets and domestic electrical appliances. These industries – and many others – make use of assembly lines, where each worker fits a single component as the product moves down the line. This system of production is commonly known as *mass production*.

Specialised production, however, is not a new development. Very early in the history of the human race, people found that the total output of a group could be greatly increased – with no extra effort – when, instead of everyone trying to provide for all their needs by their own efforts, they specialised. Each member of the group concentrated on one activity (e.g. hunting, fishing, building shelters, making simple tools and weapons, and so on).

Figure 5.3
The division of labour in manufacturing: in the assembly of cars, the fitting of each component is a specialised task

The advantages of the division of labour

1. No two people have exactly the same abilities and interests. By creating a very large number of different jobs, the division of labour makes it easier for people to find jobs which are well suited to their particular abilities and interests.
2. 'Practice makes perfect.' When a worker concentrates on a task which requires no more than a few relatively simple movements, he or she develops the ability to do the work with great speed and dexterity.
3. If a person has to carry out several operations in the process of production, he or she will have to move from one part of the workshop to another, putting down one set of tools and picking up another (or moving from one machine to another). In specialised production, it is the product which moves to the worker; no time is wasted by the movement of workers.
4. When a worker is responsible for several different operations, he or she will have a set of tools for each of the different tasks. For a large part of the time, therefore, much of the

equipment will be lying idle (since a worker cannot do two jobs at the same time). When work is specialised, each worker only needs one set of tools and these will be in constant use.

5. A most important advantage of the division of labour is that it makes it possible to mechanise the production process. When production is subdivided into many simple operations (there may be as many as a hundred operations in the production of a pair of shoes), it is not too difficult a task to devise a machine for each of these operations. Even today there is no single machine capable of converting a tree trunk into a sideboard, but when the principle of the division of labour is adopted, it becomes possible to use a whole range of powered tools and machines, such as saws, planes, drills, lathes, polishers and so on.

There is little doubt that the gradual extension of the division of labour has led to enormous increases in the productivity of labour. It has made it possible for millions of people to achieve living standards which are extremely high compared with those experienced before mass-production methods were used. At the same time, it has enabled workers to enjoy a much shorter working week. The use of machinery has also removed most of the back-breaking toil associated with work in earlier times.

The disadvantages of the division of labour

1. Constant repetition of a few simple movements is often a cause of boredom and frustration. Monotony and loss of job satisfaction are the price a worker may have to pay for the higher income and shorter working week which mass-production techniques have made possible.
2. It is said that specialisation has led to a loss of skills. Articles that used to be made by craftsmen are now made by machines. A worker does not have the satisfaction of being able to say, 'I made that'. On the other hand, modern production techniques have created demands for a whole new range of skills in the design, construction and maintenance of complex machinery, in production planning, stock control, communications and cost accountancy, in the use of computers, and so on.

3. Specialised production means that both workers and machines are required to carry out operations at great speed. This is only possible if the product is *standardised*. In other words, the system is extremely efficient at producing vast quantities of *identical* articles. Assembly lines throughout the UK are turning out thousands of identical motor cars, washing machines, television sets and so on. Many people complain, therefore, that the division of labour is responsible for a lack of variety. As against this view, it might be argued that the only reason most of us can afford to have a motor car *and* a television set *and* a washing machine *and* a refrigerator is that they are mass-produced and hence low-cost products.

4. The work done by specialist workers is often peculiar to the industry in which they are employed. If such workers are made redundant, they find that their skills cannot be used in another industry. However, the relative simplicity of much of the work in modern industry means that workers losing jobs in one industry can be quickly re-trained for jobs in another industry.

5. Specialisation makes us all very dependent upon one another. All the things we use and consume each day (e.g. food, clothing, power, transport, buildings, machines, radios, books, etc.) are the results of other people's efforts. We rely on other people buying the things we help to produce, and with our incomes we buy the things produced by other people. The fact that we are all dependent upon the efforts of other people means that what happens in one part of the economy affects all the other parts. This is brought home to us when strikes take place. A strike by a group of workers producing a particular material or component can stop production in all the firms which use that material or component.

The extent of the division of labour

The principle of the division of labour is applied at all levels of economic activity.

1 Specialisation by industry

An economy is made up of many industries, each of which tends to specialise on a particular product or process. In the UK, for example, we have industries which specialise in the production of coal, oil, chemicals, clothing, pottery, and so on.

2 Specialisation by firms

The individual firms, which together make up an industry, often specialise by making one part of the final product or by carrying out one of the several processes of production. For example, in the textile industry the production of printed fabrics is broken down into several separate processes. Firms tend to specialise on one of these processes, for example spinning, weaving, dyeing or fabric printing.

3 Specialisation by workers

This is now applied to a remarkable degree. The Census of Population lists more than 40 000 different occupations.

4 Specialisation by regions

In many countries, there is a tendency for certain regions to specialise. In the UK, some industries tend to be concentrated in particular localities. Well-known examples are cotton in Lancashire, woollen cloth in West Yorkshire, pottery in North Staffordshire, footwear in Leicester and Northampton, and tinplate in South Wales.

5 International specialisation

The principle of specialisation is applied on a world-wide scale. Some regions of the world have definite advantages over others in the production of certain commodities. These advantages may take the form of a very suitable climate, soils which favour certain crops, the existence of valuable mineral deposits, or the development of special skills by the workers of a country.

Thus, we find that Brazil is a major supplier of coffee, Malaya of tin and natural rubber, South Africa of gold, the West Indies of sugar, the Middle East of oil, Japan of cameras and motor cycles, and Switzerland of watches.

The division of labour and the size of the market

While it is *technically* possible to mass-produce most goods, for many products it would not be sensible to do so. Mass production only makes sense if there is a mass market for the product. For example, it would be technically possible to set up an assembly line which could produce thousands of identical ladies' hats every day, but no one is likely to do so.

The industries in which the principle of the division of labour is most widely applied are those which are able to sell thousands of identical products every week. Obvious examples are the industries producing cigarettes, detergents, beverages, processed foods, cars and televisions.

If the size of the market is relatively small, a firm cannot apply the principle of the division of labour to any great extent. Where people demand a variety of styles and designs (as in high-fashion clothing and jewellery), we find production in the hands of small firms. The survival of the small firm is discussed in Chapter 7.

The Main Points

- Economic activities are classified into three broad groups of industries: primary industries, secondary industries and tertiary industries.

- Productivity is measured in terms of output per unit of input. The productivity of labour, therefore, normally refers to the output per worker-hour.

- The percentages of the labour force employed in the primary, secondary and tertiary sectors in a developed country are quite different from those in a developing country. In several developed countries, more than half the labour force works in service industries.

- The division of labour (specialisation) is an important feature of modern production methods. Although it has many advantages and has been responsible for some remarkable increases in productivity, it is not without its disadvantages.

- The extent to which specialisation can be employed in the production of a good depends upon the size of the market for that good.

Test Your Understanding

1. What are the missing words in the following sentences?
   (a) .... per .... hour is the normal way of measuring the .... of labour.
   (b) Production includes the output of both .... and ....

2. Which TWO of the following are examples of secondary production?

   A serving in a shop
   B preparing and packaging frozen food
   C operating a telephone switchboard
   D bottling milk

3. Which ONE of the following does *not* occur when the division of labour is introduced?

   A productivity increases
   B more specialised machinery is used
   C work becomes more repetitive
   D workers need a wider range of skills
   E movement of workers is reduced

4. What do you consider to be the main benefits which *workers* have obtained from the widespread application of the division of labour?

5. The most famous description of the effects of the division of labour was written by the founder of modern economics, Adam Smith. The following passage appears in his book *The Wealth of Nations*, published in 1776. It describes his visit to a pin-making factory.

   A workman not educated in this business could scarce perhaps make one pin a day and certainly not twenty. But in the way this business is now carried on, not only is the whole work a peculiar trade, but it is divided into a number of branches.

   One man draws out the wire, another straightens it, a third cuts it, a fourth points it, a fifth grinds it at the top for receiving the head; to make the head requires two or three distinct operations; to put it on is a peculiar business; to whiten the pins is another; it is even a trade in itself to put them into paper.

   The important business of making a pin is, in this manner, divided into eighteen distinct operations. Ten persons therefore could make among them upwards of forty-eight thousand pins a day.

   Give three *reasons* why specialisation made possible a daily output per worker of 4800 pins, whereas without specialisation it would have been less than 20 pins per day.

BOX 5
Mass production and productivity

Automated production has helped Japan become dominant in consumer electronics. To make a television set, a Japanese firm typically uses 30 per cent fewer components than a European or American firm and it automates 80 per cent of its production – far more than its Western rivals. It requires 1.9 man-hours to produce a television set in Japan compared with 3.9 hours in West Germany and 6.1 hours in Britain.

A Japanese company has a 43 metre-long automated assembly line where six operators produce 2 million pocket calculators a month.

Source: *The Economist*, 16 March 1985

Questions
1. In Japan, labour productivity in the making of television sets is rather more than three times as great as in Britain. Does the fact that it requires only one-third as much labour to make a television set in Japan mean that its cost will be only one-third of the cost of a set made in Britain? Explain your answer.
2. The quotation refers to *automated* production. Use reference books to find out exactly what is meant by the word 'automation', and, in particular, why it does not have the same meaning as 'mechanisation'.

CHAPTER 6

Productivity and the costs of production

6.1 Fixed and variable factors of production
6.2 Short-run changes in output – average and marginal products
6.3 The costs of production
6.4 How changes in output affect costs
6.5 Some examples of production costs
6.6 Costs, revenues and profits

In the real world, the demands for different products are always changing. Firms are compelled to change their outputs in order to deal with these changes. Suppose the demand for a product is increasing. A firm making this product will be encouraged to increase its production, and the obvious way to do this is to employ more labour and buy more raw materials. In this way, a firm may be able to meet an increase in demand in a relatively short time.

It may be the case, however, that the firm is already working at full capacity, and its buildings and machinery are being fully utilised. If this is the situation, an increase in output is only possible if the firm extends its premises and installs more machinery. This may take several months or, in some cases, several years (e.g. the building of a new steelworks or chemical plant).

6.1
Fixed and variable factors of production

The factors of production are classified as variable factors and fixed factors.

Variable factors

As the name suggests, these are factors whose supply can be quickly and easily changed. They include most types of labour, raw materials, fuel, power, hand tools and so on. By employing more or less of the variable factors, a firm is able to change its output in a matter of days or weeks.

Fixed factors

The supply of fixed factors cannot be easily and quickly changed. They take a relatively long time to build, erect and install. Obvious examples of fixed factors of production are factory buildings and heavy specialised machinery.

In economics, the difference between the long run and the short run is based on the time it takes a firm to change the quantities of the fixed factors it employs.

The short run

This is the period of time over which at least one of the factors of production is fixed in supply. In this situation a firm can only change its output by using more or less of the variable factors. For example, a firm which prints textbooks may increase its output in the short run by taking on more workers, using more paper, more ink, more electricity and so on.

The long run

This is the length of time a firm needs in order to change the amounts of all the factors of production it uses (i.e. both fixed and variable). For example, if the printing firm mentioned above found that the demand for its goods was increasing steadily, it might decide to extend its premises and install more printing presses. This would be a long-run change.

Note that the term 'fixed factors' only applies in the short run; in the long run, all factors are variable.

It is not possible to define the short run in terms of a given number of days or weeks; it all depends on the type of industry. In some industries, for example those employing fairly simple types of machinery and unskilled or semi-skilled labour, the short run may be only a matter of months. In other industries such as steelmaking, oil refining and the generation of electricity, the short run will extend for several years because it will take a long time for new plants to be built.

Short-run changes in output – average and marginal products

When a firm increases or decreases its production in the short run, the changes in output are not likely to be proportional to the changes in the amounts of the variable factors employed. Each extra worker does not add exactly the same amount to the total output. The way in which the total output changes in the short run is best demonstrated with a simple arithmetical example of production changes in agriculture.

We assume that the fixed factors are land and capital (i.e. farm buildings and machinery) and the variable factor is labour. We also assume that all the workers are equally efficient. Table 6.1 shows what happens when different amounts of labour are put to work with a fixed amount of land and capital.

Table 6.1
Total, average and marginal products (tonnes per annum)

Number of workers	Total product	Marginal product	Average product
0	0	—	—
1	20	20	20
2	80	60	40
3	165	85	55
4	272	107	68
5	385	113	77
6	474	89	79
7	525	51	75
8	560	35	70
9	576	16	64

Assume that the product is wheat and the output figures represent tonnes per annum. The column headings in the table are explained below.

The *total product* is quite simply the total amount produced per annum by some given number of workers.

The *marginal product* is the change in total output brought about by increasing (or decreasing) the number of workers employed by one worker. For example, when the number employed increases from four workers to five workers, the total output increases from 272 tonnes to 385 tonnes per annum. The marginal product of the fifth worker, therefore, is 385 tonnes – 272 tonnes, or 113 tonnes per annum.

The *average product* is a measure of the output per worker employed. It is calculated by dividing the total output by the number of workers:

$$\text{Average product} = \frac{\text{Total product}}{\text{Number of workers}}$$

For example, when five workers are employed, the total product is 385 tonnes per annum. The average product, therefore, is 385 tonnes ÷ 5, or 77 tonnes per annum.

Increasing and decreasing productivity

The changes in output per worker (i.e. average product) shown in Table 6.1 are illustrated in Figure 6.1. It can be seen from the table and the diagram that, as the number of workers increases

Figure 6.1
Changes in output per worker, for the example given in Table 6.1

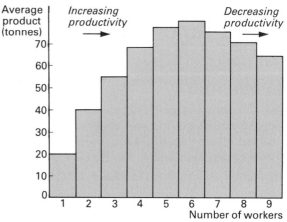

from one to six, the output per worker continues to increase. In other words, the productivity of labour is increasing.

When more than six workers are employed, the *total output* continues to increase but the *output per worker* begins to fall. Maximum productivity is achieved when six workers are employed.

These changes in productivity are not due to some workers being more efficient than others: we have assumed that they are all equally efficient. The explanation lies in the changing proportions between the fixed factors and the variable factor. At very low levels of employment, the land and capital are being underutilised; there are insufficient workers to make full use of the land and capital. In simple terms, the workers are 'too thin on the ground'. Productivity increases as more workers are employed.

As the number of workers continues to increase, however, there comes a point where the average product begins to fall. This is because the fixed amounts of land and capital are now insufficient to keep all the workers operating at their full capacity. Employing more workers will increase the total output of wheat, but the output per worker will be falling.

These changes in the average product of labour have important effects on the costs of production. If we assume that all the workers receive the same wages and that other things do not change, it should be clear that

- increasing productivity means that the cost per tonne of wheat will be falling, and
- falling productivity means that the cost per tonne of wheat will be rising.

6.3
The costs of production

The idea of opportunity cost was explained in Chapter 1. We now turn to the more familiar types of cost. These are the prices which firms have to pay in order to obtain the materials and services they need to run their businesses.

Variable costs

These are the costs of the variable factors. They are sometimes referred to as *direct* costs because they vary directly as output varies. They increase as output increases, and decrease as output decreases. Variable costs include such items as wages and the costs of raw materials, fuel, power, packaging and transport.

Fixed costs

These are the costs of the fixed factors of production. When a firm increases or decreases its output, fixed costs remain unchanged. Fixed costs include such expenses as rent, rates, insurance, interest on loans, and depreciation. These costs are sometimes described as *indirect* or *overhead* costs.

Depreciation – a fixed cost

In industries which use large amounts of capital equipment, depreciation is a major item in the costs of production. It differs from most other costs because it is not 'paid out' in the same way as rents, rates and interest on loans.

Depreciation represents the loss in the value of a firm's capital assets due to wear and tear and because they gradually become out of date. It is treated as a fixed cost because plant and machinery are assumed to lose value as time goes by, regardless of the use made of them. (This is certainly true for motor cars, as a glance at any book which lists second-hand car prices will demonstrate.)

For example, if a firm buys a new machine for £100 000 and estimates its effective life as ten years, one way in which it might depreciate this machine is by the straight-line method. This assumes that the value of the machine will decline by £10 000 each year. This £10 000 will be treated as a fixed cost and each year, for ten years, this sum of money will be placed in a depreciation fund to meet the eventual cost of replacing the machine.

Total cost

When variable costs are added to fixed costs, we obtain the total cost of production:

Variable costs + Fixed costs = Total cost

Marginal cost

This is a measure of the amount by which the total

cost changes when the output changes by one unit. For example,

Total cost of producing 20 units = £100
Total cost of producing 21 units = £106

Marginal cost of the 21st unit   =   £6

Average cost

This is the cost per unit of output. It is obtained when the total cost is divided by the number of units produced:

$$\text{Average cost} = \frac{\text{Total cost}}{\text{Number of units produced}}$$

6.4
How changes in output affect costs

Assume that an individual firm with a fixed amount of land and capital steadily increases its output by employing more of the variable factors. Table 6.2 shows how the different costs might be affected by the change in output.

Table 6.2
A firm's costs of production (£s)

Units of output (per week)	Fixed costs	Variable costs	Total cost	Marginal cost	Average cost
0	1000	—	1000	—	—
1	1000	350	1350	350	1350
2	1000	560	1560	210	780
3	1000	740	1740	180	580
4	1000	1000	2000	260	500
5	1000	1400	2400	400	480
6	1000	2000	3000	600	500
7	1000	2850	3850	850	550
8	1000	3960	4960	1110	620

Points to note on Table 6.2

1. When output falls to zero, the total cost does not fall to zero. As long as the firm remains in business, it must meet its fixed costs even if it temporarily ceases production.
2. As output increases, the total cost continues to increase. As more goods are produced, more

labour, materials, fuel and power, and other resources will be used, so the total cost must increase.
3. What is true of the total cost is not true of the marginal and average costs. As output increases, these costs tend to fall because productivity increases (see Table 6.1 and Figure 6.1). As output continues to increase, there comes a point where productivity begins to decline, and marginal and average costs begin to rise.
4. One most important reason why the average cost falls as output increases is the fact that the fixed costs are being spread over a larger output. The greater the number of units produced, the smaller the amount of fixed cost per unit. (See the example on pages 41–2.)
5. There are several reasons why, as the output increases, the average cost will begin to rise:
   – Increasing the amounts of the variable factors will eventually lead to the fixed factors being overloaded, and productivity will begin to fall.
   – It may be necessary for the firm to introduce overtime, at higher wage rates.
   – Less efficient labour may have to be recruited and less efficient stand-by equipment may be pressed into use.

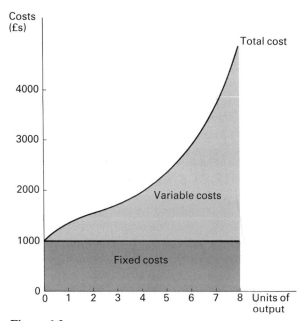

Figure 6.2
Fixed costs + Variable costs = Total cost

These changes are illustrated in Figure 6.2, which is obtained by plotting the figures in the first four columns of Table 6.2.

6.5
Some examples of production costs

Industries which use large amounts of expensive fixed capital, such as assembly lines and robots, have very high fixed costs and relatively low variable costs. In this type of industry, large-scale production leads to a great reduction in the average cost. This is because the *fixed cost per unit* falls very quickly as output increases.

For example, when pocket calculators were first introduced, they were produced on a small scale at a cost of about £100 each. Within six years, the introduction of large-scale production had reduced the average cost to less than £5.

Figure 6.3
Production using robots: high capital costs (fixed costs) and low labour costs (variable costs)

Introducing a new model or design

The remarkable way in which large-scale production can reduce the average cost may be illustrated with a simple arithmetical example. The same example can be used to demonstrate the problems faced by a firm which is trying to fix the price of a new product, or a new design of its existing product.

A firm does *not* know the average cost of production when it launches the new product or design, because it does not know how successful the product will be. The price, however, has to be decided when it starts production of the new model. These points are brought out clearly in the example. Assume the firm's costs are as follows:

Fixed costs

Research and development	£4 million
Setting up factory (e.g. re-tooling, purchase of new machines, etc.)	£15 million
Other fixed costs	£5 million
Total fixed costs	£24 million

Variable costs

Labour, materials and other variable factors amount to £20 per unit. (We assume that the variable cost per unit remains constant, i.e. every unit produced adds £20 to the total cost.)

The estimated life of the capital is eight years, hence the fixed cost per annum = £3 million.

We now look at two possibilities. In one case, sales are rather disappointing. In the other case, the product proves to be a big success.

1 Low-volume output

Total sales average 10 000 units per annum. The costs of producing this annual output will be

Fixed costs	£3 000 000
Variable costs (10 000 × £20)	£200 000
Total cost	£3 200 000

Average cost (cost per unit) = £320

2 High-volume output

Total sales average 100 000 units per annum. The costs of producing this annual output will be

Fixed costs	£3 000 000
Variable costs (100 000 × £20)	£2 000 000
Total cost	£5 000 000

Average cost (cost per unit) = £50

The very large reduction in average cost is due entirely to the spreading of the £3 million of fixed costs over the much larger output.

We can now see why the question, 'How much does it cost to produce this article?' is not a very sensible question. The answer to such a question is, 'It depends upon how many are produced.'

Costs in printing and publishing

The previous example helps to explain why books with many pages often cost less than books with far fewer pages. In the publishing industry a large part of the total cost consists of fixed costs.

The costs of editing the manuscript and redrafting it in a form suitable for the printer, the preparation of the artwork, the setting-up of the type, and the initial advertising are all fixed costs. They remain the same whether the book sells 100 copies or 100 000 copies.

Once this work is completed, the variable costs per book will be relatively small. They will include labour costs, the costs of the paper, the costs of binding, and royalties to the author. As in the previous example, with heavy fixed costs, the average cost of a book falls quite sharply as output increases.

6.6
Costs, revenues and profits

In the long run, a firm will only continue to produce if it is making profits. A simple calculation of profits and losses can be made by using the output and cost figures of Table 6.2 and assuming that the product is selling at a price of £550. We shall also assume that changes in the quantity offered for sale do not affect this price, so that the total revenue (i.e. receipts) can be obtained by multiplying the number of units sold by the price (i.e. £550).

Table 6.3 shows two ways of measuring profit:

1. If the total cost is deducted from the total revenue, we obtain the *total profit*.
2. If the average cost (cost per unit) is deducted from the price of the product, we obtain the *profit per unit*.

It can be seen from Table 6.3 that profits are earned in the range of output from four units per week to six units per week. The most profitable output is five units per week.

The relationships between costs, revenues and profits may be seen more clearly in Figure 6.4, which is based on the figures in the first three columns of Table 6.3. In this graph, the total cost curve does not begin at the origin because there are fixed costs of £1000 which have to be met even when output is zero. The total revenue curve is a straight line because the price does not change

Table 6.3

Costs, revenues and profits (£s)

Units of output (per week)	Total cost	Total revenue	Total profit	Average cost	Price	Profit per unit
0	1000	0	−1000	—	—	—
1	1350	550	−800	1350	550	−800
2	1560	1100	−460	780	550	−230
3	1740	1650	−90	580	550	−30
4	2000	2200	+200	500	550	+50
5	2400	2750	+350	480	550	+70
6	3000	3300	+300	500	550	+50
7	3850	3850	0	550	550	0
8	4960	4400	−560	620	550	−70

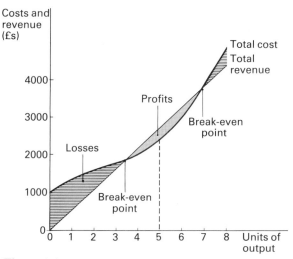

Figure 6.4
Profits and losses

when output changes. Each additional unit sold adds £550 to the total revenue.

When the output is five units per week, the vertical distance between the total revenue and total cost curves is at a maximum; this is the point at which profits are at their maximum. The break-even points show the outputs at which the firm's total revenue is just covering its total cost.

The Main Points

■ Only the amounts of the variable factors employed can be changed in the short run.

■ Changes in the amounts of the fixed factors take a relatively long time, and are described as long-run changes.

■ In the short run, increasing the amounts of the variable factors will, at first, lead to increasing productivity. As output continues to increase, however, there will come a point where productivity begins to fall.

■ Total cost = Variable costs + Fixed costs

$$\text{Average cost} = \frac{\text{Total cost}}{\text{Total output}}$$

Marginal cost = Change in total cost when output changes by one unit

Total profit = Total revenue − Total cost

■ Other things being equal, increasing productivity will reduce the average cost, and falling productivity will increase the average cost.

■ In mass-production industries with heavy fixed costs, the average cost falls very sharply as output increases.

Test Your Understanding

1. In the short run, which TWO of the following are described as fixed costs?

   A fuel and power
   B fire insurance on factory buildings
   C raw materials
   D rent

2. What are the missing quantities in the table below, which lists output in tonnes per week?

Number of workers	Total product	Average product	Marginal product
1	100	100	100
2	. . .	. . .	120
3	360	120	. . .

3. This question refers to Figure 6.5. What are the main items of (a) fixed costs, and (b) variable costs which must be met in order to keep a bus in regular service?

Figure 6.5

4. The table below shows how the output of a firm varies as more workers are employed.

Number of workers	Total output (units)
1	10
2	24
3	39
4	48
5	55

   After the employment of which number of workers does the productivity of labour begin to decline?

5. Which ONE of the following would lead to an increase in a firm's variable costs?

   A an increase in the rate of interest charged on bank loans
   B an increase in local authority rates
   C an increase in the price of raw materials
   D an increase in the rental charges on photocopiers and other office equipment

6. A publisher has to decide on the price she should charge for a new book. She estimates that the fixed costs of producing the book will be £20 000 and that the variable costs will be £3 per copy. She has agreed to pay the author a royalty equal to 10 per cent (one-tenth) of the sales revenue, and she estimates the demand for the book to be such that

   – 20 000 copies could be sold at a price of £5 per copy, and
   – 30 000 copies could be sold at a price of £4 per copy.

   On the basis of these estimates, which price would you advise the publisher to charge? Explain your answer.

BOX 6
Technical progress and productivity

Spinning ever faster: hours worked to produce ten kilograms of yarn

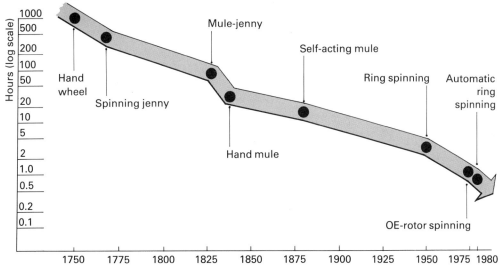

Sources: *The Economist*, 27 July 1985; Legler Stoffel

The diagram shows how, over the years, technical progress has made it possible to achieve remarkable increases in productivity in the textile industry.

Questions
1. What does the illustration tell us about the effects of technical progress on the employment of labour in this industry? Explain your answer.
2. How do you think the type of labour skills required in the textile industry has changed? Explain your answer.
3. Two important new techniques were introduced in the 1970s. How would these technical improvements affect the rate of depreciation in the textile industry?

CHAPTER 7

Large firms and small firms

Figure 7.1
Large and small firms in the footwear industry: the British Shoe Corporation's warehouse in Leicester, and a one-person business producing hand-made shoes

Economies of scale

Chapter 6 explained some of the effects on productivity and costs of a firm changing its output in the short run. In this chapter we examine some of the effects of long-run changes in output.

In the long run, a firm can change the amounts of all the factors of production it employs; that is, it can change the *scale* of its production. For example, a manufacturing firm can extend its factory, a mining company can sink a new mine, and a producer of natural rubber can bring new trees into production. All these changes alter the scale of production.

Table 7.1
Changes in the scale of production

Size of firm (units of factors employed)			Size of firm increases by	Annual output (tonnes)	Output increases by	
Land	Labour	Capital				
5	2	4		100		
			100%		150%	economies of scale
10	4	8		250		
			50%		60%	
15	6	12		400		
			33⅓%		25%	diseconomies of scale
20	8	16		500		
			25%		20%	
25	10	20		600		

A change in the scale of production does not usually lead to proportionate changes in output. If a firm doubles its size, it does not follow that its output will double. It may increase by more than 100 per cent or by less than 100 per cent. Table 7.1 shows what might happen when a firm increases its size by employing more of *all* the factors of production.

Points to note on Table 7.1

1. As the firm begins to increase in size, its output increases more than proportionately. A 100 per cent increase in size leads to a 150 per cent increase in output, and a 50 per cent increase in size leads to a 60 per cent increase in output.

2. As the firm continues to increase in size, the total output continues to increase, but the *percentage* changes in output are not the same as the *percentage* changes in the size of the firm.

3. Where the percentage increase in output is greater than the percentage increase in the size of the firm, it is said to be enjoying *economies of scale*.

4. When the percentage increase in output is less than the percentage increase in the size of the firm, *diseconomies of scale* are being experienced.

Some of the information contained in Table 7.1 is illustrated in Figure 7.2, which gives a much clearer picture of the relative changes in the size of the firm and its total output.

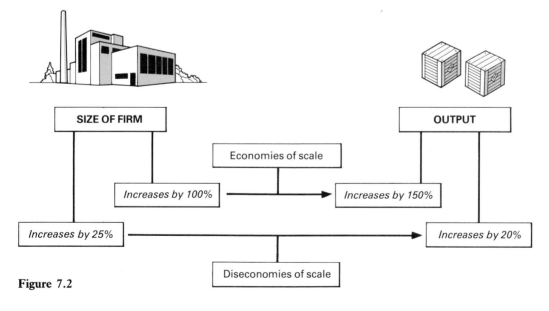

Figure 7.2

Economies of scale and average cost

If we assume that the prices of land, labour and capital do not change, economies of scale will result in lower average costs. For example, when the firm in Table 7.1 and Figure 7.2 first starts to grow, it doubles in size, but its output more than doubles. The firm uses twice as much land, labour and capital, but its output becomes two and a half times greater. If other things do not change, its cost per unit (average cost) must fall. The term *economies of scale*, therefore, refers to a situation where an increase in the size of the firm leads to a *falling* average cost.

Diseconomies of scale occur when increasing the size of the firm causes the average cost to *rise*.

When a firm achieves a size where it is producing at the lowest possible average cost, it is said to be at its *optimum size*.

All economies of scale arise from growth in the scale of production, but it is usual to classify them into two main types, internal and external.

Internal economies of scale

The total costs of a large firm will obviously be much larger than those of a small firm; we want to know why its average cost might be lower. The various features of large-scale production which can bring about a reduction in the average cost are set out in the next sections and summarised in Figure 7.3.

Technical economies

1. The large firm can make more use of the principle of the division of labour than the small firm. Production can be broken down into many more specialised operations than is possible in the smaller firm.

2. A large firm can make more effective use of large units of capital equipment which, in a small firm, would be grossly underutilised and hence costly to use. Capital equipment such as the large overhead cranes on building sites, giant presses in car production and combine harvesters in farming are extremely efficient and can be operated at low average cost when they are used to their full capacity. Where output is small, however, such equipment will be lying idle for much of the time, and the fixed cost per unit will be very high.

3. If the length, breadth and depth of a box are doubled, its volume increases by a factor of eight. This simple arithmetical fact accounts for the development of the jumbo jet, mammoth oil tankers and juggernaut lorries. The costs of producing these things, the power required to move them and the labour required to operate them do not increase proportionately with their size (see Table 7.2). Similar economies of increased dimensions apply to such things as blast furnaces, oil refineries and chemical plants.

4. In manufacturing, where a series of different machines carry out the processes of production, a problem may arise in balancing the outputs of the machines. Machine A might have an

Table 7.2
Economies of scale in transport

Carrying capacity and mileage[1]		Total operating costs per mile	Total operating costs per tonne-mile (assuming a full load)
10 tonne 500 miles per week		107.74p	10.77p
24 tonne 1000 miles per week		116.12p	4.84p

[1] In general, the larger the vehicle the greater the mileage.
Source: Based on Commercial Motor's *Tables of Operating Costs*, 1987–88

output of 50 units per hour and Machine B, which carries out the next stage in production, might have an output of 125 units per hour. In a firm with a small output, say 50 units per hour, Machine A will be fully employed, but Machine B will only be working at two-fifths of its capacity. A large firm, however, will be able to employ teams of these machines. By linking five machines of type A to two machines of type B, it can keep all the machines working at full capacity.

5. A large firm will have the resources to maintain a research and development department to help improve the quality of its product and its methods of production. Such a department may be considered an economy of scale if it helps the firm to operate more efficiently and to lower its average cost of production.

Question on Table 7.2
What is the cost per tonne-mile when the 24-tonne lorry is only carrying a load of ten tonnes?

Marketing economies

1. A large firm can buy its materials in large quantities and hence obtain them at lower prices.
2. By placing large orders with its suppliers, the large firm is also able to obtain preferential treatment regarding the quality and delivery of the goods it buys.
3. Handling and packaging costs do not increase proportionately with the size of an order. For example, the cost of typing an invoice for 1000 articles is no more than the cost of typing one for 100 articles. As point 3 above demonstrates, the cost of packaging and transporting an order for, say, 1000 articles will be much less than ten times the cost of dealing with an order for 100 articles.
4. A large firm will be able to employ specialist salesmen to maintain and expand its markets, and specialist buyers to ensure that it obtains good quality and low-cost supplies of materials.
5. The total advertising costs of a large firm will be much greater than those of a small firm, but its advertising cost *per unit sold* is likely to be much less than that of the small firm.

Financial economies

1. Since the large firm has more valuable assets and is better known than the small firm, lenders believe there is less risk in making a loan to a large firm. Larger firms are normally able to borrow money from banks and other financial institutions at lower rates of interest than those charged to smaller firms.
2. Larger firms are able to approach a much wider range of lenders than small firms (see Chapter 11).

Risk-bearing economies

Larger firms have more opportunities than smaller firms for spreading the risks of trading. The small firm is much more likely to have 'all its eggs in one basket'.

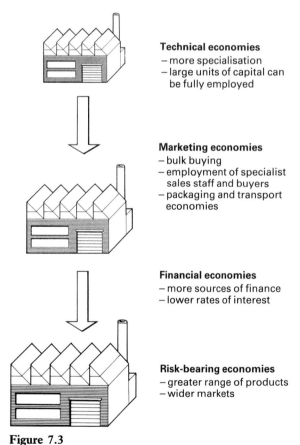

Technical economies
– more specialisation
– large units of capital can be fully employed

Marketing economies
– bulk buying
– employment of specialist sales staff and buyers
– packaging and transport economies

Financial economies
– more sources of finance
– lower rates of interest

Risk-bearing economies
– greater range of products
– wider markets

Figure 7.3
Internal economies of scale: the term 'economies of scale' refers to those advantages of larger-scale production which tend to lower a firm's average costs

1. The large firm is likely to produce a range of products so that its survival does not depend on the success of a single product. A fall in the demand for one of its products may be offset by an increase in the demand for another.
2. A small firm is likely to be dependent upon the local market or, perhaps, the national market. A large firm is likely to sell in both home and overseas markets.

Thorn EMI is a good example of a firm producing a wide range of products which it sells in both home and overseas markets. This enterprise owns and controls a large number of subsidiary companies, and employs about 70 000 people in the UK and about 20 000 overseas. Among its many activities are the renting and retailing of television sets and videos, the production and distribution of domestic electrical appliances, the production of films and recorded musical entertainment, the production of lighting equipment, and information technology and telecommunications. Some familiar names associated with this company are HMV, Ferguson, Tricity, Bendix, Kenwood, Multibroadcast and Rumbelows.

External economies of scale

External economies arise from growth in the size of the *industry*; that is, they are *external* to the firm. As an industry grows in size, certain benefits become available to all the firms in the industry. These benefits are particularly important where the industry is heavily localised, that is, concentrated in a particular region.

A supply of skilled labour

Where an industry is localised, the supply of labour in that area becomes skilled in the trades, and adapted to the working conditions, of that industry. If a firm joining the industry were to set up its factory away from the established centre of the industry, it would have to meet the costs of training people in the skills required.

Dis-integration

When an industry reaches a certain size, firms often tend to specialise in a single process or in the manufacture of a single component. When this

happens, the industry is said to have disintegrated. For example, car manufacturers *assemble* cars; they do not make every part of a complete motor car. Many of the components are purchased from specialist producers. Firms making wheels, or carburettors, or brake linings for the entire industry can produce these components on a much larger scale than any single car manufacturer. All the firms in the industry, therefore, are able to obtain components at lower cost than they could produce these articles for themselves.

Subsidiary industries

When a large industry is concentrated in a particular region, subsidiary industries establish themselves in the locality to cater for the needs of all the firms in that industry. Thus, in the area around Leicester and Northampton, where there are many footwear manufacturers, we find firms which specialise in the production of shoe-making machinery and in the maintenance and repair of this equipment.

Other examples of subsidiary industries are those which specialise in making use of the waste materials of a large industry, and those which produce containers and packaging materials specially designed to meet the requirements of firms in a major industry.

Specialised services

When a heavily localised industry has reached a certain size, it becomes worthwhile for firms to supply specialised services to that industry. Such firms may provide wholesaling services, transport services, research and information services, financial services and so on. These services will be designed to meet the particular needs of firms in a large localised industry. It would be very costly for the individual firms in the industry to supply all these services for themselves.

Local banks and insurance companies will become familiar with the needs of the firms in that industry, and offer services which are suited to their requirements. In addition, the concentration of an industry in one region will encourage local colleges to offer training courses for apprentices and other employees of firms in that industry.

7.2
Diseconomies of scale

The list of advantages of large-scale production is very impressive, but growth in the size of the firm can also create problems. For any particular industry, there seems to be an optimum size of firm, where average cost is at a minimum. When firms grow beyond the optimum size, diseconomies of scale are experienced.

Internal diseconomies of scale

The main cause of these diseconomies appears to be the increasing problems faced by management as the firm grows larger. Large firms are usually divided into several specialist departments. There are departments responsible for sales, production, stock control, accounting, buying, personnel and so on. It is not an easy task to organise and supervise the activities of several large departments and to make sure that these departments are working together as a team. Weaknesses in organisation and control can be a cause of inefficiency and hence increasing costs.

A major challenge facing the managers of large firms is to find ways of obtaining the willing cooperation of the workers. Individual workers in a labour force of several thousands may find it difficult to identify themselves with the firm; they do not feel that they are 'part of the firm'. Where management is weak and inefficient, workers may come to believe that, as far as the firm is concerned, they are little more than numbers on the wage sheet. Such a state of affairs is not likely to lead to efficient and low-cost production.

These problems can be overcome, however, because many large firms have excellent relations between managers and workers.

External diseconomies of scale

External diseconomies will affect all the firms in an industry. They can occur when the growth of an industry in a particular area reaches a stage when increasing congestion raises transport costs.

The growing concentration of an industry will lead to an increasing demand for industrial sites in the area where it is located. This, in turn, will tend to increase the price of land and the prices and rents of industrial and commercial buildings.

7.3
Why and how firms grow

Why firms grow

To reduce average cost

A most obvious and sensible reason why firms might try to grow larger is to obtain economies of scale and reduce their average costs of production.

To obtain a larger share of the market

The larger the firm, the larger its share of the market. The desire to exercise a greater control over the total market is an important reason for growth in the size of a firm. A firm which has, say, 70 per cent of the total market for a product will have far more market power (i.e. it will face weaker competition) than a firm which has only 10 per cent of the total market.

To achieve greater security

Larger firms, with their greater resources and wider range of products, are better equipped to withstand fluctuations in demand. This is an important reason for the development of firms producing several different products (i.e. multi-product firms). The total demand for a variety of products is likely to be more stable than the demand for any one of these products.

How firms grow

Firms grow in two ways, by extending the market for their existing product, or by increasing the range of their products. One way in which a firm might increase its range of products is by finding new ways of using its particular technical knowledge. Dunlop, for example, used its expertise in rubber technology to move into the markets for sports goods, footwear, upholstery materials and floor coverings. Hoover used its experience with small electric motors to move into the markets for floor polishers, spin driers and washing machines.

Figure 7.4
An example of vertical integration: the major oil companies are vertically integrated from the exploration and drilling stages to the distribution of the final product

More recently, however, the size of firms has tended to increase mainly as a result of *mergers* and *amalgamations*. The joining together of two or more firms is described as integration. There are various ways in which this integration can take place.

Vertical integration

This term describes the joining together of firms at different stages in the process of production. It may take the form of backward integration or forward integration.

Vertical integration backwards takes place when a firm takes over or merges with its suppliers. Thus, a firm making chocolate may take over a cocoa plantation, or a car manufacturer may acquire a body-building plant. A firm is likely to integrate backwards because it wishes to have a greater degree of control over the quality of its supplies and the regularity of their delivery.

Vertical integration forwards occurs when a firm takes over its market outlets. Thus, a manufacturing firm might acquire a chain of retail shops which sell its product, or an oil company may take over a number of petrol stations. Forward integration is often carried out when producers wish to improve the quality of the premises in which their goods are sold and to raise the standards of service in these premises. The major breweries have taken over many public houses and spent large sums of money on improving the accommodation and facilities. Similarly, the major oil companies have obtained control over many petrol stations and have invested heavily in schemes to modernise these outlets.

Horizontal integration

This form of integration takes place when firms producing similar products are joined together to form one organisation. The amalgamation of two or more mining companies, or the merger of firms owning chains of clothing shops, would be described as horizontal integration. There are several reasons for this type of integration:

1 Economies of scale

The scale of production of the integrated firm will be much larger than that of any of the firms before integration. The aim, of course, is to reduce average cost.

2 More market power

A merger of firms making similar products will clearly reduce the number of competitors.

3 Rationalisation

This word is used to describe the process of eliminating less efficient plants or factories, and concentrating production in the more efficient units of production. For example, suppose there are three firms, all making very similar electrical appliances. Each of the firms is working well below its full capacity, and hence producing at relatively high average cost. The integration of these firms could lead to the closing down of the least efficient factory so that the remaining factories could be worked at full capacity.

The scale of production could also be increased by reducing the number of models. If each of these three firms had been producing three different models of a particular product, the integrated firm might reduce the range from nine to, say, four or five models.

Conglomerates

Sometimes amalgamations take place between firms which do not produce similar products and which are not part of the same total production process. This type of integration is described as a conglomerate merger. The firms which join together belong to very different industries, and use different raw materials and different technical processes.

An important reason for this type of integration appears to be the desire for greater security. A conglomerate will own companies producing very different goods and, hopefully, the success of one company will tend to offset the lack of success of another company.

Although two firms may be producing very different products, there may be links between them which provide a good reason for integration. For example, a firm producing chocolates and sweets may find it advantageous to merge with a firm producing soft drinks. Economies could be obtained because they use similar raw materials (e.g. sugar) and the products are distributed through the same kinds of retail outlet (e.g. newsagents, tobacconists, grocers, supermarkets, etc.).

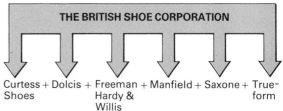

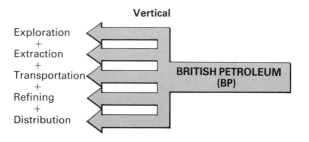

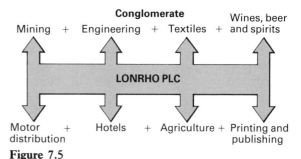

Figure 7.5
Types of integration

7.4
Multinational companies

A multinational firm is one which owns and controls enterprises in several countries. Many of the larger firms in the UK are multinational companies; Ford, Hoover, Kodak, General Motors, ICI and BP are good examples.

Some of these firms are very large indeed, and several multinational companies have annual outputs greater in value than the national outputs of many smaller countries. Multinationals account for 60 per cent of the trade in manufactured goods in the developed world. Most of them are based in the USA, but Britain, France, West Germany and Japan are also important bases for multinational companies.

These powerful organisations exert a great influence on the economies of the countries in which they operate. Decisions to invest in Country A rather than Country B, or to close a factory in Country C and expand a factory in Country D, are obvious examples of the way in which the plans of multinational companies can affect output and employment in different countries.

These companies can carry out specialisation on an international scale: a motor car manufacturer may decide to mass-produce engines in one country and gear boxes in another, and to assemble its cars in several countries, for example.

Investment decisions by multinational companies are often influenced by trade barriers. If a country places a high tariff on imported cars, a multinational company making cars may decide to set up an assembly plant inside that country in order to avoid the high cost of importing its cars.

In most of the countries in which they operate, multinational companies are usually important exporters. This is because their products have world-famous names and the companies have well-established world-wide networks of factories, agencies, distribution networks, servicing organisations and so on.

7.5
The survival of the small firm

Although there has been a fairly long-term trend towards the larger firm, there is a very large number of successful small businesses in the UK. In 1982 it was estimated that there were about 100 000 small firms in manufacturing and about 230 000 in retailing. In the 1980s there has been a considerable expansion of the small firm sector.

About 800 000 new businesses a year are set up. Many of them die, but the number of births exceeds the number of deaths. In 1987 it was estimated that there was a net increase of about 500 new businesses a week.

Today, one in ten of the workforce is self-employed and their small businesses provide a quarter of all jobs, a third of private-sector jobs and one-fifth of the country's GDP.
Source: *Economics Brief: Britain's Business*, Economist Books, 1986

Some reasons for the survival and success of small firms

In some cases, firms remain small because the proprietor may not want to take on the additional worries and responsibilities of running a larger business. There are, however, circumstances where the small firm has distinct advantages over the larger firm. Some of these circumstances are discussed below.

The size of the market

Small firms will tend to do well where the market for a particular good or service is relatively small. In such cases, firms cannot take advantage of the economies of large-scale production. There are several reasons why the markets for some goods and services may remain small:

1. There are some goods and services where people prefer to have 'something different'. People often demand some individuality in clothing, footwear and jewellery, for example. For products such as these, the market for any one design or fashion will be small, and producers cannot employ the techniques of mass production.

2. Repair work is another example of an industry where the product cannot be standardised; each job tends to be different. Hence, in trades such as the repair of property, motor cars, shoes and watches, we find a large number of small firms.

3. Personal services tend to be supplied by small firms because people prefer to deal with one person. The family doctor, the family solicitor, the local hairdresser and specialist retail shops provide examples of services where people demand individual attention.

4. Sometimes the size of the market is restricted by geographical factors. The small isolated community cannot provide a market large enough to support retail organisations such as department stores and supermarkets. This accounts for the survival of the small village store.

5. There are small markets for very expensive goods such as luxury yachts, expensive limousines and high-quality sports cars. In these cases, the market is restricted to those with very high incomes.

Specialist producers and distributors

The process of dis-integration explained earlier has enabled many small firms to prosper in manufacturing industry. Such firms supply standardised parts to large assembly plants.

Small firms also distribute the products of large firms. Television sets, washing machines and refrigerators, for example, are manufactured by large firms, but they are often installed and maintained by quite small firms.

Cooperation between small firms

It is possible for small firms to enjoy economies of scale through schemes of cooperation. They can join together in ways which enable them to obtain some of the benefits enjoyed by larger firms.

A number of small manufacturing firms may operate jointly-owned research laboratories – as in the footwear and pottery industries, for example. Many small grocery shops have forged links with wholesale organisations (e.g. Mace, VG and Spar), so that they can obtain some of the benefits of bulk buying.

Farmers have formed jointly-owned buying agencies so that they can obtain the advantages of bulk purchases of seeds, fertilisers and animal feedstuffs. Similarly, large units of capital such as combine harvesters may be collectively owned by a group of farmers.

Technical factors

In some industries, the units of capital equipment are still relatively small, so it is not possible to achieve very great technical economies of scale. The sewing machines and knitting machines used in the clothing and hosiery industries are small enough to be used economically by relatively small firms.

In some cases, technical progress has worked to the advantage of small firms, as the following quotation indicates:

The advent of microprocessors has brought with it a host of new and relatively inexpensive machines. These are easy to set up and operate, can sit comfortably on a desk top and can handle a range of common business tasks such as payrolls, stock control and word processing.
Source: *Financial Times*, 3 March 1980

Flexibility

A most important advantage of the small firm over the large organisation is its flexibility. It can adapt itself much more quickly to changes in the customers' requirements.

Government assistance

The government has several schemes which are designed to help the smaller firm. The Department of Trade and Industry has a Small Firms' Service which offers help and advice to small firms. It is also prepared to offer financial help to various local organisations which exist to help people running, or wishing to set up, small businesses. Government financial help to small firms is discussed in Chapter 15.

Measuring the size of a firm

There is no single satisfactory way of measuring the size of a firm. The most common way of measuring a firm's size is to use the *number of workers employed*. This can be misleading, however, because it underestimates the importance of very large installations such as oil refineries and chemical works which use vast amounts of expensive capital but employ relatively few workers. For this reason, statistics on the size of the firm usually include information on the *value of capital employed* by the firm.

Another way in which the relative sizes of firms can be compared is to use the *values of the outputs* of the individual firms.

The Main Points

- Economies of scale refer to those benefits of large-scale production which lead to lower average costs. These economies may arise from an increase in the size of the firm (internal economies) or from the growth in the size of the industry (external economies).

- Diseconomies of scale arise when an increase in the size of the firm (or the industry) leads to less efficient production.

■ Firms try to increase their size in order to
  - obtain economies of scale and reduce their average costs,
  - obtain a larger share of the market, and
  - reduce the risks of trading by increasing their range of products.

■ If firms making similar products join together, it is described as horizontal integration. When firms merge with, or take over, their suppliers, it is described as vertical integration backwards. If they take over market outlets, it is described as vertical integration forwards. Conglomerates are formed when firms producing quite different commodities amalgamate.

■ Small firms tend to be successful when
  - the size of the market is restricted,
  - they can act as specialist producers of parts and components for large manufacturers,
  - they distribute, and provide after-sales service on, the products of large manufacturers,
  - they cooperate to obtain economies of scale, or
  - no great technical economies of scale can be achieved.

Test Your Understanding

1. What are the missing words in the following sentences?
   (a) A firm experiences economies of scale when an increase in the scale of production leads to a fall in the .... cost of production.
   (b) If a firm engaged in weaving cloth took over a firm engaged in spinning yarn, it would be described as an example of .... integration.

2. Why is it more economical to supply breakfast cereals and detergents in large packets than in small packets?

3. A firm increases its size and as a result its output increases by 50 per cent. It finds that its total costs increase by 60 per cent. What economic term is used to describe these particular changes?

4. What is meant by the *optimum size* of a firm?

5. Which ONE of the following would be a possible reason for vertical integration by a company producing Commodity X?
   A to secure control over shops selling Commodity X
   B to take over other firms producing Commodity X so as to reduce competition
   C to acquire firms making products quite different from Commodity X in order to spread the risks of trading

6. Which TWO of the following features would be favourable to the survival of a small firm? (The features relate to situations in different industries.)
   A The product is subject to frequent changes of fashion and style.
   B Average cost falls very sharply as output increases.
   C The finished product is assembled from a large number of small standardised components.

7. A firm enjoys the following advantages:
   A It is able to place large orders for its raw materials.
   B The locality in which it is situated has an abundance of labour skilled in the type of work carried out by the firm.
   C There is a firm in the same locality which specialises in making goods from the waste materials produced by this firm.

   Which TWO of these are *external* economies of scale?

BOX 7

Integration

The following passages are adapted from an article in *The Economist*, dated 4 May 1985.

1. *The British are drinking less beer. Production fell from 41.7 million barrels in 1979 to 36.7 million barrels in 1984. The industry does not expect the production decline to be reversed.*

2. *In fact, Britain's brewers are doing well financially. Several firms owe good recent results as much to diversity as to brewing. Last year Bass derived 25 per cent of its revenues from leisure activities which include Crest Hotels, Coral Social Clubs and Pontin's Holidays. It also acquired some 80 bingo and social clubs from Thorn EMI. Guinness has bought health-care firms and a 467-shop chain of newsagents. Whitbread has bought a 20 per cent stake in TV South.*

3. *In the next three years £1.5 million or more of the brewers' capital expenditure will go in refurbishing the 47 000 brewery-owned pubs and bars. Most companies will be expanding and improving facilities for serving food as well as drink.*

Questions
1. Which of the passages above indicates that there is a great deal of vertical integration in the brewing industry? Explain your answer.
2. What policies have the brewers adopted in order to offset the effects of the decline in the demand for beer?
3. To which type of integration do the examples in the second extract belong?

CHAPTER 8

Prices and markets

8.1
The meanings of price and value

In economics the word 'value' has a particular meaning; it refers to *value in exchange*. In other words, the value of something is expressed in terms of the things for which it can be exchanged.

Money prices are really measures of exchange value – they measure what one thing is worth in terms of other things. Since nearly all goods and services have money prices, it is very easy to find out what one thing is worth in terms of another. For example, if the price of Good A is £4 and the price of Good B is £2, we know that one unit of Good A is worth two units of Good B.

Wages are the price of labour. If the price of a person's labour is £4 per hour, then the exchange value of one hour of that labour is the variety of goods and services which £4 will buy.

The prices of most of the things we buy are determined by *market forces* – the forces of supply and demand. Supply refers to the willingness and ability of people to offer goods for sale, and demand describes the willingness and ability of people to buy them.

Before we look more closely at the way in which these market forces work, it is necessary to know something about markets.

8.2
Types of market

Old and new markets

The oldest form of market – the traditional market – is a place where buyers meet sellers to do business with one another. Most of our towns still have a market square or market hall where buying and selling take place in a manner which has not changed for centuries.

In the modern world, however, a market can take many forms. A market is best defined as any arrangement which enables buyers and sellers to transact business in such a way that prices can be established and exchanges can take place. The buyers and sellers do not have to meet face to face. A telephone network can provide an effective link between people wishing to buy and sell. The 'small ads' column in the local newspaper is another effective means of putting buyers and sellers in touch with one another.

In the foreign exchange market, dealers buy and sell foreign currencies. These dealers do not meet one another – in many cases they are separated by thousands of miles. Modern systems of communication enable them to know exactly what is happening to the prices of foreign currencies in different parts of the world. Dealers in London can do business with dealers in New York just as effectively as if they were in the same room.

Figure 8.1
Markets

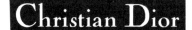

There are world-wide markets for the products of many firms

A traditional market

A market in foreign currencies

Local newspapers help to provide local markets in labour, houses, cars, etc.

▶ GOODS FOR SALE

ABSOLUTE bargains, dishwasher, £90; electric typewriter, £45; Open University books/tapes, complete A101/T101, £30 each. — Tel. ██ ██. f 143350

A CALL on Impress Crafts, High Street, ████ (near Post Office), will reward those seeking that unusual quality gift. — Tel. ██. z 148305

ALKO saw bench, bargain, £100. — Tel. ████████ (anytime). f 102045

A MATCHING cabin style bed, wardrobe and chest of drawers in immaculate condition, £100 ono. — Tel. ████. 133960

ANTIQUE, furniture, mahogany, pine etc., bought and sold, top quality three piece suites on

▶ MOTOR MART

A BARGAIN!! at Leyton, saloons from £1,495, hatchbacks, Minis, come and view, no obligation, 388 ██████. — Tel. ██ (mobile) (T) f 101353

ACCLAIM CD auto, 1983, 35,000 miles only, full history, long MOT, immaculate, £3,500. Private sale but PX possible. — Tel. ██████ after 6pm. 104617

ALLEGRO 1300 DL, 1978, blue, low mileage, gold seal engine, no rust, long MOT and tax. — Tel. ██████ evenings. p 148972

ALPINE 5-door hatchback, 1978, 1500cc, long MOT, taxed, radio, reliable, £395. — Tel. ██. 940466

A SIERRA, 1984, A reg, 2.0GL, automatic, five door, metallic blue,

▶ SITUATIONS VACANT

AAAA. Earn cash, £25 to £50 in a couple of hours, selling perfume, very simple, anybody can do it, five vacancies left — Tel. ██. 151571

A BAR person wanted for part-time evenings and weekends. — Apply The Retreat, Retreat Way, ██████. z 137565

A BASE for your job search, friendly assistance, experienced temporaries always required, Office Services Bureau, Old Church Road, ██████ (near Post Office). — Tel. ██. p 107082

A BASE for your job search, friendly assistance, experienced temporaries always required. Office Services Bureau, Old Church Road, Chingford (near post office). — Tel. ██. p 133901

ACCOUNTANT or experienced book-keeper wanted able to prepare books up to trial balance. — Tel. ██████. 102051

ACCOUNTANTS assistant £9,000! liaise at all levels! expanding co! — Tel. HMS Rec Cons ██████. 103724

ACCOUNT book-keeper for bank reconciliation, E17, £7,000 plus. — b

▶ PROPERTY FOR SALE

ACACIA ROAD, ██████, modernised and very well maintained two bedroomed mid terreced house, keenly priced at £62,500, for quick sale, must be seen. — Tel. ██. 147175

ARE you looking for a secure investment with good capital growth, or first time purchaser wanting to break into the porperty market? Look no further. Expanding Essex market town, only 55 mins Liverpool Street station, 25 mins M11, 20 mins Stansted, large flats just released, ready Christmas, from £51,250. — Tel. ██████. z 102170

BRAND new house by Berkley Homes, ██████, four bedrooms, two bathrooms, three reception, £205,000. — Tel. ██████. z 104423

BUCKHURST HILL, spacious semi-detached Victorian cottage, central heating, good condition throughout, three bedrooms, two receptions, five minutes Central Line, shops and schools, £89,950. — Tel. ██████. x 101607

Local, national and international markets

In earlier times most markets were local. People provided for most of their wants by their own efforts, and very few of the things they needed were purchased from other people. Primitive means of transport made it difficult or impossible to produce goods for sale over a wide area.

Improvements in transport and communications and the use of advertising made it possible to create national markets for many goods. Most of the goods we buy are now marketed throughout the UK.

These same developments have also led to the creation of world markets. In the UK, for example, we are almost as familiar with the names of leading American, Japanese, West German, French and Italian manufacturers as we are with the leading British firms. Primary products such as rubber, tin, oil, wheat, sugar, coffee and tea have been sold on world markets for many years. And we should not overlook the fact that many services such as banking and insurance services are bought and sold on world markets.

8.3
Demand

In the early chapters of this book, quite a lot has been said about people's *wants*. We now turn to a rather different idea, namely, people's *demands* for goods and services.

In economics, the word 'demand' refers to a desire for a good which is backed up by the willingness and ability to pay the price of that good or service. The important point is that firms will only continue to supply goods and services if they can sell them at prices which cover their costs. In other words, there will be a supply of a good or service only if there is a *demand* for it – firms will not supply goods and services simply because people *want* them.

Demand is defined as the quantity demanded at any given price over some given period of time. For example, we could say that the demand for Good X at a price of £5 is 1000 units per week.

How changes in price affect demand

Experience shows that, with very few exceptions, the quantity demanded of a good increases as the price decreases. This fact is normally stated in the form of a 'law' of demand: *'Other things being equal, more will be demanded at lower prices than at higher prices.'*

The expression 'other things being equal' is a very important part of this statement. We can say with some certainty that more of a good will be demanded when its price falls *if* (and only if) we assume that other things do not change. If, when the price of a good falls, consumers' incomes, or consumers' tastes, or the prices of other goods are also changing, the effects of the fall in price become very uncertain.

For example, the effect of a fall in the price of beef on the quantity demanded could not be forecast if falls in the prices of pork and lamb were taking place at the same time. If, however, the prices of other types of meat were not expected to change, we could say with some certainty that more beef would be demanded at the lower price.

It is important to remember that whenever a statement is made about the effect of a change in price on the quantity demanded, we are always assuming that other things do not change. Figure 8.2 shows how a change in the price of a commodity affects the quantity demanded if other things do *not* change. The table on the right of Figure 8.2 shows how much will be demanded at different prices; it is described as a *demand schedule*. The graph on the left of Figure 8.2 represents a *demand curve*. It is obtained by plotting the figures in the demand schedule.

The shape of the demand curve

Why do demand curves slope downwards from left to right? Why do people buy more of a good when its price falls and less when its price rises? There are several ways of explaining the shape of a demand curve. We shall consider a fairly simple and straightforward explanation which deals with two effects of a change in price.

1. If the price of a good falls while consumers' incomes and the prices of other goods remain unchanged, consumers will be better off. They

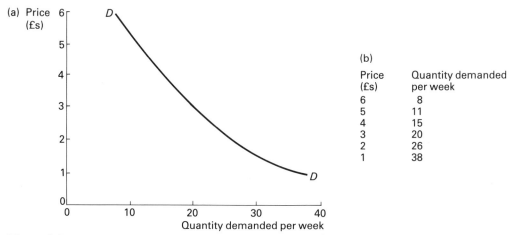

Figure 8.2
(a) Demand curve   (b) Demand schedule

can now buy more of this good without having to buy less of the other goods.

2. When we make purchases we usually have to choose from a number of very similar products. Most goods have closely competing substitutes. When the price of a commodity falls, therefore, its price will become relatively more attractive compared with the prices of its substitutes. More of the commodity will be demanded as consumers switch some of their purchases away from the substitutes, which are now *relatively* dearer. For example, if the price of butter falls, many people will buy more butter and less margarine. If the price of apples falls, many people will buy more apples and less of other fruits such as pears.

A rise in the price of a commodity will have opposite effects to those described above.

8.4
Supply

Supply does *not* mean the existing stock of a good; it refers to the amounts which traders are prepared to offer for sale.

Supply is defined as the quantity of a commodity which is supplied at any given price over some given period of time. For example, we could say that at a price of £5 per unit, 1000 units of Commodity X will be supplied each week.

The amounts which firms are prepared to supply will depend upon the prices which people are prepared to pay. When farmers consider market prices to be too low, they will sometimes plough vegetables back into the ground or dump fruit crops, rather than take these products to the market (see Figure 8.3). In such cases, the vegetables and fruit were produced, but they were not part of the *supply* of these things because they were not offered for sale.

Figure 8.3
Peaches being dumped into a giant pit: since these peaches were not offered for sale, they did not form part of the supply of peaches

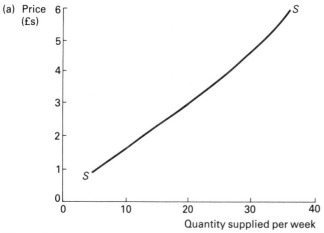

Figure 8.4
(a) Supply curve   (b) Supply schedule

Another of the 'laws' of economics states, '*More will be supplied at higher prices than at lower prices.*' This is illustrated in Figure 8.4. The table on the right of Figure 8.4 is described as a *supply schedule*; it shows the quantities which will be supplied at different prices. The graph on the left of Figure 8.4 is a *supply curve*, which is obtained by plotting the figures in the supply schedule.

The shape of the supply curve

The shape of the supply curve is based on the idea that firms will always try to earn the maximum profit. This assumption helps us to understand why supply curves slope upwards from left to right, that is, why firms are prepared to supply more at higher prices.

If the demand for a commodity increases, it will become more scarce and its price will rise. This will make it more profitable to produce. The amount supplied will increase, because the increased profitability will encourage firms to increase production. The higher prices and greater profits will also tempt more firms to enter the industry.

A fall in the demand for a product will tend to lower its price. The fall in demand will mean that, at the existing price, there will be excess supplies in the market. Firms will be obliged to lower the price in order to dispose of their goods. At the lower price, production will be less profitable and

firms will reduce their outputs; there will be a reduction in supply. The fall in price may also force some less efficient firms to leave the industry.

8.5
The market price

If we bring together the supply and demand curves on to one diagram, we find that they intersect at only one price. This is the *market* or *equilibrium price*. Only at this price is the quantity demanded equal to the quantity supplied. Figure 8.5 brings together the demand curve of Figure 8.2 and the supply curve of Figure 8.4. It shows that, under the existing conditions of supply and demand, the equilibrium price will be £3.

This equilibrium or market price is arrived at by a gradual process. If trading takes place at prices other than the market price, there will be either a shortage or a surplus, which will cause the price to move until it settles at the equilibrium level. We can use Figure 8.5 to demonstrate the process.

Suppose trading in the market begins at a price of £4. This price will soon change, because firms will find themselves with unsold stocks. At a price of £4, the quantity supplied is much greater than the quantity demanded, so the price will be forced downwards.

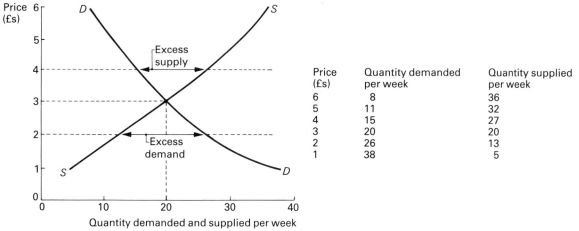

Figure 8.5

Now suppose trading begins at a price of £2. At this price, the quantity demanded greatly exceeds the quantity supplied. There will be a shortage, which will cause the price to be bid upwards.

Only at the price of £3 is the quantity demanded equal to the quantity supplied. At this price, there is no shortage and no surplus in the market. Therefore, £3 is the equilibrium price.

8.6
Changes in demand

A demand curve describes what happens to the quantity demanded when the price changes and other things do not change. In the real world, however, these 'other things' do change. They are described as the conditions of demand. When these conditions change, the whole demand curve moves.

Students beginning the study of supply and demand are often puzzled by the term 'changes in demand'. Unfortunately, this term is often used to describe both
– a movement *along* the demand curve, and
– a movement *of* the demand curve.

In fact, these two movements have very different causes. Table 8.1 and Figure 8.6 (over the page) should help to remove any misunderstanding about these two different movements.

A movement along the demand curve

In Table 8.1, the first two columns represent a normal demand schedule, and this appears as the demand curve *DD* in Figure 8.6(a). This curve can be used to read off the quantities demanded when the price changes. For example, a fall in price from £5 to £4 leads to an increase in quantity demanded from 120 units to 150 units (see Table 8.1). This is described as an *increase in the quantity demanded* or an *extension of demand*. Similarly, a rise in price from £4 to £5 leads to a *decrease in the quantity demanded* or a *contraction of demand* from 150 units to 120 units. (These movements assume that nothing else changes when the price of the product changes.)

A movement of the demand curve

An entirely different situation is demonstrated in Figure 8.6(b), which shows the effects of a *change in demand*.

The third column in Table 8.1 shows the effects of an increase in demand – more is now demanded at each and every price. This increase in demand is portrayed in Figure 8.6(b) as a movement of the whole demand curve to the right.

DD is the original demand curve, and D_1D_1 is the position of the demand curve after the increase in demand. At any given price, more is demanded. For example, whereas a quantity of 150 units was previously demanded at a price of

Table 8.1

Price (£s)	Quantity demanded per week	Quantity demanded per week after increase in demand
10	20	50
9	30	70
8	50	90
7	70	110
6	90	140
5	120	170
4	150	220
3	190	270
2	240	340

Figure 8.6

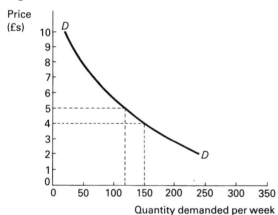

(a) A change in price causes a change in the quantity demanded

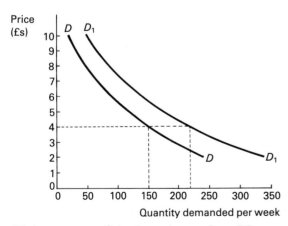

(b) A movement of the demand curve from *DD* to *D₁D₁* represents an increase in demand; a movement from *D₁D₁* to *DD* represents a fall in demand

£4, the quantity demanded at that price after the increase in demand is 220 units (see Table 8.1).

Figure 8.6 can be also used to show the effects of a fall in demand. All we need to do is to assume that D_1D_1 now represents the original demand curve. A fall in demand means that less is demanded at each and every price, so the demand curve moves to *DD*.

1. *An increase in demand means that the demand curve moves to the right, causing more to be demanded at each price.*
2. *A fall in demand means that the demand curve moves to the left, causing less to be demanded at each price.*

Causes of movements of the demand curve

1 Changes in income

An increase in real income will, in most cases, increase the demand for goods and services; a fall in income will reduce the demand for most goods and services. Strictly speaking, it is changes in disposable income which affect demand. This means that changes in income tax and social security benefits will have important effects on demand and change the position of demand curves.

There are some circumstances, however, where an increase in real income might cause the demand for a good or service to fall. Some commodities are described as *inferior goods* because an increase in real income causes people to buy less of them. Which goods happen to be 'inferior' depends upon the existing standard of living. In Western Europe and North America, for example, there has been a serious decline in the demand for public transport as incomes have risen and more people have been able to afford motor cars. In the same regions, the demand for bread has been falling for many years. As standards of living have risen, bread has become a much smaller part of people's diet. When real incomes were much lower, bread represented a major part of the food consumed by many people.

An increase in real income will reduce the demands for inferior goods and move their demand curves to the left.

2 Changes in the prices of other goods

Substitutes

As pointed out earlier, many goods have close substitutes. A change in the price of one of these goods will affect the demands for the substitutes. Different brands of margarine are close substitutes for one another. An increase in the price of one brand will undoubtedly lead to an increase in the demand for the others. Similarly, a fall in the price of one brand of paint is likely to reduce the demands for other brands of paint.

Complementary goods

These are goods in joint demand, where the use of one good requires the use of another. Obvious examples are cameras and films, cars and petrol, and cassette players and tapes. In these cases, the demand for one of the goods will be affected by changes in the price of its complement. An increase in the price of gas will affect the demands for gas cookers and gas fires, and if cameras became much cheaper, there would be an increased demand for films.

3 Changes in taste and fashion

The demands for some products are subject to large and frequent changes in demand. This is especially true of those goods and services which are affected by changes in taste and fashion. The clothing, footwear and entertainment industries are good examples. In recent years, publicity about dangers to health has had important effects on the demands for certain foods. Those which have received bad publicity have experienced falling demands; those which have received favourable publicity have experienced increased demands.

4 Advertising

The aim of most advertising is to move the demand curve for the advertised product to the right. If a successful advertising campaign is carried out on behalf of a good which has a number of close substitutes (e.g. a particular brand of instant coffee), it may also have the effect of moving the demand curves for the competing products to the left.

5 Hire purchase

Many durable consumer goods are bought on hire purchase. The demand for such goods will be seriously affected if there are changes in the terms on which hire-purchase facilities are available. If they are made easier (by means of smaller deposits and longer periods for repayment), the demand curves for many goods will move to the right. The opposite will happen when hire-purchase terms are made less favourable. The demands for cars, motor cycles, electrical appliances and furniture are very much influenced by changes in hire-purchase terms.

The effects of changes in demand

We can look at the effects of changes in demand by assuming that the conditions of supply do not change. For this purpose we can make use of Figure 8.7, which can be used to show the effects of an increase in demand and of a decrease in demand.

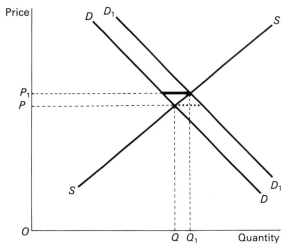

Figure 8.7
An *increase* in demand raises the price and increases the quantity supplied. A *fall* in demand lowers the price and reduces the quantity supplied

1 An increase in demand

Assume that the original demand curve in Figure 8.7 is *DD*, so that the equilibrium price is *OP*, and a quantity *OQ* is demanded and supplied. An increase in demand moves the demand curve to D_1D_1. The immediate effect is to cause a shortage at the existing price, because the quantity demanded at price OP is now greater than the quantity supplied. This shortage, which is shown by the dotted line, will force the price upwards. As the price rises, more will be supplied, until a new equilibrium price of OP_1 is arrived at. At this price, the quantity demanded (OQ_1) is equal to the quantity supplied (OQ_1).

Other things being equal, an increase in demand will raise the price and increase the quantity supplied.

2 A decrease in demand

In this case, we assume that the original demand curve is D_1D_1, so that the equilibrium price is OP_1 and a quantity OQ_1 is demanded and supplied. A fall in demand now moves the demand curve to DD. The immediate effect of this change is to cause a surplus at the existing price, because the quantity demanded at price OP_1 is now less than the quantity supplied. This surplus, which is equal to the heavier section of the price line, will force the price downwards. As the price falls, the quantity supplied will decrease until a new equilibrium price of OP is established. At this price, the quantity demanded (OQ) is equal to the quantity supplied (OQ).

Other things being equal, a fall in demand will lower the price and reduce the quantity supplied.

8.7
Changes in supply

We can use the same kind of reasoning as we used to explain the effects of changes in demand, to deal with changes in supply.

Movements *along* the supply curve are caused by changes in the price of the product when other things do not change. These changes in the quantity supplied are described as *extensions* or *contractions of supply*.

Movements *of* the supply curve are caused by changes in the conditions of supply. Movements of the supply curve represent *increases* or *decreases in supply*.

These two kinds of changes are illustrated in Figure 8.8.

Figure 8.8

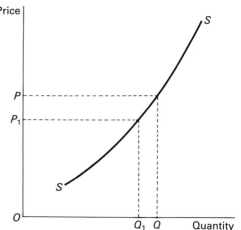

(a) A change in price causes a change in the quantity supplied

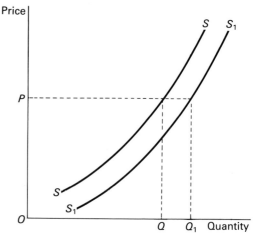

(b) A movement of the supply curve from SS to S_1S_1 represents an increase in supply; a movement from S_1S_1 to SS represents a fall in supply

A movement along the supply curve

Figure 8.8(a) shows the effect of a change in the price of the product when other things do not change. An increase in price from OP_1 to OP will cause the quantity supplied to increase from OQ_1 to OQ (i.e. there will be an extension of supply). A fall in price from OP to OP_1 will cause the quantity supplied to fall from OQ to OQ_1 (i.e. there will be a contraction of supply).

A movement of the supply curve

Figure 8.8(b) shows the effects of a change in the conditions of supply. This diagram can be used to demonstrate the effects of an increase or a decrease in supply. If we assume that SS is the original supply curve, a movement to S_1S_1 represents an *increase in supply* because more is now supplied at each and every price. If we assume that S_1S_1 is the original supply curve, a movement to SS represents a *fall in supply*, because less is now supplied at each and every price.

Causes of movements of the supply curve

The changes which cause the supply curve to move must be changes which affect the costs of production. If firms are prepared to supply more at the existing price, some changes must have taken place which have enabled them to produce at lower cost. Alternatively, we can say that firms are now prepared to supply any given quantity at a lower price. Similarly, a fall in supply means that costs of production have increased, because firms now require a higher price in order to persuade them to supply any given quantity.

The more likely causes of movements of the supply curve are set out below.

1 Changes in the prices of the factors of production

The prices paid for labour, land and capital are clearly costs to the firms which employ these factors. If other things do not change, increases or decreases in the prices of the factors of production will affect the firms' costs and cause the supply curve to move. For example, if wage rates increase and there is no increase in productivity, production costs will increase and the supply curve will move to the left. A fall in the prices of raw materials will reduce costs and move the supply curve to the right.

2 Technical progress and productivity

Changes in the techniques of production will affect the costs of production. The use of more efficient machinery, better organisation of work and the introduction of new technology (e.g. robots) will tend to increase productivity and lower the costs of production. If the productivity of labour rises faster than the wage rates, labour costs will fall.

Other things being equal, improvements in productivity will move the supply curve to the right.

3 Weather conditions

The outputs of farmers are very much influenced by variations in the weather. Extremely favourable weather conditions will lead to bumper crops, and unfavourable weather will have the opposite effect. Variations in weather conditions will have an important effect on a farmer's costs of production. If good weather increases the number of tonnes of barley yielded by one hectare of land, the cost of producing each tonne will be reduced. The increased output is a gift of nature and has not involved the farmer in any extra costs, as the costs of ploughing, harrowing, seeding and fertilising the land are the same whether it yields a bumper crop or a poor crop. Favourable weather will move the supply curves for agricultural products to the right; unfavourable weather will move them to the left.

4 Taxes and subsidies

The costs of bringing goods to the market can be changed by imposing taxes on them or by granting subsidies to producers.

The placing of a tax, such as VAT, on a good or service has the same effect as an increase in the costs of production: it moves the supply curve to the left.

Subsidies are grants paid by the government to suppliers. They may take the form of a lump sum payment or, more likely, a payment of so much per unit (for example, £5 per tonne or £1 per gallon). A subsidy has exactly the same effect as a reduction in the costs of production: it moves the supply curve to the right.

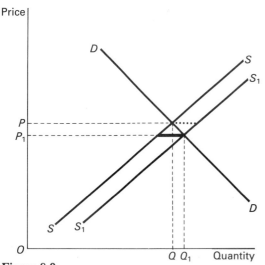

Figure 8.9

An *increase* in supply lowers the price and increases the quantity demanded. A *fall* in supply raises the price and reduces the quantity demanded

The effects of a change in supply

The effects of a movement of the supply curve are illustrated in Figure 8.9.

1 An increase in supply

Assume that the original supply curve is SS. The equilibrium price is OP and the quantity demanded and supplied is OQ. Now supply increases, and the supply curve moves to S_1S_1. The immediate effect is to cause a surplus at the existing price. This surplus, which is shown by the dotted line, will force the price downwards. As the price falls, the quantity demanded increases until a new equilibrium price of OP_1 is established. At the price OP_1, the quantity demanded is again equal to the quantity supplied.

Other things being equal, an increase in supply will lower the price and increase the quantity demanded.

2 A reduction in supply

Now assume that the original supply curve is S_1S_1. The equilibrium price is OP_1 and the quantity demanded and supplied is OQ_1. Now supply falls, and the supply curve moves to SS. The immediate effect is to cause a shortage at the existing price. This shortage, which is shown by the heavier section of the price line, will cause the price to be bid upwards. As the price rises, the

quantity demanded falls until a new equilibrium price of OP is arrived at. At this price, the quantity demanded is equal to the quantity supplied.

Other things being equal, a fall in supply will increase the price and reduce the quantity demanded.

Demand and supply – some important relationships

1 Competitive demand

Goods which are close substitutes for one another are said to be in competitive demand. The different brands of coffee, tea, butter, margarine and detergents which are displayed on the shelves in the supermarket are in competitive demand. One brand of detergent is a close substitute for another brand, and the same is true of the other products mentioned.

Another good example of competitive demand is found in the market for domestic heating. Gas, electricity, oil and coal all compete strongly in this market. The main competitors, however, are gas and electricity. A change in the price of one of these sources of energy will have important effects on the demand for the other. For example, an increase in the costs of producing gas will raise its price. The quantity of gas demanded will fall, and there will be an increase in the demand for electricity.

2 Joint demand

Goods are said to be in joint demand when the use of one good requires the use of the other. Obvious examples are cameras and films, record players and records, and cars and petrol. As mentioned earlier in the chapter, these goods are usually described as *complementary goods*.

When two goods are in joint demand, an increase in the price of one good will reduce the demand for the other good. For example, an increase in the price of video recorders will reduce the demand for tapes. Similarly, a reduction in the price of one good will increase the demand for the complementary good. A fall in the price of electric fires will tend to increase the demand for electricity.

Figure 8.10
Examples of goods in competitive demand

Figure 8.11
Examples of goods in joint demand (complementary goods)

Figure 8.12
A problem of joint supply: these transporters will have to make their return journey without a paying load

3 Joint supply

When goods are in joint supply, the production of one of the goods automatically creates a supply of the other good. For example, it is not possible to produce mutton without producing sheepskins, and beef cannot be produced without creating a supply of hides.

Problems arise when the demand for *one* of the goods in joint supply increases. For example, lead and zinc are found in the same ore. An increased demand for lead will cause more of it to be produced. But because more lead is being produced, more zinc is also being produced, even though the demand for zinc has not changed. The increased supply of zinc will cause its price to fall.

Another interesting example of joint supply occurs in the transport industry. An outward journey cannot be supplied without supplying an inward journey. This means that, on many return journeys, vehicles are running empty. A petrol tanker will almost certainly return empty to the oil refinery, and lorries which have carried coal will return empty to the pits. 'Empty running' raises the costs of transporting goods and people. The transport charges for the outward journey must cover the costs of any return journey which does not have a paying load.

8.9
Demand and supply – some real examples

1 Non-market prices

Holding down food prices during an emergency

In times of a severe shortage, for example in wartime, the government will fix the prices of essentials, such as certain foodstuffs, at levels which the great majority of the population can afford to pay. It does this because, owing to the shortage, the free market price of the goods would be so high that many people would not be able to buy the goods. However, fixing prices below the true market or equilibrium prices can cause problems, as Figure 8.13 demonstrates.

The true market price for the commodity in Figure 8.13 is OP, but the government makes an order fixing the price at OP_1. Unfortunately, at the price OP_1, the quantity demanded (OQ_2) is greater than the quantity supplied (OQ_1). People are willing and able to buy more than is being supplied.

Unless some further action is taken, there will be a situation of 'first come, first served'. There will be queues and waiting lists, and some people will be left without any supplies of this good. In these circumstances, the government will be obliged to introduce some form of rationing.

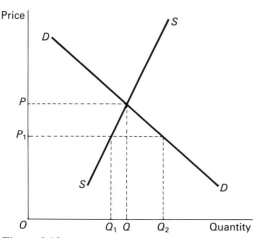

Figure 8.13
The government fixes the maximum price at OP_1, causing a shortage equal to Q_1Q_2

Figure 8.14
The government guarantees farmers a price of OP_1, causing a surplus equal to Q_1Q_2

Everyone will receive coupons which entitle them to a certain amount of the good. In most cases, however, the amounts they receive will be much less than they would like to buy, and can afford to buy, at the price set by the government.

Offering farmers a guaranteed price higher than the free market price

In the European Economic Community (EEC) and in many other parts of the world, governments guarantee minimum prices for certain agricultural products. These guaranteed prices are often higher than the prices the farmers would receive if they had to sell the products on a free market. When this is the case, the government has to deal with the problem of surpluses. Figure 8.14 shows how these surpluses are created.

In Figure 8.14, the free market price of the product (say, wheat), is OP, but the government guarantees that farmers will receive a minimum price of OP_1. At this guaranteed price, however, farmers supply more than the quantity demanded. There is a surplus equal to Q_1Q_2. At the price OP_1, households and firms will buy a quantity equal to OQ_1. The excess supply, equal to Q_1Q_2, will be purchased by the government and stored in granaries. It may hold these stocks in the hope of releasing them if there is a shortage in the near future, or it may sell them in overseas markets, most probably at a loss.

2 A fixed supply – Cup Final tickets

This is another example of price fixing, but in this case the price is not fixed by the government. The supply of Cup Final tickets is strictly limited to the capacity of Wembley Stadium. The supply

Figure 8.15
Fixing the price for Cup Final tickets below the market price causes an annual problem of unsatisfied demand

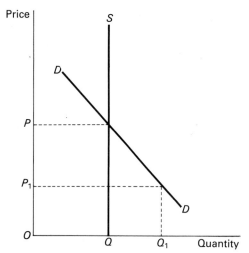

Figure 8.16
The number of tickets demanded at the fixed price
(OP_1) is greatly in excess of the capacity of the
stadium (OQ)

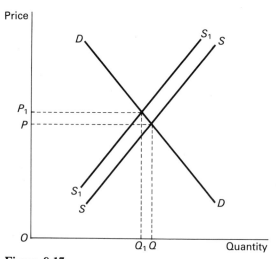

Figure 8.17
A *tax* moves the supply curve to the left (from SS to
S_1S_1). A *subsidy* moves the curve to the right (from
S_1S_1 to SS)

curve, therefore, will be a vertical line because the
supply of seats cannot change, no matter what
happens to the price. The price of tickets, which
is fixed by the Football Association, is held well
below the true market price. Figure 8.16 shows
how this creates an annual problem for the FA.

In Figure 8.16, the true market price of tickets
is OP, where the quantity demanded is equal to
the quantity supplied (OQ). The price fixed by the
FA is OP_1 and at this price the quantity
demanded (OQ_1) greatly exceeds the number of
tickets available. There is a shortage equal to QQ_1.
The FA is obliged to introduce some form of
rationing which means, of course, that there are
many thousands of disappointed football fans.

3 Taxes and subsidies

A government is able to influence market prices
by means of taxes and subsidies. In the UK, the
most familiar of the taxes on goods and services
is VAT, but taxes in the form of customs and
excise duties are also levied on many goods. The
effect of these taxes is to increase the cost of
bringing the goods to the consumer; they
represent an increase in the costs of production.
Taxes on goods and services, therefore, move the
supply curves to the left.

Subsidies have exactly the opposite effect. They
have the effect of reducing the costs of bringing
goods to the consumer, and move the supply
curves to the right.

Figure 8.17 can be used to show the effect of
both taxes and subsidies.

The effect of placing a tax on a commodity

Assume that SS in Figure 8.17 is the original
supply curve, so that the equilibrium price is OP
and the quantity demanded and supplied is OQ.
When a tax is placed on the commodity, the
supply curve moves to S_1S_1. The effect of the tax,
therefore, is to raise the price from OP to OP_1
and to reduce the quantity demanded from OQ to
OQ_1.

The effect of a subsidy

Now assume that S_1S_1 is the original supply
curve, so that the equilibrium price is OP_1 and the
quantity demanded and supplied is OQ_1. When
a subsidy is granted to the producers of this
commodity, the supply curve moves to SS. This
has the effect of reducing the price from OP_1 to
OP, causing the quantity demanded to increase
from OQ_1 to OQ.

The Main Points

- Markets are arrangements which enable buyers and sellers to transact business with one another. They can take many forms, and range in size from the traditional local markets to world-wide markets.

- Market prices are determined by the forces of supply and demand.

- Demand refers to effective demand – desire that is backed up by the ability to pay the price. Supply refers to the goods and services which are offered for sale.

- Demand curves show the quantities demanded at different prices – they slope downwards from left to right. Supply curves show the quantities offered for sale at different prices – they slope upwards from left to right. Demand and supply curves are drawn on the assumption that price is the only thing which changes.

- Only at the equilibrium price is the quantity demanded equal to the quantity supplied.

- An increase in demand
  - means that more is demanded at each price,
  - moves the demand curve to the right, and
  - causes price to increase and the quantity supplied to increase.

  A fall in demand has the opposite effects.

- An increase in supply
  - means that more is supplied at each price,
  - moves the supply curve to the right, and
  - causes the price to fall and the quantity demanded to increase.

  A fall in supply has the opposite effects.

- If the market price is above the equilibrium price, there will be a surplus in the market. If it is below the equilibrium price, there will be a shortage in the market.

Test Your Understanding

1. What name is given to an arrangement which enables buyers and sellers to do business with one another?

2. Give *two* reasons why people will tend to buy more of a good when its price falls.

3. 'With so many poor people living in the area, there is bound to be a great demand for all kinds of consumer goods.' Is this a sensible statement? Explain your answer.

4. Tennis rackets and tennis balls are purchased together. Of what kind of demand is this an example?

5. Figure 8.18 shows the demand for beef.

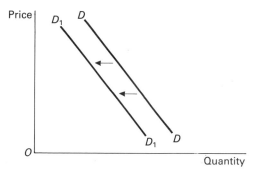

Figure 8.18

Which ONE of the following is likely to cause the movement of the demand curve from *DD* to D_1D_1, as shown in the diagram?

A a fall in the price of beef
B an increase in the prices of pork and lamb
C a fall in consumers' incomes
D a fall in the supply of beef

6. Figure 8.19 shows the supply of television sets.

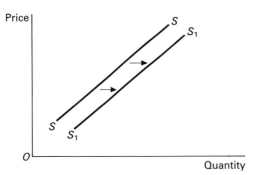

Figure 8.19

Which ONE of the following is likely to cause the movement of the supply curve from SS to S_1S_1, as shown in the diagram?

A an increase in the prices of the materials used to make television sets

B an increase in VAT

C a fall in the price of television sets

D an increase in the productivity of the factories making television sets

7. The graph in Figure 8.20 is taken from an article on house prices which appeared in *The Economist* on 18 July 1987.

Figure 8.20
Ratio of house prices to earnings

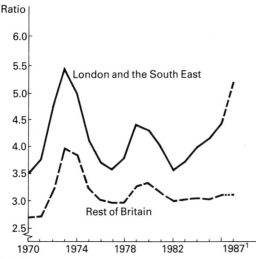

[1] Estimate
Sources: *The Economist*, 18 July 1987; Bank of England; Halifax Building Society

It shows the average cost of a house in terms of what people earn in one year. In 1987, for example, the average price of a house in London and the South East was rather more than five times the average annual earnings.

Some of the points made in the article are summarised below:

– Compared with the situation a few years ago, house-buyers can obtain mortgages more easily and can borrow larger sums of money.

– An increasing number of houses and flats are being bought jointly by young single people who, individually, could not afford to buy them.

– The supply of houses in the South East is limited by the Green Belt.

– People in London, on average, take loans for house purchase equal to more than three times their annual incomes, whereas northerners, on average, borrow just over twice their annual incomes.

(a) What is a mortgage?

(b) What determines the size of the mortgage which a building society or bank will grant to a house-buyer?

(c) What is a 'green belt', and why should it limit the supply of houses in a particular region?

(d) Which of the points listed above is likely to have the greatest effect on the demand for houses? Explain your answer.

8. The table below shows the demand and supply schedules for a particular commodity.

Price (£s)	Quantity demanded per week (units)	Quantity supplied per week (units)
10	20	80
9	25	70
8	30	60
7	35	50
6	40	40
5	45	30
4	50	20

(a) Plot the supply and demand curves on a sheet of graph paper.

(b) Draw horizontal and vertical lines to show the equilibrium price and the quantity demanded and supplied at this price.

(c) What is the total revenue at the equilibrium price?

Now assume demand doubles at all prices, with the supply remaining unchanged.

(d) Plot the new demand curve.

(e) What is the new equilibrium price?

(f) What is the quantity demanded and supplied at this price?

BOX 8
A full house, or maximum receipts?

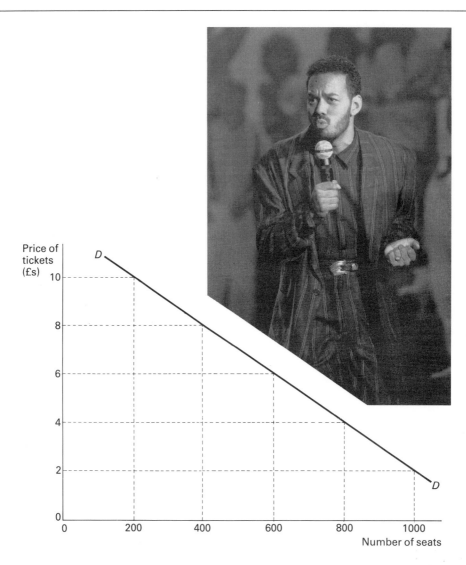

A concert hall has a seating capacity of 800 seats. The graph shows the estimated demand for tickets when a popular singer is booked to give a performance in the hall. The organisers of the concert will choose the price for the tickets from those shown on the graph.

Questions
1. What is the shape and position of the supply curve?
2. What is the equilibrium price for the tickets?
3. If the organisers of the concert wish to obtain the maximum possible revenue, what price should they charge for the tickets? Explain your answers.

CHAPTER 9

Elasticity of demand and elasticity of supply

9.1 Elasticity of demand
9.2 Why is demand elastic for some commodities but inelastic for others?
9.3 Elasticity of supply
9.4 Why is supply elastic for some commodities but inelastic for others?

9.1
Elasticity of demand

All firms know that they will sell more goods if they lower their prices, and that they are likely to sell less if they raise their prices. What these firms would like to know, however, is how any change in price will affect their total revenue (i.e. total receipts). Will cutting prices, and therefore increasing the amount sold, increase or decrease their total revenue? Will raising prices, and therefore reducing the amount sold, increase or decrease their total revenue? The answers to these questions depend on the way in which the quantity sold varies when the price changes. Whether total revenue will increase or decrease depends upon the *elasticity of demand*.

The meaning of elasticity of demand

Elasticity of demand describes the responsiveness of the quantity demanded to a change in price:
- If a small change in price causes a relatively large change in the quantity demanded, we say that demand is *elastic*.
- If a small change in price causes a relatively small change in the quantity demanded, we say that demand is *inelastic*.

Elasticity of demand can be measured by making use of the following formula:

Elasticity of demand

$$= \frac{\text{Percentage change in the quantity demanded}}{\text{Percentage change in the price}}$$

1 When demand is elastic

Demand is elastic when the percentage change in the quantity demanded is greater than the percentage change in the price, i.e. when

$$\frac{\text{Percentage change in the quantity demanded}}{\text{Percentage change in the price}} > 1$$

Example
Figure 9.1 shows a situation where a fall in price from 20p to 18p causes the quantity demanded to increase from 100 units to 150 units.

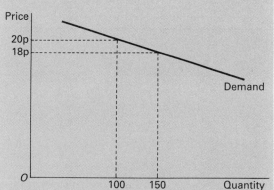

Figure 9.1
In the price range 20p to 18p, demand is elastic

Percentage change in the quantity demanded
$$= \frac{50}{100} \times \frac{100}{1} = 50\%$$
Percentage change in the price
$$= \frac{2}{20} \times \frac{100}{1} = 10\%$$

(continued)

Elasticity of demand $= \dfrac{50}{10} = 5$

Therefore, in the price range 20p to 18p, the *demand is elastic.*

What happens to the total revenue?

When the price is 20p, total revenue
$= 20\text{p} \times 100 = 2000\text{p}$

When the price is 18p, total revenue
$= 18\text{p} \times 150 = 2700\text{p}$

So when demand is elastic,
– a fall in price increases total revenue, and
– a rise in price reduces total revenue.

2 When demand is inelastic

Demand is inelastic when the percentage change in quantity demanded is less than the percentage change in price, i.e. when

$$\dfrac{\text{Percentage change in the quantity demanded}}{\text{Percentage change in the price}} < 1$$

Example

Figure 9.2 shows a situation where a rise in price from £4 to £6 causes the quantity demanded to fall from 200 units to 160 units.

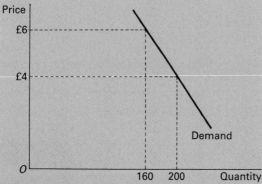

Figure 9.2
In the price range £4 to £6, demand is inelastic

Percentage change in the quantity demanded
$$= \dfrac{40}{200} \times \dfrac{100}{1} = 20\%$$

(continued)

Percentage change in the price
$$= \dfrac{2}{4} \times \dfrac{100}{1} = 50\%$$

Elasticity of demand $= \dfrac{20}{50} = \dfrac{2}{5}$ or 0.4

Therefore, in the price range £4 to £6, the *demand is inelastic.*

What happens to the total revenue?

When the price is £4, total revenue
$= £4 \times 200 = £800$

When the price is £6, total revenue
$= £6 \times 160 = £960$

So when demand is inelastic,
– a rise in price increases total revenue, and
– a fall in price reduces total revenue.

3 Two exceptional cases

1. Figure 9.3 illustrates a situation where a change in price has no effect on the quantity demanded. The same amount is demanded whatever the price. Demand is said to be *perfectly inelastic,* i.e.

Elasticity of demand $= 0$

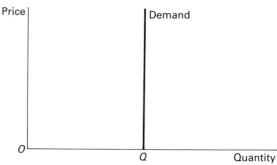

Figure 9.3
Perfectly inelastic demand; elasticity = 0

2. Figure 9.4 illustrates another extreme case. At the price *OP*, people are prepared to buy all that they can obtain. They would buy an infinite amount if it were obtainable. Demand is said to be *perfectly elastic,* i.e.

Elasticity of demand $=$ infinity

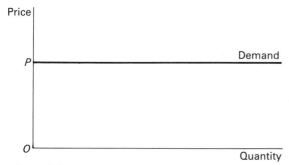

Figure 9.4
Perfectly elastic demand; elasticity = infinity

9.2
Why is demand elastic for some commodities but inelastic for others?

1 The availability of substitutes

If a commodity has a number of close substitutes, all at similar prices, the demand for it will be elastic. A small price increase will cause many consumers to switch to the substitutes, which are now *relatively* cheaper, and a small reduction in price will attract many consumers who were formerly buying the substitute goods. For example, we would expect the demand for *any one brand* of coffee, or soap powder, or pet food to be elastic, because other brands are close substitutes.

Where a commodity has no close substitute, demand will be inelastic. When the price of such a commodity changes, consumers cannot switch to or away from other similar competing goods. A price change will have a relatively small effect on the quantity demanded. For example, the *total* demands for petrol and paint will be inelastic. These products have no close substitutes.

2 Habit-forming goods

People can become addicted to certain products; tobacco and alcohol are obvious examples. Where this is the case, demand will be inelastic. For the addict, such goods have no substitutes.

3 'Luxuries' and 'necessities'

It is often said that the demands for necessities are inelastic because we cannot manage without them. The demands for luxuries are said to be elastic because the amounts people buy will be very much influenced by their prices. It is true that the demands for necessities such as water, food, clothing and shelter are inelastic. If the prices of

Figure 9.5

There is no close substitute for petrol, and the demand for it is inelastic

Different brands of petrol are close substitutes for one another, and the demand for any one brand is elastic

such things increase, people will continue to buy them, even if it means having to sacrifice other desirable goods.

But households' demands for such goods as petrol, tobacco and alcoholic drinks are also very inelastic. It is difficult to regard these goods as necessities in the same way as food and clothing are. The problem here is the meaning given to the word 'necessity'. What people regard as necessities depends upon their present standard of living. For example, domestic appliances such as electric irons, washing machines and refrigerators are widely regarded as necessities in most developed countries.

All we can say is that the demands will be inelastic for those goods which are *generally regarded* as necessities.

4 The proportion of income which is spent on the commodity

Where the total spending (per week or per month) on a good or service amounts to a small fraction of a household's income, the demand for it will be inelastic. For example, an increase of 1p in the price of a box of matches would be described as a small increase in price. It would, in fact, represent quite a large *percentage* increase in price. There would, however, be very little effect on the quantity demanded. The demand for matches, therefore, is inelastic, and the same is true of such items as table salt, shoe laces and hair grips.

9.3
Elasticity of supply

This term refers to the way in which the quantity supplied responds to a change in price. Elasticity of supply can be treated in much the same way as elasticity of demand, but remembering that, in this case, the quantity supplied moves in the same direction as price.

The measurement of elasticity of supply makes use of a formula similar to that used to measure elasticity of demand:

Elasticity of supply

$$= \frac{\text{Percentage change in the quantity supplied}}{\text{Percentage change in the price}}$$

1 When supply is elastic

Supply is elastic when the percentage change in the quantity supplied is greater than the percentage change in price, i.e. when

$$\frac{\text{Percentage change in the quantity supplied}}{\text{Percentage change in the price}} > 1$$

Example
In Figure 9.6, when the price increases from £10 to £11, the quantity supplied increases from 1000 units to 1300 units.

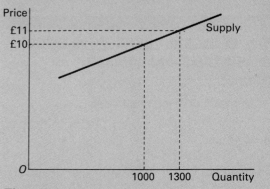

Figure 9.6
In the price range £10 to £11, supply is elastic

Percentage change in the quantity supplied
$$= \frac{300}{1000} \times \frac{100}{1} = 30\%$$
Percentage change in price
$$= \frac{1}{10} \times \frac{100}{1} = 10\%$$
Elasticity of supply $= \dfrac{30}{10} = 3$

Therefore, in the price range £10 to £11, the *supply is elastic*.

2 When supply is inelastic

Supply is inelastic when the percentage change in the quantity supplied is less than the percentage change in the price, i.e. when

$$\frac{\text{Percentage change in the quantity supplied}}{\text{Percentage change in the price}} < 1$$

Example

Figure 9.7 shows a situation where a fall in price from £5 to £4 causes the quantity supplied to fall from 200 units to 180 units.

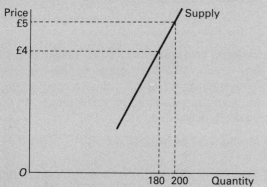

Figure 9.7
In the price range £5 to £4, supply is inelastic

Percentage change in quantity supplied
$$= \frac{20}{200} \times \frac{100}{1} = 10\%$$

Percentage change in price
$$= \frac{1}{5} \times \frac{100}{1} = 20\%$$

Elasticity of supply $= \dfrac{10}{20} = \dfrac{1}{2}$ or 0.5

Therefore, in the price range £5 to £4, the *supply is inelastic*.

3 Two exceptional cases

1. Figure 9.8 illustrates a situation where a change in price has no effect on the quantity supplied.

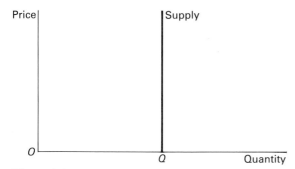

Figure 9.8
Perfectly inelastic supply; elasticity = 0

The amount offered for sale is the same at all prices. In this case, supply is said to be *perfectly inelastic*, i.e.

Elasticity of supply = 0

2. In Figure 9.9 it can be seen that, at the price *OP*, firms are prepared to supply whatever quantities are demanded – an infinite amount if necessary.

In this case, supply is *perfectly elastic*, i.e.

Elasticity of supply = infinity

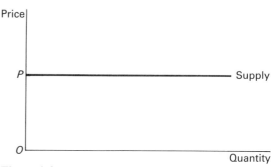

Figure 9.9
Perfectly elastic supply; elasticity = infinity

Why is supply elastic for some commodities but inelastic for others?

Supply is elastic when firms can easily and quickly change the amounts supplied in response to a change in price. Supply is inelastic when the quantity supplied cannot be easily and quickly changed when price changes.

How long it takes to adjust supply to changes in price depends upon the following factors.

1 Whether or not there is any excess capacity

When an industry is working below capacity, machines will be lying idle and labour will be unemployed or working short-time. In this case, supply will be elastic. An increase in demand can be met fairly quickly by taking on more labour and putting the idle machines to work. If the industry is fully employed, however, supply will be inelastic, at least in the short run. It may take a long time to build new factories or extend the existing ones. Even if there is unemployed labour, supply may still be inelastic if there is a shortage of labour with particular skills.

2 The level of stocks

If an industry is holding large stocks of its products, an increase in demand can be met by running down the stocks. While the stocks last, supply will be elastic.

3 Manufactured goods and agricultural products

In the case of farm products, elasticity of supply is affected by the length of the growing season. For things like vegetables and cereals, no great change in supply can be brought about for at least a year. Some plantation products such as natural rubber, tea, coffee and cocoa will be inelastic in supply over even longer periods of time, because it takes several years for new trees and bushes to reach maturity.

In general, manufactured products are more elastic in supply than agricultural products. In manufacturing, it is often possible to deal with a fall in demand by dismissing labour or working short-time and switching off machinery. An increase in demand can be met by bringing idle machinery into production, hiring more labour or working overtime.

The Main Points

- Elasticity of demand compares the percentage change in the price with the percentage change in the quantity demanded.

- Demand is *elastic* when a small change in price has a relatively large effect on the quantity demanded; it is *inelastic* when a small change in price has a relatively small effect on the quantity demanded.

- Elasticity of demand (E_d)

$$= \frac{\text{Percentage change in quantity demanded}}{\text{Percentage change in the price}}$$

If $E_d > 1$, demand is elastic.

If $E_d < 1$, demand is inelastic.

- If demand is *elastic*,
  - a rise in price will reduce total revenue, and
  - a fall in price will increase total revenue.

- If demand is *inelastic*,
  - a rise in price will increase total revenue, and
  - a fall in price will reduce total revenue.

- The demand for a good or service will be elastic when there are a number of close substitutes in the same price range.

- The demands for things which people regard as necessities will tend to be inelastic.

- Elasticity of supply compares the percentage change in price with the percentage change in the quantity supplied.

- Supply is *elastic* when a small price change has a relatively large effect on the amount supplied; it is *inelastic* when a small price change has a relatively small effect on the amount supplied.

- Elasticity of supply (E_s)

$$= \frac{\text{Percentage change in the quantity supplied}}{\text{Percentage change in the price}}$$

If $E_s > 1$, supply is elastic.

If $E_s < 1$, supply is inelastic.

- The supply of a good or service is elastic when the amounts offered for sale can be easily and quickly changed. This is true of many manufactured goods (unless the industry is working at full capacity).

- The supply of a good or service will be inelastic when the supply of it cannot be easily and quickly changed. This is true of the supply of labour to occupations which require long periods of training. It is also true of agricultural products, where supplies cannot be increased for at least one year or, in some cases, for several years.

- In the long run, the supplies of most goods and services will be elastic.

Test Your Understanding

1. For which TWO of the following goods is demand likely to be elastic?

   A electricity used for lighting
   B a particular brand of butter
   C one of the cheaper makes of ball-point pens
   D bread

2. A firm selling refrigerators lowered the price of the product from £200 to £180. Its sales increased from 400 refrigerators per week to 480 per week. Calculate the elasticity of demand for this product.

3. A local bus company lowered its bus fares. Although the number of passengers increased, there was a fall in the weekly receipts from bus fares. Was the demand for bus services elastic or inelastic? Explain your answer.

4. In which TWO of the following cases is supply *perfectly inelastic*?

   A seats in a London theatre
   B cars produced by Jaguar
   C paintings by Rembrandt

5. In which TWO of the following cases is supply likely to be elastic?

   A the supply of razor blades when the firms producing them are on short-time working
   B the supply of natural rubber when world demand is equal to world supply
   C the supply of oil when the oil companies' storage tanks are full

BOX 9
Coffee – world supply and demand

Coffee-picking in India

Coffee is produced in a large number of countries in Latin America, Asia and Africa. Latin America is the major source of supply and Brazil is by far the most important of the Latin American producers. Large-scale plantings in recent years will lead eventually to a substantial increase in the supply of coffee. Coffee trees take about six years to reach full maturity.

Growth in the demand for coffee is expected to be low world-wide. This is because of the relatively slow growth of incomes and populations in the major consuming regions – North America and Western Europe. It is also due to the fact that consumption levels are reaching saturation in many of the countries in these regions.

Coffee faces the prospect of increasing supply and slow growth in demand. The demand for coffee tends to be inelastic. It is estimated that for world consumption to go up by 1 per cent, the world price of coffee would have to fall by 4 per cent. By producing more coffee, the export revenues of the producing countries as a whole may well go down.

Source: Adapted from *Finance and Development*, IMF and the World Bank, vol. 20, no. 1

Questions
1. Which sentence indicates that, in the short run, the supply of coffee is likely to be inelastic?
2. What is meant by the statement that the consumption levels of coffee in some regions are reaching *saturation*?
3. From the estimates given, calculate the elasticity of demand for coffee.

Figure 10.1
All the activities which play a part in moving goods
(in this case, frozen foods) from producers to
consumers are included in *distribution*

In the UK, about three million people are employed in what are described as the *distributive trades*. These people are employed in jobs which help to move goods from producers to consumers.

10.1
The chain of distribution

1. The traditional method of distribution is for producers to supply goods in bulk to independent wholesalers, who hold stocks and distribute relatively small quantities to individual retailers.

2. There are, however, many very large retail organisations which each own a large number of retail shops. These organisations are large enough to buy in bulk and they deal directly with the manufacturers. They do not make use of the independent wholesalers because they operate their own warehouses and have their own transport departments.

3. In some cases, the manufacturing, wholesale and retail stages are integrated within a single firm. As described in Chapter 7, breweries often sell through their own public houses, and oil companies both manufacture petrol and sell it through their own petrol stations.

4. Small-scale producers often deal directly with retailers. For example, local bakeries usually supply bread and cakes directly to retail shops.
5. One chain of distribution bypasses the retail shop: mail-order firms deal directly with house-holders. They use local agents to obtain orders and collect payments, and the goods are supplied by post.

10.2
The wholesale trade

The wholesale stage is a most important link in the chain of distribution. The wholesaler helps to solve the basic problem of distribution. This problem arises because
– producers wish to supply in large quantities and to dispose of their goods as quickly as possible, and
– consumers wish to buy small quantities of a variety of goods as and when they need them.

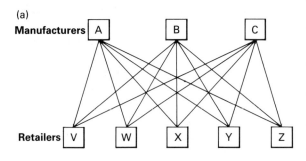

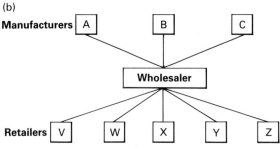

Figure 10.2
(a) Direct distribution from manufacturers to retailers
(b) Distribution with a wholesale stage

To overcome this problem, wholesalers provide a number of important services.

1 Breaking bulk

Wholesalers buy large quantities from a variety of producers and divide these into smaller quantities for distribution to retailers. A single delivery from a wholesaler can supply a retailer with a range of goods made by different manufacturers. The existence of the wholesale stage leads to a saving in transport costs as Figure 10.2 shows very clearly. Figure 10.2(a) shows the number of journeys required if each manufacturer makes a delivery to each retailer, and there is no wholesale stage. Figure 10.2(b) shows the number of journeys required when distribution takes place through a wholesale stage.

2 Holding stocks

Consumers usually expect to be able to purchase a commodity just when they need it. To meet this kind of demand someone must be prepared to hold stocks. Most retailers do not have the space to hold large stocks, and could not afford the expense of holding them even if they had the space. By holding large stocks, wholesalers make it possible for retailers to obtain supplies when they require them. Frequent (often daily) deliveries from wholesalers enable retailers to meet consumers' demands without having to hold excessive stocks.

3 Information and advice

The wholesaler's warehouse is an important source of information to retailers. They can visit the warehouse and inspect the range of goods available, obtain advice on these goods and keep themselves informed of new developments.

4 Bearing risks

The holding of large stocks can be a risky undertaking. The value of goods may fall while large stocks are being held. A change of fashion, the development of a superior product or, in some cases, deterioration may reduce the value of goods held by the wholesaler. On the other hand, if prices rise, the value of the stocks held will increase, and the wholesaler will enjoy higher profits.

The retail trade

Retailers are the last link in the chain of distribution. They provide the following services:
- They make a variety of goods available in locations convenient to the consumer.
- They provide producers with a large number of market outlets for their products.
- They perform an important advertising function for producers by displaying goods and offering advice on them.
- When goods are bulky and heavy, they normally offer a delivery service.
- For products of a technical nature, they offer after-sales services.

Types of retail outlet

Retailing covers all the activities which supply goods directly to the general public. Apart from retail shops, therefore, it includes public houses, petrol stations, street markets, door-to-door selling and so on. In this section, however, we shall deal only with the main types of retail shop and mail-order houses.

1 Independent retailers

Independent retailers are usually sole traders or 'one-shop' firms. There are far more independent retailers than any other form of retail outlet. Figure 10.3 shows that their share of the retail trade has been steadily declining. They remain, however, a very important part of the retail trade.

Because there are so many of them, independent retailers offer the public the great convenience of having a shop within easy reach of home. They often remain open for longer hours than other types of retail shop, and usually offer a personal service which is sometimes lacking in larger stores.

2 Multiple shops

These are shops which belong to chains of very similar shops that are owned by large companies. Each of the organisations has its own particular style of shop front and interior layout. They are easily identifiable in the centres of the larger towns. Some of them, such as Burton, Dixons, Halfords and W. H. Smith, tend to specialise in a particular range of goods. Others, such as Marks and Spencer, Woolworths, Boots and Littlewoods, deal in a much wider range of products.

Figure 10.3 demonstrates the success of the multiples in capturing a growing share of the total retail market. This success is based largely on the ability of large firms to achieve economies of scale. Organisations which own multiple shops usually have the following features:
- They buy in large quantities and obtain their supplies at lower prices.
- They carry out their own wholesaling.
- They employ specialist buyers and marketing experts.
- They market their own brands.
- They advertise extensively (Marks and Spencer is an exception).
- They exercise close control over the shops from 'head office'.

Figure 10.3
Changing shares of the retail trade, by type of store

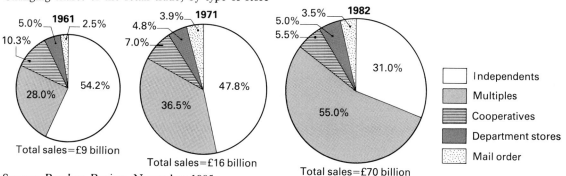

Source: *Barclays Review*, November 1985

3 Voluntary groups

Severe competition from the multiples and super-markets forced independent wholesalers and retailers to form voluntary associations such as Mace, Spar and VG. The shops belonging to one of these groups all trade under the same name, but each shop remains independently owned and controlled. To qualify for membership of such a group, a shop usually has to be of a certain minimum size.

These groups are usually organised by whole-salers, and they make it possible for independents to obtain some of the economies of scale enjoyed by larger firms. Retailers undertake to obtain supplies from the group wholesalers, who can then place large orders with producers and obtain important discounts. These discounts can be passed on to the retailers in the form of lower prices. Voluntary groups market many of their own brands.

Voluntary groups offer advice and assistance to retailers on matters relating to the management and organisation of their shops. They are most common in the grocery trade, but similar organ-isations exist for chemists and for the newspapers, tobacco and confectionery trade.

4 Department stores

Most large towns have one or more department stores. In effect, a department store consists of several specialist shops under one roof. Harrods, Selfridges, Lewis's and Debenhams are well-known department stores. Most of the larger cooperative societies (see Chapter 11) also have department stores.

These shops carry a wide range of goods which are sold in specialist departments. For example, one usually finds departments specialising in furniture, bedding, carpets, electrical goods, food and so on. Department stores also offer many services, such as catering facilities, banking, hair-dressing, and booking agencies for theatre tickets and holidays. The variety of goods and services available offers customers the attractive prospect of doing most of their shopping in one building.

5 Supermarkets

A supermarket is defined as a self-service food store with a sales area in excess of 2000 square feet (190 m^2). In this type of store, the techniques of self service and self selection have enabled retailers to obtain impressive gains in productivity.

Both the number and the average size of super-markets have been increasing in recent years. Many of the larger ones, such as Sainsbury's, Tesco, Asda and Waitrose, are controlled by multiples, and many supermarkets are owned by the cooperative societies.

Supermarkets, however, are now much more than grocery shops, because they have diversified into wines and spirits, electrical goods, clothing, DIY materials and a wide range of household goods. This has led to the development of the *superstore*, which is defined as a supermarket with a sales area in excess of 25 000 square feet (2300 m^2), in which food might occupy no more than half the selling space.

A further development of the supermarket is the *hypermarket*, which is defined as a single-storey retail outlet with at least 50 000 square feet (4650 m^2) of selling space. These very large self-service stores are usually located on the outskirts of towns, where adequate car-parking facilities can be provided.

6 Discount stores

Discount stores are large 'retail warehouses'. They usually occupy large single-storey premises away from city centres and sell on a 'cash and carry' basis. They deal in durable consumer goods, many of them specialising in electrical appliances.

By providing very little in the way of personal service they are able to operate with low labour costs. Their premises are relatively cheap to build, equip and maintain compared with the large city-centre stores.

7 Mail-order houses

Mail-order firms sell a range of goods very similar to those found in department stores. All trans-actions are carried out by post. Local agents, working on a part-time basis, use colourful and attractive catalogues to obtain orders which can be purchased by instalments. Agents are paid by commission; that is, they receive a certain percentage of the value of the orders they obtain.

Customers are offered the convenience of 'shopping in their own homes'. Although postal distribution is relatively expensive, mail-order firms obtain economies of scale by bulk buying, and they obtain the wholesaler's and retailer's profit margins. They use out-of-town warehouses, which are normally cheaper to buy or rent and have lower rates than premises in city centres.

10.4
The changing structure of retailing

Over the past two decades there has been something of a revolution in retailing. The most obvious changes have been the increasing importance of the multiples and the increase in size and number of the supermarkets. There are several reasons why such changes have taken place.

1 Price competition

For many years prior to 1964, manufacturers were able to fix the prices at which their products were sold to the general public. Shopkeepers had to sell their goods at prices that were laid down by the manufacturers. This practice was known as *resale price maintenance* (RPM). The effect of RPM was

Figure 10.4
In recent years there have been some very great changes in the retail trade

that there was no price competition for many goods at the retail stage. They were sold at the same price in all shops. The more efficient shops could not cut their prices and take business away from the less efficient shops.

The Resale Prices Act of 1964 made it much more difficult for firms to practice RPM. The result was that almost all manufacturers decided not to continue the practice of fixing the resale prices of their products. The abandonment of RPM gave retailers the freedom to compete by cutting prices. The larger and more efficient firms could now pass on the benefits they obtained from bulk purchases and better organisation, in the form of lower prices. The freedom to engage in price competition greatly benefited the multiples and supermarkets.

2 Improvements in the methods of marketing goods

The introduction of cheap, lightweight, transparent wrapping materials has had a great influence on the retailing of many goods, especially foodstuffs. It has made it possible to standardise and pre-pack goods so that consumers can make their own selection. The result has been a great saving in labour costs.

Large-scale advertising, the familiarity of brand names and the pre-packing and labelling of all kinds of goods have made possible a great expansion of self-service retailing. 'Over-the-counter' shopping has been increasingly superseded by self-

A small independent retailer   A hypermarket

service shopping in very large stores which offer a great variety of products.

3 Social changes

Bulk buying has now become a feature of household shopping. Two developments have been particularly important in bringing about changes in the shopping habits of many households.

There has been a steady increase in the number of married women who go out to work. In 1961 about 30 per cent of married women had jobs outside the home. In 1986 rather more than 50 per cent of married women went out to work. For many working women, a weekly visit to the supermarket is more convenient than the older custom of shopping for small quantities in a variety of local shops every day.

The second important development has been the increasing extent of car ownership. Rather more than 60 per cent of UK households have the use of a car. One shopping expedition to the supermarket, using the car as the means of transport, is sufficient for a family to satisfy its demands for groceries and household goods for a week or even longer. This is especially true where the household possesses a deep freezer.

10.5
Advertising

In order to sell goods, it is not sufficient simply to move the goods to places where people can easily obtain them. Potential customers have to be made aware of what goods are available and then be persuaded to buy them. It is the function of advertising to *inform and persuade*.

In most Western industrialised countries, advertising is a major industry. In the UK in 1986, the total annual expenditure on advertising was more than £5117 million. This is a very large figure, although it amounts to less than $2\frac{1}{4}$ per cent of total consumer spending.

Forms of advertising

We encounter advertising in many different forms and many different places. The relative importance of the different forms is shown in Figure 10.5.

Figure 10.5
Total advertising expenditure, UK, 1986

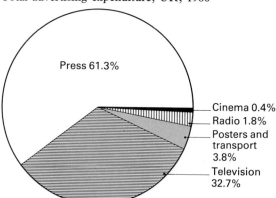

Total expenditure = £5117m

Source: The Advertising Association, 15 May 1987

1 Television and radio

Television advertising is powerful and effective, since it reaches millions of people within their own homes. There is a kind of 'captive audience', since the people watching the programmes can hardly avoid seeing the advertisements.

2 Newspapers and magazines

The press is by far the most important advertising medium. A major part of the costs of newspapers and magazines is covered by the revenue from advertisements. Advertisements in the press have the great advantage that they can be read and re-read at leisure, while television advertisements rely on an instant impression (but they can, of course, be repeated at regular intervals).

3 Posters

These are one of the oldest forms of advertising. Their effectiveness depends very much on their location.

4 Circulars

Door-to-door delivery of circulars, which usually advertise 'special offers' for various goods, is a very popular form of advertising.

5 Packaging

Many manufacturers package their goods in attractive cartons or wrappers, which give prominence to the name of the product.

6 Transport

Advertisements appear on the sides of buses, and many firms use the sides of their lorries and vans as a means of advertising their products.

7 Exhibitions

Trade fairs and exhibitions, for example the Motor Show, the Boat Show and the Ideal Home Exhibition, are staged in large exhibition halls to advertise the products of certain industries.

The purpose of advertising

The main purpose of advertising is clearly to influence the demand for a good or service. Advertising aims to increase demand, that is, to move the demand curve to the right. There is no doubt that a well planned and cleverly presented advertising campaign can increase the demand for a product. Producers are keen to point out, however, that such an increase in demand cannot be maintained unless consumers are satisfied with the good. People will not continue to buy a well advertised commodity unless it lives up to their expectations.

Most advertising is linked to some particular brand name. Its purpose is to increase brand loyalty by trying to convince consumers that competing brands are *not* close substitutes.

Informative advertising

Some advertising is essential. Without it, consumers would not be fully aware of the variety of goods available to them, and their choices would be restricted. It is also necessary to inform consumers of the existence and features of new products when they become available.

Economists describe this as informative advertising. The government itself has to undertake a great deal of informative advertising in order to make people aware of new regulations, changes in the law, changes in taxation and social security benefits, etc.

Persuasive advertising

Critics of advertising argue that much advertising is merely persuasive and does not add to people's knowledge. They point out that, in the case of many heavily advertised products, consumers are already fully aware of the features of those products. Advertisements which make exaggerated claims can mislead consumers rather than help them to make a sensible choice.

Does advertising raise costs?

There is a widely-held view that advertising is simply an additional cost of production and must, therefore, keep prices higher than they would be if there were no advertising.

It has already been pointed out that mass-production techniques can lower average costs of production. But mass-production methods cannot be used unless there is a mass market for the product. It would be very difficult, or take a very long time, to establish a mass market for a good without advertising. It might be argued, therefore, that if advertising succeeds in establishing a large market for a product, economies of scale might offset the costs of advertising.

On the other hand, suppose Firm A advertises in order to steal customers from Firm B, and then Firm B advertises to counter the effects of Firm A's advertising. The end result might be that the sales of both firms change very little. In this case, it would seem that the advertising will have the effect of raising the average costs of production.

The Main Points

■ The movement of goods from producers to consumers makes use of transport services, communication services and the work of wholesalers and retailers.

■ In some cases, each of the different stages of distribution is carried out by independent firms. In other cases, two or more of these stages may be carried out by a single firm (for example, multiples do their own wholesaling).

■ Wholesalers assist producers and retailers by buying large quantities, breaking bulk, holding stocks, providing information and advice, and by carrying the risks of holding stocks.

■ Retailers assist producers and consumers by displaying goods and making them available in convenient locations, giving advice to consumers, and by providing delivery and after-sales services.

■ Multiples have been gaining ground at the expense of independent retailers. Over the last 25 years, multiples have doubled their share of the retail trade.

■ There is a trend towards larger stores. In 1963 there were only two superstores in Great Britain. There are now more than 400. There has also been a steady increase in the range of products sold in supermarkets and superstores.

■ Changes in the structure of retailing have been encouraged by
  – increased freedom for retailers to engage in price competition,
  – technical changes which made it cheaper and easier to pre-pack goods, leading to a great increase in self-service retailing, and
  – social changes, such as the growing percentage of married women working outside the home and the wider ownership of motor cars.

■ Advertising aims to increase the demand for a product. There are many different forms of advertising, of which the press and television are the most important.

■ Advertising is sometimes classified as either informative or persuasive.

■ Whether advertising raises average costs depends upon the extent to which it increases the total market. Economies of scale may offset the costs of advertising. On the other hand, if two or more companies are fighting for larger shares of a market which is not growing, advertising will probably raise average costs.

Test Your Understanding

1. The main purpose of the chain of distribution is to place the product in the hands of the .... What is the missing word?

2. Of what type of retail outlet are British Home Stores, MFI, Next, Currys and Rumbelows examples?

3. What does the term 'breaking bulk' mean when it is used to describe the work of wholesalers?

4. This question relates to the following types of retail outlet:
   A a department store
   B an independent retailer
   C a multiple store
   D a superstore
   Which of the above retail outlets
   (a) is defined in terms of its selling space?
   (b) is sometimes described as 'many shops within a shop'?
   (c) may also be defined as a chain store?

5. How does the existence of a wholesale stage reduce the costs of moving goods from producers to retailers?

6. The sales manager of a firm which makes high-quality children's toys is planning a national advertising campaign. Which form of advertising would you advise him to use? Explain your answer.

7. How would you explain the survival of so many small independent retailers in spite of the competition from multiples and supermarkets?

BOX 10
The distribution of footwear

The British Shoe Corporation's distribution warehouse, located in Leicester, has one million square feet of floor space. It can hold 11 million pairs of shoes, plus handbags and other accessories. Shoes from all over the world are delivered to this warehouse.

From this distribution centre, deliveries are made to some 2500 shoe shops in 600 towns located in every region in the UK. These shops include the British Shoe Corporation's own subsidiaries such as Curtess, Dolcis, Manfield and Freeman Hardy & Willis. In addition, deliveries are made to other stores, including department stores.

Each lorry leaving the warehouse carries stock for nine or ten shops in one locality. Major stores have their stocks replenished at least twice a week.

Questions
1. Why do you think the British Shoe Corporation chose to locate its distribution warehouse in Leicester?
2. What will be the main difference between the type of loads carried by lorries making deliveries *to* the warehouse and those carried by the lorries making deliveries *from* the warehouse?
3. What part of the account above indicates that both horizontal and vertical integration have taken place? Explain your answer.

CHAPTER 11
Types of business organisation

11.1
What is a firm?

A firm is a *unit of management*. It is an organisation which trades under a particular name, and which controls the way in which land, labour and capital are used. It takes decisions on such matters as the methods of production, the design of its products and the way the products are marketed. A firm must be distinguished from a *unit of production* such as a factory, a farm, a mine or a quarry. One firm may own and control several units of production.

Firms vary in size, from a sole trader to companies which employ thousands of workers, and they may be organised in different ways.

11.2
The sole trader

This type of firm is also described as a one-person business, or a sole proprietor. It is the oldest form of business organisation, and there are more sole traders than any other type of firm.

It is fairly easy to become a sole trader. There are no complicated legal arrangements to be made, and it usually requires very little money to set up this kind of firm. Many hundreds of such businesses are set up every day and, although many of them are successful, there is a large number of such firms closing down every day. Lack of experience by people setting up in business for the

Figure 11.1
There are many one-person businesses in window cleaning

first time, and insufficient money to carry them through 'a bad patch', are probably the main reasons for the large number of failures.

The main features of the one-person business are summarised below.

1. It is relatively easy and inexpensive to establish oneself as a sole trader.
2. It is a flexible organisation. Decisions about what should be done, and how it should be done, do not have to wait for meetings of partners or directors.

3. The owner can provide a personal service to the customers.
4. There is a great incentive to be efficient. The owner gets all the rewards of success, and bears all the losses of failure.
5. It suffers from the great disadvantage of unlimited liability. If the business goes bankrupt, the owner is personally liable for the debts of the firm. His or her personal possessions may have to be sold to pay off the debts.
6. It may be difficult for a sole trader to obtain loans, because such businesses are often thought to be a bigger risk than large well-known firms. The main sources of money are likely to be the proprietor's own savings, and loans from friends and relatives. In recent years, however, the government has introduced schemes to provide financial assistance to people wishing to set up their own businesses.
7. Sole traders are common in retailing, farming, personal services (e.g. hairdressing), craft work and repair work.

11.3
Partnerships

The Partnership Act of 1890 defined a partnership as a voluntary association of from two to twenty people which is formed to carry on business with a view to profit. However, in some professions such as law, accountancy and stockbroking, more than twenty people are now allowed to form a partnership.

Some important features of partnerships are listed below.

1. With several people putting money into the business, a partnership can raise more capital than a sole trader.
2. The management of the firm can be more specialised. Different partners can be made responsible for different departments, such as sales, administration, production and so on.
3. Partnerships also suffer from the disadvantage of unlimited liability. In ordinary partnerships, each partner is fully liable for the debts of the firm.

Business Opportunities

NEWLY redundant gent seeks partner interested in starting new video photography business venture. Must have enthusiasm, ideas, contacts and some working capital. Business experience an advantage. — Apply giving details to Box ▮▮, Leicester Mercury, St. George St., Leicester.

Business Opportunities

PARTNER

REQUIRED for medical and distribution company, a division of an existing research establishment. Age between 28 and 50. You will probably already be involved in medical, sales, marketing or distribution. Experience in medical, road haulage would be an advantage, but is not essential.

APPLY in the first instance to Box ▮▮ Leicester Mercury, St. George St., Leicester.

Figure 11.2
Partnerships are easy to set up

4. It is possible to form a limited partnership, where a partner's liability is limited to the amount of money he or she has put into the firm. But limited partners can take no part in running the business, and at least one partner must have unlimited liability.
5. Partnerships can be unstable, because they are easy to set up and easy to break up.
6. Partnerships are commonly found in farming, catering, retailing and building, and in professions such as law, medicine and accountancy.

11.4
Limited companies

The word 'limited' is used in the description of these companies to indicate that, unlike one-person businesses and partnerships, the liability of the owners is strictly limited. This is explained on the next page.

Limited companies are often described as *joint stock companies*, and they are far more important than any other form of business organisation. The term 'joint stock' refers to the fact that a number of people have contributed to a common stock of capital which is to be used for setting up and running the company. This stock of capital is divided into many small units called *shares*, and the people who buy these shares – the *shareholders* – are the owners of the company.

Profits are divided among the shareholders according to the number and types of shares they hold. The profits paid to shareholders are known as *dividends*.

Limited liability

A shareholder's liability for the debts of a joint stock company is strictly limited to the value of the shares he or she has agreed to buy. Once shareholders have fully paid for their shares, they have no further liability for the company's debts.

Public and private companies

There are two kinds of limited company, public companies and private companies. An important difference between them is that public companies can invite the general public to buy their shares, but private companies cannot. Also important is the fact that shares in a public company are freely transferable; holders of such shares can sell them at any time. Shares in private companies are not freely transferable; they can normally only be sold with the permission of the other shareholders.

Public companies are usually large firms, but private companies tend to be small, and are often family firms. Forming a private company is a way of obtaining the advantage of limited liability and, at the same time, keeping control of the firm in relatively few hands.

There are about 850 000 limited companies in the UK, of which some 6000 are public limited companies. Although there are far fewer public companies, they are much more important than private companies in terms of the numbers employed, the assets owned and the value of output.

Companies, both private and public, must have at least two members, and a public company must have a minimum share capital of £50 000.

The formation of companies

All limited companies must be registered with the Registrar of Companies. Before a company can commence business, it must submit certain documents to the Registrar for his approval. Among the more important of these documents are the following.

The memorandum of association

This must contain the company's name, the address of its registered office, the objects for which the company is being formed, and the amount of capital which the company wishes to raise by issuing shares. The name of the company must include the word 'limited' or, in the case of a public company, the words 'public limited company' (plc).

The articles of association

These must give details of how the company will be controlled and organised. For example, there must be information on the rights of the shareholders, the rights and duties of the directors, and the procedure for calling meetings of shareholders.

If the various documents submitted by the promoters of the company are acceptable to the Registrar, he will issue a *certificate of incorporation*, which gives the company a legal existence.

A public limited company must also submit a copy of its *prospectus*. This is the document which invites the general public to buy shares in the company. This prospectus must also be published in one or more newspapers. If the prospectus meets with the Registrar's approval, he will issue a *certificate of trading*, which allows the company to commence trading.

The law requires all registered companies to publish annual accounts, and copies of these accounts must be sent to the Registrar.

Some important features of limited companies

1 Limited liability makes it easier to obtain capital

A person buying shares in a limited company is not risking the loss of his or her personal possessions. This fact has encouraged very large numbers of people to buy shares, and has made it possible to raise the vast amounts of money required to finance large-scale enterprises.

2 Transferability of shares encourages share ownership

When a company sells shares, it requires the permanent use of the money it receives. But few, if any, people are prepared to make a permanent loan. This problem is solved because shares in a public company are transferable. There is a market – the Stock Exchange – where, if they so wish, people can sell the shares they hold. This means that companies can have permanent use of their share capital, while shareholders can always convert their shareholdings into money. Market prices of shares change from day to day, so that shareholders selling their shares may make a profit or a loss.

3 The life of a company is independent of the lives of its members

Unlike sole proprietors and partnerships, the life of a limited company is not tied to the lives of its owners. If shareholders die or sell their shares, it has no effect on the life of the company. This is important because many firms have to make large investments in plant and machinery which will take many years to pay for itself. People will only put money into this type of project if they believe that the firm will have a continued existence over many years.

4 Ownership and control may be in different hands

In a large company, the management of the firm is in the hands of a board of directors. The owners of the company are the shareholders, but they play no part in the running of the enterprise. This is because
– they are too numerous,
– they live in different parts of the country, or different parts of the world, and
– they do not have the time, knowledge or skills required to run a large company.

The shareholders have the right to elect the directors. They can show their approval or disapproval of the way the company is being run when the directors come up for re-election at the annual general meetings. In most cases, however, relatively few shareholders attend these meetings.

5 One company can take over another company

The fact that one company can own another company makes it possible for a whole group of companies to be controlled by relatively few people. Take-overs are discussed later in this chapter.

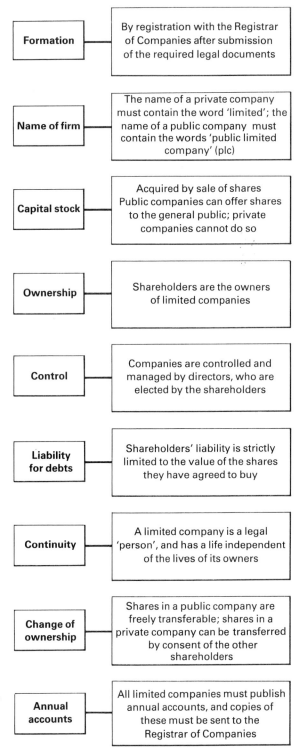

Figure 11.3
Limited companies (joint stock companies)

11.5
Company shares and debentures

Public companies can raise money by selling shares and debentures to the general public. The money raised in this way is used to purchase the buildings, machinery and materials which the company needs to carry on business.

There are two main types of share, but there are several varieties of each type.

Preference shares

As the name suggests, the holders of these shares get preferential treatment. They have the right to a share in profits before the holders of other types of share. Preference shares normally carry a fixed rate of interest (see the example on page 99).

Cumulative preference shares carry a right to any arrears of interest which have accumulated during years when the company did not earn enough profit to pay the fixed rate of interest. Some firms issue *participating preference shares*, which carry the right to a fixed rate of interest and additional payments out of profits when the company has a particularly good year.

Preference shareholders do not normally have a vote at the annual general meeting, but they may be entitled to vote when the company has not been able to make payments on these shares.

Ordinary shares

Owners of ordinary shares bear most of the risks because they have no guaranteed income and they are 'at the end of the queue' for a share in the profits. They are entitled to what remains of the distributed profits after all the other people with a claim to profits have been paid. This means that in bad years they will receive no dividends, but in good years they might receive quite large dividends.

Because they are the main risk-bearers, holders of ordinary shares normally have voting rights. This means that they have the power to change the management and, perhaps, the policy of the company, at the annual general meeting. As explained later, the fact that ordinary shares carry voting rights makes these shares very important in take-over bids.

Figure 11.4
Shares and debentures

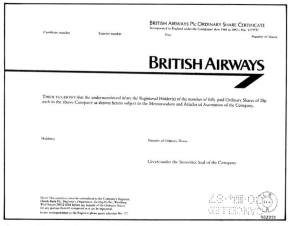

An ordinary share certificate

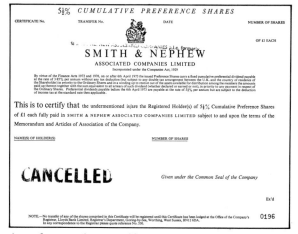

A preference share certificate

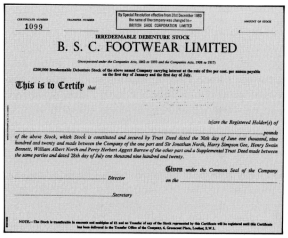

A debenture certificate

Debentures

In addition to issuing shares, a company can obtain capital by issuing debentures. These are not shares but documents which acknowledge a loan to the company. A debenture is, in fact, a kind of IOU.

Debenture capital is defined as *loan capital*. Unlike the shareholder, the debenture holder is not an owner of the company. Debentures carry a fixed rate of interest which must be paid whether the company makes a profit or not. The claims of debenture holders must be met before those of shareholders.

Sometimes debentures are secured by claims on the property of the company. This means that, if the company defaults on its payments to them, the debenture holders can seize certain assets of the company and sell them in order to obtain the money due to them. Such debentures are described as *secured debentures*.

Payments to debenture holders and shareholders

The following is a very simplified example of how a company distributes interest and dividends to debenture holders and shareholders.

Share capital	*Company's capital*
20 000 5 per cent preference shares of £1 each	£20 000
40 000 ordinary shares of £1 each	£40 000
Loan capital	
20 000 10 per cent debentures of £1 each	£20 000
	£80 000

Assume that the company has £7000 available for distribution to debenture holders and shareholders. It will distribute this money as follows:

1. Total payments on debentures
   = 10 per cent of £20 000 = £2000

2. Total payments on preference shares
   = 5 per cent of £20 000 = £1000

   £3000

3. Ordinary shareholders will receive £4000.

$$\text{Dividend} = \frac{\text{Total payment on ordinary shares}}{\text{Ordinary share capital}} \times \frac{100}{1}$$

$$= \frac{£4000}{£40\ 000} \times \frac{100}{1}$$

$$= 10 \text{ per cent}$$

Take-overs and holding companies

A company is a legal 'person' and can, therefore, take over the ownership of another company. Since the owners of a company are the shareholders, a company can be purchased by buying the shares in that company – whoever owns the shares owns the company.

It is not necessary to buy all the shares in a company in order to control it. Effective control can be obtained by buying a majority of the voting shares. One company can acquire the ownership of another by exchanging shares instead of paying cash for the shares it wishes to obtain. For example, suppose Company A wishes to obtain control of Company B. It might approach the shareholders of Company B and offer them shares in Company A in exchange for the shares they hold in Company B.

A company may be formed for the sole purpose of holding shares in other companies. Such a company is known as a *holding company*. If it holds the majority of the voting shares in the subsidiary companies it will, of course, have control over these companies.

11.6
Cooperative societies

There are two main types of cooperative society, worker cooperatives (or producer cooperatives) and consumer cooperatives (or retail cooperatives).

Worker cooperatives

The main idea behind worker cooperatives is that the business should be owned and controlled by those who work in it. The workers provide, or borrow, the money to set up the business. They take all the management decisions, either collectively or by electing managers from their own ranks. Profits are shared out between the workers on some basis agreed amongst themselves.

Worker cooperatives have a long history, and the idea of cooperative production continues to have a strong appeal for large numbers of people. Unfortunately, most of the early experiments did not meet with a great deal of success. These enterprises probably failed for one or more of the following reasons:

- a lack of management experience among the workers;
- insufficient reserves of money to keep the business going until its products had become established in the market;
- most of the enterprises were set up by workers who were extremely poor, and there was a natural desire to distribute the profits rather than plough them back into the business;
- workers tended to elect popular rather than effective managers.

At the beginning of the twentieth century there were about 200 worker cooperatives in the UK, and they were strongly supported by the retail cooperatives which bought most of their output. By the early 1960s, however, the number had fallen to about 30, most of them in printing, clothing and footwear.

In recent years there has been a great revival of interest in this form of business organisation. In 1986 there were rather more than 900 worker cooperatives listed in the directory of the Cooperative Development Agency. Many of them are very small and an increasing number are in service industries. In 1978 the government established a special agency to help worker cooperatives with technical advice.

Worker cooperatives have proved to be very successful in Spain and France.

Consumer cooperatives

In this type of cooperative the owners are the consumers, that is, those who purchase the goods, rather than those who make them.

The first cooperative retail society was formed by a group of poor weavers who set up a small shop in Rochdale in 1844. From these humble beginnings the movement has grown to become one of the largest retail organisations in the UK, with some ten million members and about 10 000 shops.

The basic principles of the cooperative society have changed relatively little since the days of the Rochdale pioneers.

1 Open membership

There is no maximum number of members, and members are free to join or leave at any time.

2 Distribution of the surplus or profits

For many years members received a cash dividend, payable at regular intervals. This dividend amounted to a percentage of the amount of money spent at the cooperative. Later the system changed to the issuing of dividend stamps whenever purchases were made. Some societies no longer issue these stamps but offer members discounts on certain items instead.

3 Democratic control

The minimum shareholding is £1 and the maximum £5000, but the rule is 'one member, one vote'. This is very different from the joint stock company, where voting rights depend upon the number of shares held.

4 Payment of interest on share capital

Members receive a fixed rate of interest on their share capital.

The management of a consumer cooperative is the responsibility of a committee – usually part-timers – elected by the members. The day-to-day operations of the business, however, are controlled by full-time managers, who are appointed by the elected committee.

In the UK in recent years, there have been some great changes in the structure of the consumer cooperatives. For a long time, most towns, both large and small, had their own local cooperative society. A large number of these societies have now disappeared, as the societies have been amalgamated to form larger units. The purpose of these amalgamations has been to obtain economies of scale so that the cooperatives could deal with the fierce competition from large retail organisations such as the multiples, supermarkets and discount stores. The formation of large societies, each covering a wide area, has meant that the idea of local ownership and control has been sacrificed in some areas, and this has tended to weaken local loyalties.

Cooperatives account for about 6 per cent of the national retail trade in the UK, about 15 per cent of the grocery trade and about one-third of the country's milk. The retail societies own and control the Cooperative Wholesale Society, which supplies a large proportion of the goods sold by the retail societies. The CWS is a large-scale importer and manufacturer; it is also Britain's largest farmer. The cooperative movement in the UK is also an important supplier of services such as banking and insurance.

Traditionally, the cooperative societies have seen themselves as something more than a particular form of business organisation. They started as a working-class organisation, and one of their important aims was (and is) to help the working class, not only financially, but socially and politically. They finance and organise educational and social activities and they support political movements which seek to encourage the idea of worker and consumer control of industry.

11.7
Publicly-owned enterprises

If we take the word 'government' to mean both central and local government, then we can say that the government is easily the biggest 'business' in the UK. It is by far the largest employer, and its income and expenditure are many times greater than those of the largest limited company.

In this chapter, however, we are dealing with *trading* enterprises, that is, businesses which *sell* the goods and services they produce. This means that we cannot include those central and local government departments which are responsible for such things as education, health, law and order, and social security. Although these and several other publicly-owned organisations supply households and firms with a great variety of goods and services, they are not trading organisations. The things they supply do not have market prices.

There are, however, many publicly-owned enterprises which, like privately-owned firms, sell what they produce. The most familar of these are the nationalised industries such as those supplying coal, electricity and rail transport. These enterprises are run by public corporations.

The public corporation

1 Ownership

The public corporation is the form of business organisation which is used for the management of a nationalised industry. Like a limited company, a public corporation is a legal 'person', but unlike the limited company, there are no shareholders. The public corporations are owned by the state. In effect, they are owned by the citizens of a country.

2 Management

Each public corporation has a board of managers. These managers have duties and responsibilities which are similar to those of the directors of a company. An important difference lies in the way the managers are selected. In a public corporation they are *appointed* by a Minister of the Crown, whereas in a limited company they are *elected* by the shareholders.

The managers of a public corporation are responsible for the day-to-day running of the enterprise but they are accountable to the government and not to a body of shareholders. The overall responsibility for the performance of a public corporation lies with a Minister of the Crown. For example, the Secretary of State for Energy has responsibility for British Coal, and the Secretary of State for Transport is responsible for British Rail.

3 Finance

Since there are no shareholders, a public corporation cannot raise capital by issuing shares. In the UK, the public corporations obtain long-term loans directly from the government, and short-term loans from the banks. In recent years some public corporations have obtained loans from overseas, and the Treasury normally guarantees these loans. The government finances any losses incurred by the public corporations.

Each public corporation must publish an annual report and accounts. These reports and accounts are reviewed by Parliament.

4 Aims

The main objective of a limited company is to make a profit, but this is not the main purpose of a public corporation. The public corporations which run the nationalised industries are expected to 'pay their way'; that is, they should not make persistent losses. Their main objective, however, is to operate 'in the public interest'. This means that the managers should run these businesses in such a way as to bring benefits to the whole country.

A public corporation, therefore, should take far more account of the social effects of its activities than would be the case with a limited company. For example, British Rail would be very reluctant to close down loss-making lines to some rural areas. The closure of such lines would, in some cases, deprive residents and firms in those areas of a valuable service. If such lines are kept open, however, British Rail might incur heavy losses (which it is supposed to avoid). The present policy of the government, therefore, is to provide public corporations with subsidies to cover losses on services which are thought to have great social benefits even though they are run at a loss.

The subject of nationalisation is discussed in Chapter 12.

Municipal enterprises

Local authorities are also involved in running trading enterprises. Probably the most familiar of these are the local bus services operated by local authorities in the larger towns. But facilities such as swimming baths, golf courses, restaurants, seaside piers and a variety of entertainments are typical of the services produced and sold by local authorities.

Some of these leisure services may be subsidised from the rates and sold at prices which do not cover the full cost of providing them.

The Main Points

- *The sole trader* is the most common form of business organisation. A one-person business is easy to establish and is a very flexible organisation. The owner obtains all the profits and bears all the losses, so there is a strong personal incentive to succeed. A major disadvantage is that the owner has unlimited liability for the debts of the business.

- *Partnerships* can raise more capital than a sole trader can, and the partners can share the management duties (i.e. they can specialise). Active partners have unlimited liability but inactive partners may have their liability limited. Partnerships are commonly found in agriculture, catering, retailing and building, and in professional services such as law, accountancy and medicine.

- *Limited companies* must comply with the Companies Acts and be registered with the Registrar of Companies. Public limited companies can invite the general public to subscribe for their shares, but private limited companies cannot do so. Public companies are generally large enterprises; private companies are usually small enterprises and are often owned by members of one family. A company's shareholders have no further liability for the debts of the company once they have fully paid for their shares. Shares in a public company are freely transferable. The profits of companies are distributed in the form of dividends which are expressed as a percentage of the nominal value of the shares. A dividend of 15 per cent means that 15p is paid out on every £1 share. All companies must publish annual accounts.

- *Cooperative societies* fall into two types:
  - Worker cooperatives are owned and controlled by the people who work in them. The managers of these enterprises are elected by the workers.
  - Consumer or retail cooperative societies are owned by the members who, in this case, are the customers. Anyone can become a

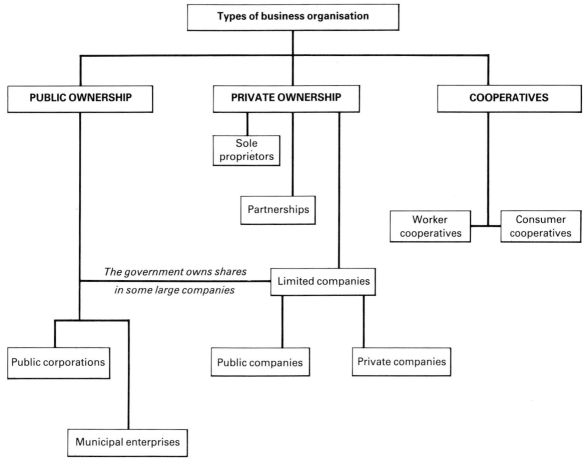

Figure 11.5
Types of business organisation

member of a cooperative society by purchasing one £1 share. Control is democratic – each member has one vote. Members elect a management committe to run the enterprise. Profits are shared out according to the value of a customer's purchases, and members receive additional benefits in the form of bonuses or special offers. The retail cooperative societies own the Cooperative Wholesale Society which supplies many of the goods sold by these societies.

■ *Public corporations* are organisations which manage the day-to-day operations of the nationalised industries. Since these industries are owned by the state, there are no shareholders, and the members of the boards of management are appointed by a Minister of the Crown. Long-term loans are provided by the government, which also finances any losses. Public corporations do not try to maximise profits, but they are expected to cover their costs and to earn a reasonable surplus to help finance their new investment. Parliament reviews the performance of the nationalised industries.

Test Your Understanding

1. Figure 11.6 shows the symbols or trade marks used by some large well-known public companies. Can you identify the companies?

Figure 11.6

2. Give some examples of industries and occupations in which there are many sole traders.

3. Many of the firms supplying professional services are organised as partnerships. Give some examples of these professional services.

4. What is meant when it is said that a firm has *unlimited liability*?

5. This question refers to the following groups of investors:

   A preference shareholders
   B ordinary shareholders
   C debenture holders

   (a) Which TWO of the above groups are owners of the company?
   (b) Which ONE of the groups will experience the most variable income from the company?
   (c) Which ONE of the groups holds the safest (least risky) form of investment?

6. Which ONE of the following enterprises is a public corporation?

   A GEC
   B ICI
   C CEGB
   D BP

7. This question refers to the following types of business organisation:

   A a sole trader
   B a retail cooperative society
   C a private joint stock company
   D a public joint stock company
   E a public corporation

   Which ONE of the above
   (a) limits its voting rights to 'one member, one vote'?
   (b) is the easiest type of business organisation to set up?
   (c) has its managers appointed rather than elected?
   (d) cannot offer its shares to the general public?

BOX 11
Getting started – the birth of a business

John Smith is a skilled engineer who spends much of his spare time in his small workshop making gadgets for the home and toys for his children. One of his toys performs very successfully. It is an electrically powered motor car which, with a few simple adjustments, can be converted into a form of powered motor boat.

Susan Jones, a friend and neighbour, is a businesswoman and she persuades John that he has invented something which could be a big success in the market for toys. John makes more of these 'car–boats', and local shops have no difficulty in selling them.

Susan believes that if John gave up his job and worked full-time producing this new toy, he could have a successful business. But this would mean producing the toys much more quickly and more cheaply. In order to market more toys at lower prices, John will require a much larger workshop and some machines. This will require an investment of about £20 000, but John has only about £4000 in his savings account.

Questions
1. How might John obtain the money he needs in order to obtain the larger workshop and the machines?
2. Would the methods you have suggested leave John with unlimited liability? Explain your answer.
3. Suppose John wishes to keep control of the firm in the hands of his family and a few friends and, at the same time, have limited liability. What steps should he take? Explain your answer.
4. How might John prevent other firms from copying his invention?

CHAPTER 12
Competition and monopoly

12.1 Competition
12.2 Monopoly
12.3 The control of monopoly
12.4 Protecting the consumer
12.5 Nationalisation and privatisation

12.1
Competition

In the markets for most of the things we buy we
have a choice. Whether we are buying a motor
car, a tube of toothpaste or a holiday abroad, we
find several firms competing for our custom.
Firms compete with each other in different ways.

Price competition

The main form of competition is price competition, where firms try to 'under-price' their
competitors. This is very common in the markets
for groceries and other household goods. It is
probably most noticeable in the competition
between supermarkets, the large DIY stores and
discount stores selling electrical appliances.

Non-price competition

Competition between firms, however, is not
confined to price competition; it can take many
other forms. Firms may compete by
- branding their goods and making the brand
  name familiar by means of advertising,
- using attractive packaging,
- offering improved services to customers, such
  as better after-sales service and better guarantees,
- creating more attractive retail outlets,
- offering 'free' gifts (e.g. drinking glasses),
  special offers (e.g. gifts in exchange for collec-
  tions of packet tops or wrappers) or the chance
  to win prizes in competitions,
- providing easier and cheaper hire-purchase
  facilities.

Figure 12.1
Types of competition

Price competition is a common feature in the markets
for household goods

Another form of competition

Some features of competition

1. In a competitive market, firms are not free to set any price they wish. They have to take account of the prices being charged by other firms selling very similar goods and services.
2. If the competition between firms is very fierce, prices will be forced downwards to levels which are very close to the firms' costs of production.
3. An important feature of a market in which several firms are competing is the fact that consumers will have a choice.
4. Competition may force firms to cut the quality of their goods as a way of reducing costs and prices.
5. If a market is being supplied by many small firms, each trying to produce something slightly different from the products of other firms,
   - there may be an excessive variety of products, and
   - small-scale production could mean relatively high average costs.
6. Supporters of competition argue that it forces firms to be efficient. The penalty for being inefficient is to be driven from the market by more efficient firms.

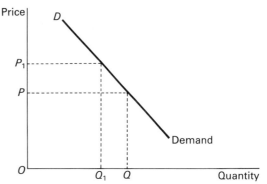

Figure 12.2
A monopoly can control the supply of a good or service, but it cannot control the demand for it. If the firm sets a price of OP_1, then the demand curve fixes the quantity demanded at OQ_1. If the firm decides to place the quantity OQ on the market, it will have to accept a price of OP

3. A monopoly is free to set *either* the price of its product *or* the quantity it wishes to sell (it cannot set both, because it cannot control the demand curve). If it decides to set the price, the demand curve will determine the quantity it can sell. If the monopoly decides to place a certain quantity on the market, the demand curve will determine the price at which it can sell that quantity (see Figure 12.2).
4. The fact that a monopoly can control the quantity supplied to the market means that it can influence the price. By deliberately restricting the amount supplied, a monopoly will be able to force the price upwards.
5. A monopoly can only continue to exist if other firms are prevented from entering the market. Monopolies are protected from competition by what are known as 'barriers to entry'. These are described below.

12.2

Monopoly

A monopoly exists when there is a sole supplier of a good or service. In this type of market there is an absence of competition – there *are* no competitors. Examples of monopoly can be found in the markets for electricity, rail transport and postal services. All these are supplied by publicly-owned industries which have monopoly powers.

Some features of monopoly

1. In theory, monopoly means that there is only one supplier of a particular good or service. A monopolist supplies the total market. (We shall see later that the legal definition of monopoly is rather different from this.)
2. A monopolist, therefore, does not have to worry about the prices charged by competitors, because there are no competitors.

How monopolies are created

1 By law

The government can grant monopoly powers to a firm by making it illegal for other firms to enter the industry. Most of the nationalised industries are legal monopolies. The law can also grant the holders of patents the sole right to supply the products they have patented.

2 By competition

Fierce competition will drive the weaker and less efficient firms out of an industry. It is possible that, eventually, one firm could come to dominate a whole industry.

3 By mergers and amalgamations

When an industry is made up of a few relatively large firms, a series of mergers or take-overs could lead to a monopoly situation.

4 By forming a cartel

A cartel is created when the individual firms in an industry make an agreement to restrict their outputs to some agreed amounts, and to charge a common price. The Organisation of Petroleum Exporting Countries (OPEC) is a form of cartel, and so is the Milk Marketing Board in the UK.

5 By ownership of scarce resources

Where the workable deposits of certain minerals are concentrated in a particular region, the owners of such deposits will have considerable monopoly power. This is the case with gold deposits in South Africa.

Monopoly and the barriers to entry

It has already been noted that a firm can only hold a monopoly position if other firms are prevented from competing with it. The barriers which prevent other firms from entering the industry can take several forms.

1 The law

This was explained in the previous section.

2 Economies of scale

A very large firm may be protected from competition by the sheer size of its operations. Large-scale production may enable it to produce at very low average cost. Any new firm thinking of entering the same industry would find it difficult or impossible to achieve such a low average cost. It would be unlikely to have the resources or be prepared to take the risks of starting production on the same scale as the existing firm.

3 Advertising

The products of some large firms have well-established brand names whose familiarity is maintained by continuous and expensive advertising. It is difficult for new firms to enter these markets because they would have to undertake very costly advertising campaigns in order to establish a new brand name.

4 Geography

As explained above, owners of scarce and valuable mineral deposits are protected from competition until some new deposits are discovered or some substitute product is invented. For example, the monopoly powers of OPEC were seriously weakened by the discovery of new oilfields.

5 Restrictive trade practices

The existing firms in an industry may act together so as to make it difficult for new firms to enter the industry. For example, manufacturers may form an association and make agreements with wholesalers and retailers whereby these distributors will only stock the goods made by the existing manufacturers. Any new firm trying to compete with the existing firms would find it very difficult to market its products. This type of agreement is now illegal in the UK.

Some arguments for monopoly

1. In some industries, competition would lead to a wasteful duplication of capital equipment. The most obvious examples are in the distribution of gas, electricity, water and telephone services. Competition would mean the installation of several competing networks of pipes or cables.
2. In many industries, a large dominant firm will be able to obtain economies of scale which could not be achieved by small competing firms. The fact that a monopoly can produce at lower cost, however, does not necessarily mean that prices will be lower: it could mean higher profits.
3. A monopoly is likely to have more resources for research and development than the small firms in a competitive industry. It also has a greater

incentive to spend money on research, since it will obtain all the profits of any successful invention. In a competitive industry, new ideas are quickly copied by other firms.

Some arguments against monopoly

1. A monopoly is capable of restricting the supply of a product. It can, therefore, raise prices well above the average cost of production.
2. Monopolies are not under constant pressure from competitors. This lack of competition could well result in them being less efficient than firms which have to compete with other firms.
3. When an industry is monopolised, there is only one source of supply. The variety of goods available to consumers will tend to be less than that which would be supplied by a number of competing firms.
4. New techniques and new products are often introduced by small newly-established firms. The fact that monopolies can prevent other firms from entering an industry means that the flow of new ideas and new products will probably be restricted.

12.3
The control of monopoly

There is a widely-held belief that monopolies will use their market power to charge prices which are much higher than costs, and so make excessive profits. Many people also believe that actions which restrict competition are generally harmful to the economy. These views, and others, have persuaded governments to control the activities of monopolies.

The fact that monopoly situations can have advantages for the general public as well as disadvantages has meant that monopolies have not been banned. In the UK, the government's policy is designed to remove the disadvantages of monopolies, while retaining, where possible, the advantages.

There are two kinds of monopoly organisations which are subject to government control:
– where there is a single-firm monopoly, and

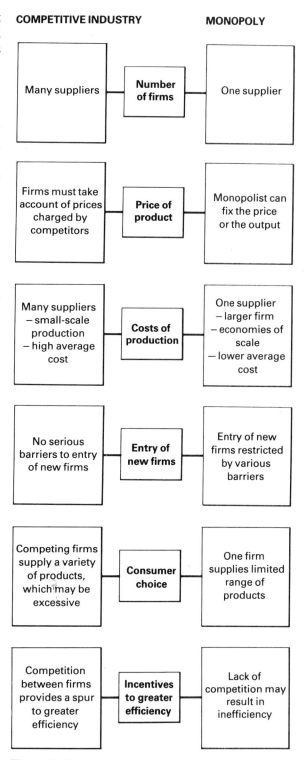

Figure 12.3

Features of a competitive industry and a monopoly

– where the firms in an industry make an agreement not to compete with one another, and take action to restrict the entry of new firms. (Such agreements are known as restrictive trade practices, and were discussed above.)

Government controls apply to monopolies in the supply of services as well as goods. In British law, a firm (or group of firms acting together) does not have to control 100 per cent of the supply of a good or service in order to be classed as a monopoly. If it controls more than 25 per cent of the total supply it counts as a monopoly.

The government has established a number of institutions which have the task of investigating monopolies in order to discover whether or not they are acting against the public interest. These include the following.

The Director-General of Fair Trading

This important official has the main responsibility for seeing that the government's policy on monopolies and competition is carried out. His department, the Office of Fair Trading, collects information on the way in which companies and trade associations are conducting their business, and recommends action when it appears that firms are doing things which are against the public interest.

The Monopolies and Mergers Commission (MMC)

This commission consists of men and women drawn from different occupations, who serve on a part-time basis. The task of the MMC is to investigate monopolies, and to publish reports on their findings. In these reports, the MMC sets out any changes it would like to see in the organisation of the industry, the way in which the goods and services are marketed, the way in which the prices are fixed, and so on. After considering such a report, the government decides what action should be taken. It may advise or, if necessary, order firms to make changes in the way they are running their businesses.

The MMC can also be asked to investigate and report on the likely effect of proposed mergers. A merger can be vetoed by the government if it thinks it will lead to an unsatisfactory monopoly situation.

The Restrictive Practices Court

This is a branch of the High Court which was set up to deal with restrictive trade practices. A decision of the Court becomes part of UK law.

Agreements between firms which have the effect of restricting competition have to be registered with the Director-General of Fair Trading, who can then refer them to the Restrictive Practices Court. The task of the Court is to look at the way a restrictive practice is working, and then to decide whether it is harmful to the public interest. It may, for example, decide that a restrictive practice should be made illegal because
– it is restricting competition and enables the firms to keep prices higher than they would be without such an agreement, or
– it is preventing other firms from entering the industry, or
– it is restricting consumers' freedom of choice.

12.4
Protecting the consumer

In a perfectly free market, the individual consumer is in a weak position when dealing with suppliers of goods and services. He or she does not have the technical knowledge or the experience of the business world which is usually possessed by sellers of goods and services. For this reason, the government has taken powers to protect consumers and to make sure that they are not deliberately misled or dealt with unfairly by firms selling goods and services.

The Director-General of Fair Trading acts as the consumers' watchdog. His duties include the following:
– proposing new laws to end unfair trading practices,
– encouraging trade associations to draw up codes of good conduct for their member firms,
– dealing with manufacturers and traders who persistently commit offences,
– keeping the public informed of their rights by publishing pamphlets and booklets.

The major Acts of Parliament which deal with consumers' rights are as follows.

The Sale and Supply of Goods Acts

This legislation requires that the goods supplied must satisfy three conditions:

1. They must be of merchantable quality. For example, if a consumer buys a pre-packed garment and finds a hole in it when it is unpacked, he or she has the right to return the garment.
2. The goods must be fit for the purpose for which goods of that kind are normally used. A lawn-mower must be capable of cutting grass, a dish-washer must be capable of washing dishes, and so on.
3. The goods must be as described on the package, on a display sign or by the seller in person.

If any of these conditions is not met, the buyer has the right to reclaim money spent on the goods. But the buyer must exercise due care. If he or she examined the goods when making the purchase and the faults were apparent or were pointed out by the seller, the buyer has no rights against the seller.

The Trade Descriptions Act

This Act makes it an offence for traders to describe inaccurately the goods or services being sold. For example, it is an offence for a retailer to label a garment 'all wool' if it consists of a mixture of wool and nylon. A spoken inaccurate description is just as much an offence as a written one.

The Unsolicited Goods and Services Act

This Act makes it an offence for a firm to demand payment for goods which have not been ordered. Such goods are usually sent by post. The consumer is under no obligation to return goods which he or she has not ordered: it is up to the firm which sent them to collect them.

The Weights and Measures Act

Traders' weights, measures and scales must be accurate, and it is an offence to give short measure or inadequate quantity, or to mark pre-packed goods with a wrong indication of their quantity.

The Food and Drugs Act

This Act makes it an offence to sell unfit food, or to describe food falsely, or to mislead people as to its nature, substance or quality. The Act also includes regulations governing hygiene in all places where food is prepared or sold.

The Consumer Safety Act

This legislation aims to protect consumers from unsafe goods, and to reduce the risk of death or injury. Regulations have been made in respect of the design and materials used in such things as electrical appliances, room heaters and cooking utensils, and the flammability of clothing materials.

The Consumer Credit Act

Many goods and services, especially durable consumer goods, are now bought on credit; that is, they are purchased by instalments. This Act makes it compulsory for traders to supply full information about their credit and hire-purchase schemes, so that purchasers will not be misled about the terms on which they are buying the goods and services.

Other sources of help for consumers

There is a large number of organisations which offer help and advice to consumers. Three examples are described below.

Local authorities

Local authorities have Trading Standards, Consumer Protection, and Health departments, whose job it is to make sure that most of the laws described above are enforced. They investigate complaints about unfair advertising, misleading descriptions of goods, products which are unsafe, unhygienic conditions in food shops and restaurants, and so on. Offenders are prosecuted. Many local authorities also have *Consumer Advice Centres*, to which shoppers can take complaints and which offer information and advice.

Citizens' Advice Bureaux

These provide a 'walk-in' service and offer help and advice on all aspects of shopping. They also deal with queries on such matters as housing, health and legal matters.

The Consumers' Association

This is a private organisation which is paid for by members' subscriptions. Membership is open to everyone. Its monthly magazine, *Which?*, publishes the results of tests carried out on a wide range of goods and services. Since the association gets no money from industry or advertising, it can offer independent advice and is free to criticise anything which it thinks is unsafe, of inferior quality or poor value for money.

12.5
Nationalisation and privatisation

Nationalisation

The term 'nationalisation' describes the process of transferring industry from private ownership to public ownership. The state buys the companies in an industry by paying shareholders a price which approximates to the market value of their shares. Nationalisation is included in this chapter because most of the nationalised industries have some degree of monopoly power.

During the course of this century many large and important industries were nationalised. In 1979 the nationalised industries employed nearly two million people and accounted for about 10 per cent of the total output of the UK. They dominated the industries supplying coal, gas, electricity, steel, rail transport, telecommunications and postal services.

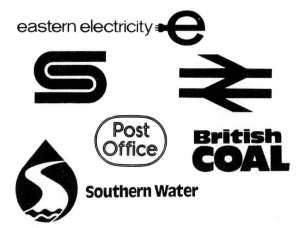

Figure 12.4
Some state-owned companies

Table 12.1
Privatisation in the UK

The nationalised industries that will remain in the public sector at the end of 1987–88 are:
British Coal
Electricity (England and Wales)
North of Scotland Hydro-Electric Board
South of Scotland Electricity Board
British Steel Corporation
The Post Office
Girobank
British Railways Board
Scottish Transport Group
British Shipbuilders (Merchant)
Civil Aviation Authority
Water (England and Wales)
London Regional Transport

The following industries have been privatised since 1979:
British Telecom
British Gas Corporation
British National Oil Corporation
British Airways
British Airports Authority
British Aerospace
British Shipbuilders (Warships)
British Transport Docks Board
National Freight Company
Enterprise Oil
National Bus Company

Source: *Economic Progress Report*, HMSO, December 1987

Privatisation

Since 1979 the picture has greatly changed. The Conservative government elected in 1979 and re-elected in 1983 and 1987 carried out a major programme of privatisation. In other words, it returned many state-owned industries to the private sector. The public corporations which ran these industries were converted into limited companies, and the shares were sold to the general public. Among the better-known industries which were privatised were British Gas, British Telecom and British Airways. (See Table 12.1 and Box 12.)

The nationalised industries

Table 12.1 lists the major nationalised industries in the UK in 1987.

Nationalisation, of course, is not peculiar to the UK. The public ownership of industries supplying gas, electricity, coal, railway transport, and postal and telephone services is a common feature of many economies.

Arguments for nationalisation

1 To avoid wasteful competition

As explained earlier, the industries supplying gas, water, electricity and telephone services need vast networks of pipes and cables in order to supply their customers. To allow several firms to compete with one another in such industries would lead to a wasteful duplication of overhead and underground equipment. However, this is an argument for monopoly rather than for nationalisation. The argument for nationalisation says that these monopolies should be publicly owned because the goods and services they supply are so important to the economy that they should be run in the national interest and not for private profit.

2 Economies of scale

In industries such as those mentioned above, the full benefits of economies of scale can only be obtained if there is one large firm in each industry. Many people believe that the quickest and most certain way of achieving a monopoly in these industries is to nationalise them.

3 To help manage the economy

The ownership and control of major industries gives the government a powerful instrument for influencing the performance of the economy. For example, the prices of coal and electricity are important elements in the costs of industry and they are major items in the spending of households. In times of rising prices, therefore, the government may hold down the prices charged by the nationalised industries in an attempt to slow down the rate of inflation.

4 Political arguments

Nationalisation is seen by many people as an important part of a policy for reducing inequalities of income and wealth. They believe that industry should belong to, and be run for the benefit of, all the people. Nationalised industries, for example, will take far more account of social costs and benefits than private firms would.

Some criticisms of nationalisation

1 It does not encourage efficiency

Lack of competition

Many nationalised industries are protected from competition by law. Without the spur of competition, it is argued, management will become complacent and inefficient. Lack of competition also reduces consumers' choice.

No fear of bankruptcy

Nationalised industries cannot go bankrupt, because the government is obliged to cover any losses they may make. Opponents of nationalisation believe that this is another reason why nationalised industries are likely to be less efficient than privately-owned firms.

2 It is difficult to measure the efficiency of nationalised industries

Some idea of the efficiency of a privately-owned firm can be obtained by comparing its performance with those of other firms in the same industry. This is not possible with a nationalised industry. If nationalised industries make profits, it does not follow that they are efficient, because they may be using their monopoly powers to raise prices. If they make losses, it does not follow that they are inefficient, because the government may be forcing them to hold down their prices.

The Main Points

- The main form of competition is price competition, but there are many forms of non-price competition, such as advertising, 'free' gifts, special offers, improved services, and competitions.

- Keen competition probably encourages efficiency, and is likely to drive prices down to levels close to the costs of production.

- In an industry with many competing firms, production will be on a small scale, with relatively high average costs. There could also be an excessive variety of products.

■ In theory, a monopoly exists where there is just one supplier of a product. In British law a monopoly exists when more than 25 per cent of the total supply of a product is controlled by one firm or a group of firms acting together.

■ A monopolist can control either the price or the output, but not both. A monopoly can only exist where there are barriers to the entry of other firms.

■ Monopolies can be advantageous where competition would result in wasteful duplication of capital equipment and where important economies of scale are possible. On the other hand, they have the power to raise prices well above the costs of production and, because they have no competitors, they may be inefficient. By preventing other firms from entering the industry, they restrict consumers' choice.

■ The Director-General of Fair Trading is responsible for seeing that the government's policy on competition and monopoly is carried out. The Monopolies and Mergers Commission and the Restrictive Practices Court exist to ensure that monopoly power is not being used in ways harmful to the public interest, and that firms are not making use of unfair trading practices.

■ Nationalised industries tend to be monopolies, and the arguments for and against monopolies can be applied to these industries. They have been nationalised for many reasons; among these are widely-held views that powerful monopolies should not be run for private profit and that public ownership is more democratic than private ownership.

Test Your Understanding

1. What is the main form of competition between supermarkets?

2. In what different ways do petrol companies compete with one another?

3. Why is competition supposed to encourage efficiency?

4. A village has one grocery store. Its prices, on average, are at least 10 per cent higher than the prices in the nearest supermarket, which is situated five miles from the village. What is protecting this store from competition?

5. Why is the managing director of a monopoly very unlikely to make the following statement (or one very similar to it) to his sales manager: 'I intend to produce a thousand of these articles each week, and I want you to sell them at £5 each'?

6. (a) What is the title of the official who has overall responsibility for carrying out government policy on competition and monopoly?
   (b) Which official body will he ask to investigate
      (i) a situation where one firm is believed to control 40 per cent of the market in frozen food?
      (ii) a situation where a group of manufacturers have agreed not to supply their goods to 'cut-price' retailers?

7. In choosing a hotel for its summer holiday, a family was influenced by a local travel agent who told them: 'In my opinion, this is a very good hotel. I have stayed there and I thoroughly enjoyed my visit.' In fact, the hotel was not what the family expected, and they found it very unsatisfactory. Was the travel agent guilty under the Trade Descriptions Act?

8. The sale of British Telecom by issuing shares to employees and the general public was an example of the process known as .... What is the missing word?

9. One of the reasons for nationalisation is the belief that nationalised industries would be much more concerned with social costs and benefits than privately-owned companies. Give some examples of how concern with social costs and benefits has influenced the activities of *one* of the following: British Rail, British Coal, the Post Office.

BOX 12
Privatisation

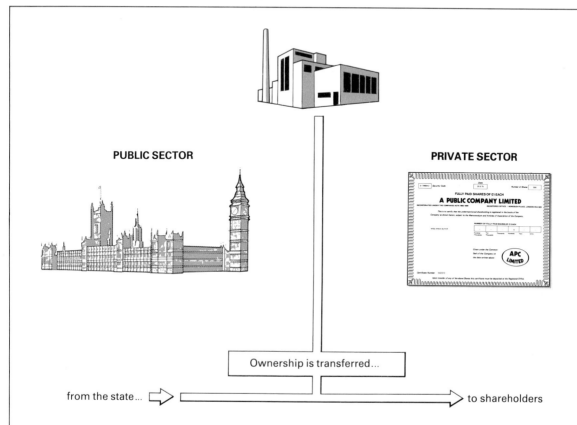

PUBLIC SECTOR

PRIVATE SECTOR

Ownership is transferred...

from the state... ⟹ ⟶ to shareholders

The Conservative government elected in 1979 set out to reduce the size of the public sector by transferring publicly-owned assets to private ownership. This policy is described as *privatisation*, and includes
– de-nationalisation (the sale of nationalised industries),
– the sale of government-owned shares in large public companies, and
– the sale of council houses to their tenants.

By 1987, one third of the industry which had been state-owned in 1979 had been privatised. By this time, the policy of privatisation had brought in more than £10 billion in revenue for the government, and some 600 000 jobs had been transferred from the public sector to the private sector. It had also increased the number of private shareholders from about $2\frac{1}{2}$ million in 1979 to around 9 million in 1987.

Questions
1. Privatisation refers to a transfer of ownership. Explain how the ownership of an industry may be transferred from the public sector to the private sector.
2. Give some arguments for, and some against, the privatisation of one of the following: British Telecom, British Gas, British Airways.

CHAPTER 13

The location of industry

13.1 Factors that influence the location of industry
13.2 Why governments influence industrial location
13.3 Regional policy – assisted areas

Factors that influence the location of industry

One of the most important decisions to be taken when an entrepreneur is setting up in business, or thinking about expanding the firm, is where to locate the firm (or the new branch of the firm).

For different industries, different locations have advantages or disadvantages which will affect the firm's costs of production. If we assume that firms try to earn the maximum profit, they will be drawn to locations where they believe average cost will be relatively low. There are many factors which may influence a firm's choice of location.

1 Availability of land

The availability and, perhaps more important, the price of land will have an important influence on the choice of location. For example, modern factories are often single-storey buildings which use up a lot of land. This is one reason why many new factories are found in industrial estates situated on the outskirts of towns, where land tends to be relatively cheap.

2 Access to raw materials, power and water

Raw materials

Some industries process heavy, bulky raw materials which are costly to transport. The products of these industries generally weigh much less than the raw materials from which they are made. For example, it takes many tonnes of sugar beet

to make one tonne of sugar, and many tonnes of iron ore to make one tonne of iron. In these cases, locating the firm near to the source of the raw materials greatly reduces transport costs.

Where heavy and bulky raw materials have to be imported, locations at or near major ports will have obvious advantages. In the UK, for example, we find that steelworks are located on iron-ore fields or at major ports.

Power

In the early days of industrialisation, the main source of energy was coal, which is costly to handle and to transport. For this reason, most industries sited themselves on the coalfields. Nowadays, the coalfields have little or no influence on location decisions because electricity, gas and oil are available in all parts of the UK.

Water

Although supplies of water are available in all areas of the UK, some industries use vast quantities of water in their production processes. The generation of electricity and the production of chemicals, steel and paper are examples of such industries. A location on the banks of a river or on an estuary is essential where water plays such an important part in the industrial process.

3 The locations of the main markets

A site near the major markets for the product will obviously reduce the costs of transporting the finished product. It may not, however, minimise the total transport costs. If the raw materials are very costly to transport, a site near the source of these materials may still be the most favourable location. A location near to the market will tend to have advantages when the finished product is more costly to transport than the raw materials. For example, planks of wood can be moved at less cost than pieces of furniture, and thin sheets of steel are more easily transported than washing machines and refrigerators.

Products which are heavy or bulky in relation to their value will also tend to be produced near to their markets in order to reduce transport costs. Brewing, brickmaking and the baking of bread are examples of such industries.

The attraction of sites near to major markets helps to explain why so many firms are located in the London area.

4 Labour

All firms need a supply of labour. When there is heavy unemployment, labour will be available in all areas. In more prosperous times, however, it is not unusual to find labour shortages in some areas and surpluses in other areas. Firms will be attracted to areas which have a surplus of labour.

When the demand is for some particular types of skilled labour, some areas have advantages over others. For example, Coventry has a labour force skilled in the manufacture of motor cars, and Sheffield has workers skilled in making things from steel.

Firms deciding on their location will also take into account any differences in the costs of labour in different parts of the country. Although trade unions try to negotiate *national* wage rates for their members, there are significant differences in average earnings in different regions of the UK.

5 Transport facilities

In the nineteenth century the railway network exerted a powerful influence on the location of industry. Firms depended heavily on the railways for the transport of their raw materials and their products. Most factories were sited near to a railway line. Nowadays, most goods are moved by road and, since the the road network is much more extensive than the rail network, firms now have a much wider choice of location. In more recent times, sites near to the motorway network have become popular locations.

Many firms assemble finished products from parts and components manufactured by several different firms located in different parts of the country. This means that good transport links are likely to play a large part in the choosing of a location for an assembly plant.

6 Regional specialisation

Once an industry becomes well established in a particular region, that area acquires advantages from which all the firms in that industry can benefit. Firms wishing to enter the industry, therefore, tend to be attracted to this particular location. The advantages enjoyed by firms in localised industries have been described earlier under the heading 'external economies of scale' (see page 50): they are also described as *economies of concentration.*

Several British industries are heavily concentrated in certain regions. Well-known examples are

- shipbuilding on the Clyde, and in Tyneside, Merseyside and Belfast,
- the manufacture of woollen cloth in West Yorkshire,
- the cotton industry in Lancashire,
- the pottery industry in North Staffordshire,
- the car industry in Coventry, Luton, Oxford and Dagenham,
- the footwear industry in Leicester and Northampton,
- the manufacture of steel products in Sheffield.

The original reasons for the localisation of these and other industries were the natural advantages of an area, such as

- local deposits of iron ore or clay,
- easy access to supplies of coal and water,
- adequate local supplies of wool or leather, or
- nearness to a port where raw materials were imported and the products exported.

But long after these natural advantages either disappeared or became much less important, industries remained in the same area because other advantages – the economies of concentration – had become very important.

7 The government

In the UK, and in most other countries, the

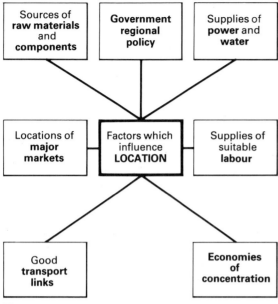

Figure 13.1

government exerts a great influence on the location of industry. Why it does so, and how it does so, are the subjects of the rest of this chapter.

13.2
Why governments influence industrial location

1 Regional differences in unemployment rates

After the First World War, the decline of several major British industries caused serious unemployment problems in the areas where they were concentrated. Shipbuilding, coal, steel and cotton were among the industries which experienced serious falls in the demands for their products. The areas most affected were Central Scotland, Northern England and Wales. Among the reasons for the decline of these industries were the following:

– Some of them, for example coal, cotton and shipbuilding, lost important export markets.
– In some cases, the industry's product was replaced by a superior substitute. For example, oil became an important source of energy at the expense of coal and, in later years, synthetic fibres such as nylon affected the demand for cotton.

Figure 13.2
Regional unemployment in the UK, November 1987

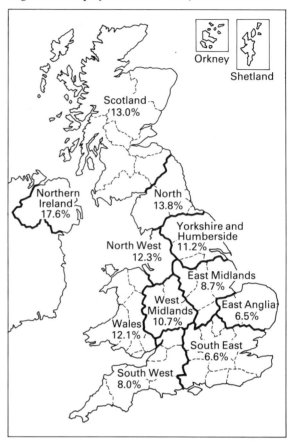

Source: *Department of Employment Gazette*, January 1988

The problem was made worse because the newer industries, such as the manufacture of motor cars, electrical goods and processed foods, tended to choose locations in the Midlands and the South East. The result of these developments was that unemployment rates were very much higher in some regions than in others. The high levels of unemployment in the 1980s affected the whole country, but Figure 13.2 shows that regional differences in unemployment rates still persist.

2 Industrial concentration makes a region too dependent on one industry

The concentration of an industry in one region means that the prosperity of that region depends mainly on the success of that industry. If the industry declines, it will have a kind of 'snowball effect' – not only will the workers in that industry lose their jobs, but workers in local firms which supply the industry with materials and services will also suffer unemployment. Shops, garages, cafés, public houses and places of entertainment will all experience a loss of trade, as the incomes and spending of local people are reduced.

3 Urban sprawl

Heavy concentrations of industry lead to the growth of sprawling built-up areas such as those around London, Glasgow, Birmingham and Manchester. These *conurbations*, as they are called, create heavy social costs in the form of congestion and pollution. Such areas are regarded as unsatisfactory environments, and they have given rise to increasing social problems. These are particularly serious when the centres of large cities are allowed to decay as people and industry move out to the suburbs.

13.3
Regional policy – assisted areas

The features described above make up what is described as the *regional problem*. The government's regional policy aims to
- reduce the differences in regional unemployment rates,
- reduce an area's dependence on the prosperity of one major industry, and
- restrict the growth of the great conurbations.

Regional unemployment

There are two possible ways of dealing with this problem:

1 'Taking workers to the work'

The movement of unemployed people from areas which have high unemployment rates to more prosperous areas is a difficult task. Housing shortages and people's reluctance to leave relatives and friends in the areas where they have grown up are serious barriers to the movement of labour from one area to another. Although the government does offer financial assistance to those who can move, this policy is not regarded as the best solution to the problem.

2 'Taking work to the workers'

Most of the government's attempts to deal with regional unemployment concentrate on persuading firms to move to, or set up new branches in, the areas of relatively high unemployment. The measures used by the government are described below.

Assisted areas

Certain parts of the country, where unemployment is much higher than the national average, have been identified as being in need of special government aid. They are described as assisted areas.

Until 1979, large areas of Scotland, Wales, Northern England and some parts of Devon and Cornwall were classed as assisted areas. The size of the assisted areas has since been reduced, but in 1986 they still contained about 35 per cent of the working population.

Figure 13.3
Assisted areas in the UK

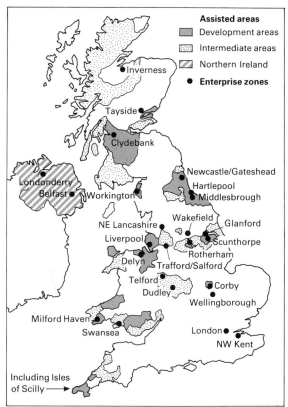

Source: *The Economist*, 26 October 1985

There are two types of assisted area, *development areas* and *intermediate areas*. Development areas are regions where the unemployment problems are particularly serious, and they qualify for more assistance than intermediate areas. Figure 13.3 (on page 119) shows the distribution of assisted areas in 1986.

Government help to assisted areas

In order to encourage firms to move to or expand in assisted areas, the government offers several forms of assistance:

1 Capital grants

These are intended to help towards the cost of purchasing land, buildings, machinery and equipment. Additional grants are available in development areas.

2 Training grants

Firms setting up in or expanding in assisted areas can obtain grants to cover part of the cost of training local labour.

3 New factories

The government has built new factories in the assisted areas. These are made available to firms for rent or sale on very favourable terms.

4 Preferential treatment

Firms in assisted areas are sometimes given preference when government contracts are being awarded.

The grants are available for service industries, as well as manufacturing industries. Government aid is usually only available for projects which will definitely create new jobs or safeguard existing jobs. In addition to this aid from the central government, assisted areas also receive help in the form of loans and grants from the European Economic Community (EEC).

Local authorities, anxious to attract firms to their areas, also offer various incentives, such as reduced rent and rates for limited periods, and grants to assist with the development of a new industrial site and to cover some part of the cost of fitting out new industrial buildings.

Enterprise zones

In 1980 the government announced plans to deal with the serious problems of decline and decay in the centres of several large industrial cities. It established enterprise zones in a number of cities, and provided several inducements to attract firms back into these areas. Firms setting up in enterprise zones are offered tax allowances on industrial buildings, exemptions from local rates and a relaxation of certain planning controls.

New towns

As a means of restricting the growth of the large conurbations, a number of new towns have been built. These have been sited so as to draw people and industry away from the more densely populated regions. About 20 of these new towns have now been built.

Effects of regional policy

Although the policy has not succeeded in removing the differences in regional unemployment rates, there is no doubt that it has had an important effect. It is estimated that between 1964 and 1984 it was responsible for creating some 400 000 new jobs and probably safeguarded a further million jobs.

It must be borne in mind that the true cost of the government measures to create jobs is much less than the amount the government spends on subsidies and grants. When jobs are created, the government has to spend less on unemployment pay and social security benefits.

The Main Points

■ Different locations have advantages and disadvantages for different industries. A favourable location can reduce a firm's average costs of production.

■ A particular location may be desirable because it has either natural or acquired advantages, or both.

■ Natural advantages are features such as access to raw materials and power supplies, nearness to markets, and good transport links.

■ Acquired advantages are those which develop gradually, owing to the concentration of an industry in a particular location. They include such features as a supply of skilled labour, the presence of firms which specialise in supplying the industry with services and components, and training courses provided by local colleges which are specially designed for workers in the industry.

■ The government's regional policy aims to
  – reduce the differences in regional unemployment rates,
  – reduce a region's dependence on one major industry,
  – restrict the growth of the large conurbations.

■ The main features of regional policy are:
  – grants and other benefits are offered to firms which move to or expand in the assisted areas (additional aid is available in the development areas);
  – firms are offered tax concessions and other benefits if they move to enterprise zones, which have been established in urban areas where there are serious problems of decay and decline;
  – new towns have been built to draw people and industry away from the great conurbations.

Test Your Understanding

1. (a) Why were the coalfields the most important influence on the location of industry in the early days of industrialisation?
   (b) Why are the coalfields no longer an important influence on industrial location?

2. A firm's raw materials and components are easily transported, but its finished product is very bulky. Other things being equal, the firm will choose a location near to its .... What are the missing words (or word)?

3. Why does the government wish to see a greater variety of industries in all the regions of the UK?

4. This question refers to the following features which might influence the location of a firm:

   A In the area there is a supply of labour which has the skills required by the firm.
   B There are easily accessible deposits of the raw materials needed by the firm.
   C The locality already has several firms providing repair, maintenance and other technical services which the firm will need.
   D The firm requires large amounts of water for cooling purposes, and sites on a river bank are available in the locality.

   (a) Which TWO of these features can be described as *natural* advantages?
   (b) Which TWO of these features can be described as *acquired* advantages (or economies of concentration)?

5. A 'Taking workers to the work'
   B 'Taking work to the workers'

   Which of these alternatives is the main aim of regional policy? Why is it preferred to the other?

6. Why is the *net* cost of government financial help to the assisted areas less than the *total* cost?

BOX 13
Industrial location

The extracts below are taken from the *Mid Glamorgan Fact File*.

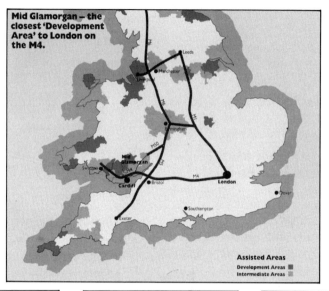

Mid Glamorgan – the closest 'Development Area' to London on the M4.

Assisted Areas
Development Areas ■
Intermediate Areas ▧

Cash grants, cheap loans, training and relocation assistance, new factory rentals from £2.00p per square foot, these are just some of the incentives available to businesses setting up in Mid Glamorgan.

You will be in good company in Mid Glamorgan. Some of the companies already here include Sony, Ford, Hitachi, A.B.Electronics, The Royal Mint, Hoover, Sekisui, Sheer Pride, Revlon, Christie-Tyler, Catnic Components, Fram Europe, A&A Electronics, Align-Rite and Ferrero.

But the Guide is not only about sites and premises. It will tell you something about the other key assets that are important to a businessman and his family.

Assets such as our skilled and adaptable labour force, our education and training resources, our wide range of leisure and recreational facilities, good executive housing and the attractive and rich cultural environment to be found in South East Wales.

■ **15 million people** are within a 100 mile radius of Mid Glamorgan and you will have access to 4.5 million people within 50 miles.

The Miskin Interchange (no.34) on the M4 motorway gives access to a range of nearby industrial estates and greenfield sites.

The Severn Bridge and the M4 motorway give fast passage for road distribution to British markets.

Cardiff-Wales Airport, on the doorstep of Mid Glamorgan, services national and international travel and has an inter-port removal facility.

Cardiff Docks, close to the County, is one of five ports along the South Wales Coast.

On the '125' inter-city high speed train Bridgend is about two hours away from Central London.

Questions
1. What is a development area?
2. Why does the *Business Location Guide* include the names of firms which have already located in Mid Glamorgan?
3. What does the *Business Location Guide* say about the availability of factors of production?
4. Explain the importance of the information which is provided on
   (a) communications by road, rail, sea and air.
   (b) population distribution.

CHAPTER 14

Money and banking

14.1
What is money?

The answer which many people would give to this question would probably be 'Notes, coins and cheques'. However, this is not a very satisfactory answer, for two reasons. Firstly, notes and coins make up quite a small part of the total money supply. Secondly, as explained later, cheques are not money.

A simple answer to the question is that money is whatever is generally acceptable in exchange for goods and services. In the past, many things have been used as money – shells, beads, ivory and salt are just a few examples. If people willingly accept something as a means of payment, then it is money. For example, we freely accept pieces of paper (banknotes) in exchange for goods and services. But banknotes are not valuable in themselves – they are simply pieces of paper! *They are valuable only because everyone accepts them as a means of payment.*

Even more remarkable is the fact that the most important form of money in use today has no physical existence – we cannot touch it or handle it, as we can notes and coins. This money is in the form of bank deposits, which consist of bookkeeping entries in a bank's accounts. Nowadays these bank deposits take the form of records in a bank's computer. They are explained in more detail in Section 14.4.

14.2
The functions and qualities of money

The functions of money

1 A medium of exchange

The earliest form of exchange was *barter* – the direct swapping of goods for other goods. This is a time-consuming and inconvenient process because it depends upon a *double coincidence of wants*. Put very simply this means that, under a barter system, if you have something you wish to exchange, you must find someone who not only wants what you have to offer but, at the same time, also has a supply of the goods you want to obtain.

The use of money as a medium of exchange removes the difficulties of barter. It enables sellers to exchange goods and services for money and then use the money to obtain whatever goods and services they desire.

2 A measure of value

Even under a barter system, exchange can only take place when there is some agreement on what one thing is worth in terms of another. For example, a lot of bargaining will have to take place before it is decided how many sheep will be exchanged for one cow, or how many metres of cloth should be given up for a tonne of potatoes.

When all goods and services have money prices, it is easy to measure the value of one thing in terms of another – we simply compare their money prices. If the price of Good X is £1 and the price of Good Y is £5, then we know that one unit of Y is worth five units of X.

3 A store of value

People may not wish to spend all their income as soon as they earn it; they may wish to save some for future consumption. In a society which does not use money, this may be very difficult. It would mean that a farmer would have to store some of the harvest and a woodworker would have to store tables and chairs. These things would then have to be exchanged for whatever was

wanted at some future date. It is costly to store things in this way, and there is also the risk of deterioration. In any case, people who produce services, for example doctors, accountants and lawyers, cannot 'store' what they produce.

Money solves these problems, because we can sell our services or the things we have produced and save the money for spending in the future. Money, however, is not such a good store of value when prices are rising, because its value will be falling.

4 A standard for deferred payments

Just as it would be difficult to carry on trade in goods and services without money, so borrowing and lending would be difficult to organise without

Figure 14.1
The functions of money

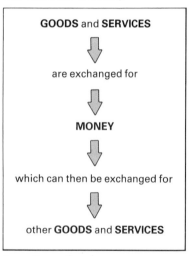

A medium of exchange

A store of value

A measure of value

A standard of deferred payments

money. If money did not exist, borrowers would have to find people willing and able to lend the actual goods they required. The debt would have to be repaid with similar goods, either by instalments, or in full at the end of the loan period.

Nowadays people borrow money (that is, purchasing power), and this can be used to buy whatever goods and services they require. Money, therefore, is a very convenient way of measuring debt and repaying debt.

The qualities of money

A commodity will only be generally acceptable as money if it possesses certain properties:

1 Durability

People will not accept as money something which is perishable, or which rusts or deteriorates in some other way.

2 Portability

It must be possible for a person to carry quite a lot of purchasing power without any great inconvenience. The commodity, therefore, must not be bulky or heavy in relation to its money value.

3 Divisibility

It must be able to be divided into smaller units without any loss in value, so that there will be no problem in making both small and large payments.

4 Limited in supply

Anything which is unlimited in supply will have no economic value and could not, therefore, serve as money.

Coins

The list of desirable qualities set out above helps to explain why gold and silver came to be so widely used as money. These metals are relatively durable, they are divisible, portable and limited in supply, and they are greatly valued for their own sakes.

For a long time, the metals were weighed out in scales every time a price was agreed. The introduction of coins, therefore, greatly increased the convenience of using gold and silver as money. For centuries they had virtually no competition from other kinds of money. Only in relatively recent times have coins with no gold or silver content come into general use.

14.3
Paper money

During the seventeenth century, people began to leave their valuables, especially their gold and silver, in the strongrooms of goldsmiths for safe keeping. The goldsmiths issued receipts for the precious metal deposited with them. These receipts were *paper claims* to gold – they could be exchanged for gold at any time. In time, the depositors began to use these receipts as a means of settling their debts. They would write on the receipts a note to the goldsmith informing him that they had transferred ownership of the gold to someone else. As this practice became more popular, the goldsmiths began to issue receipts in convenient denominations, such as £1, £5, £10, £20 and so on. They also made the receipts *payable to the bearer*, which meant that anyone possessing such a receipt could exchange it for gold. When these claims to gold became payable to the bearer, they became the first fully-fledged banknotes. They were acceptable as money because people knew that they could convert them into gold at any time. The notes were *fully backed* by the gold in the goldsmiths' strongrooms.

The next stage in the development of paper money came when the goldsmith-bankers began to issue banknotes in excess of the value of the gold they held. They found that they could do this because more and more people were using banknotes, and fewer and fewer were withdrawing gold in order to make payments. Although, on any one day, there would be people coming in to exchange their banknotes for gold, others would be coming in to deposit gold. Most of the gold was lying idle in the strongrooms. The goldsmith-bankers believed that they could safely increase the issue of banknotes and still meet all likely demands for gold from the people holding their banknotes.

Up to this point, the goldsmith-bankers had not been creating money. People had simply exchanged one form of money (gold) for another form of money (banknotes). Now, however, money was being created, because the bankers were issuing banknotes to a greater value than the gold they held. This additional money was used to make loans, on which the banks charged a rate of interest. That part of a note issue which is not backed by gold is described as a *fiduciary issue*.

In these early days, anyone could set up in business as a banker and issue banknotes. This led to many bank failures because bankers were tempted to over-issue banknotes and then found themselves unable to meet exceptional demands from people wishing to exchange their banknotes for gold. The government was obliged to regulate banking, and the Bank of England is now the only note-issuing bank in England and Wales. A few banks in Scotland and Northern Ireland still retain the right to issue notes.

Token money

Until the outbreak of the First World War, a British banknote was convertible into gold. This is no longer the case, although the wording on our banknotes has remained unchanged (see Figure 14.2). The whole of our note issue is fiduciary. Similarly, the value of the metal content of our coins is only a very small percentage of their money value. Our currency, both notes and coins, is token money.

Figure 14.2
This wording on our banknotes
has remained unchanged from the time when they were convertible into gold

14.4
Bank deposits

Table 14.1 shows that bank deposits account for the greater part of the money supply. Almost all

Table 14.1
UK money supply, 30 September 1987

	£ million
Notes and coin	13 206
Sterling bank deposits	
Sight deposits (see page 128)	76 050
Time deposits	87 343
	176 599

Source: *Bank of England Quarterly Bulletin*, November 1987

the larger payments of money take the form of a transfer of bank deposits. These transfers are made by means of cheques. A cheque itself is not money; it is an order to a banker to transfer money from one bank deposit to another. Clearly a cheque which is drawn on a bank deposit in which there is no money is worthless.

Bank deposits are claims to cash

Bank deposits may be seen as claims to cash (notes and coin) because they can be converted into cash, either on demand or after some period of notice. The banks, however, do not have to keep cash reserves equal to the total value of their deposits. People with bank deposits normally use cash for smaller payments; for larger payments they tend to use their cheque books. This means that bank depositors will normally only demand a small percentage of their bank deposits in the form of cash.

Just as the goldsmith-bankers were able to issue banknotes to a greater value than their gold reserves, so modern bankers are able to create bank deposits to a much greater value than their cash reserves.

A bank's assets and liabilities

Assets

Although banks possess valuable real assets in the form of property and technical equipment (e.g. computers), most of their assets are financial assets. These financial assets take the form of claims against individuals or firms. Thus, when a bank makes a loan, it has acquired an asset – it

Notes and coins

– are descibed as 'cash'

– are a minor part of the total money supply

– are issued by the Bank of England (notes) and the Royal Mint (coins)

Bank deposits

– form the major part of the total money supply

– are created by the banking system

– can be transferred by cheque (current accounts and sight deposits)

Figure 14.3
Money

has *a claim against the borrower*. To the person borrowing money, of course, the loan is a liability; it is a debt which has to be repaid.

Liabilities

Most of a bank's liabilities consist of its deposits, because these bank deposits are *claims against the bank*. If the depositors demand cash, the bank must supply it. If they draw cheques on their deposits, the banks must honour them, that is, make the necessary payments. To a depositor, of course, a bank deposit is an asset.

How bank deposits are created

1 When cash is deposited in a bank

A bank deposit is created when someone deposits notes and coin in a bank. For example, suppose Mr A makes a deposit of £100 in banknotes. The

bank's assets and liabilities will both increase by £100:

Liabilities	*Assets*
Deposits +£100	Cash +£100

No money has been created; all that has happened is that Mr A has changed the form in which he holds some of his money, from cash to a bank deposit.

2 When a bank makes a loan

Suppose Mrs B obtains a bank loan of £500. The bank will supply this loan in the form of a bank deposit, and Mrs B's account will be credited with £500. If she had, say, £50 in her account before the loan was granted, she will now have £550 in her account. The effect on the bank's total assets and liabilities will be as follows:

Liabilities	*Assets*
Deposits +£500	Loans +£500

In this case, however, money has been created.

The new deposit increases the money supply by £500; this money has not been taken from anyone else's deposit. Bank deposits are created when banks make loans. The size of the money supply, therefore, depends very much on the extent of the banks' lending.

Bank lending and the cash reserves

The banks cannot create deposits to an unlimited extent. They must always be in a position to meet their depositors' demands for notes and coins. This means that they must keep some safe ratio between the amount of cash they hold and the total level of bank deposits.

For example, suppose that the banking system has discovered by long experience that, if banks hold notes and coins equal to 10 per cent of the total value of deposits, it will be more than sufficient to meet all likely demands for cash. The banking system, therefore, decides to operate with a 10 per cent cash ratio. In other words, it will not allow the level of bank deposits to exceed ten times the value of cash in the banks.

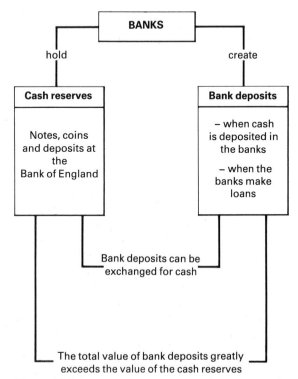

Figure 14.4

A cash ratio of 10 per cent means that for each £1 of cash they hold, the banks will be able to maintain £10 in the form of bank deposits. Thus, if the cash in this banking system rose by £5 million, total bank deposits could be increased by £50 million. If the banks' holdings of cash fell by £10 million, bank deposits would have to be reduced by £100 million.

In fact, UK banks operate with a cash ratio much smaller than 10 per cent.

Types of bank deposit

1 Current accounts

A person who holds money in a current account can withdraw cash on demand. Holders of current accounts are given cheque books and can make payments from their bank deposits by cheque. Interest is not usually paid on money in current accounts. These accounts are often described as *sight deposits* or *demand deposits*.

2 Time deposits

Money placed in a time deposit earns interest. It cannot be withdrawn on demand or transferred by means of a cheque. The bank normally requires several days' notice of withdrawal.

Money and near money

This chapter began with the question, 'What is money?' In fact, there is no general agreement on what should be counted as money. If we define money as something which can be directly exchanged for goods and services, then we can only count those things which are 'immediately spendable'. We can only include, therefore, notes and coins, and bank deposits which can be transferred by cheque.

Money, however, also acts as a store of value. Most people would include, as part of their stock of money, time deposits in banks, deposits in building societies and deposits in various savings banks. These deposits cannot be *directly* exchanged for goods and services, but they can usually be converted into cash fairly quickly and easily. These deposits are frequently described as *near money*.

14.5
Banking services

1 Receiving deposits

Bank deposits are a safe and convenient way of holding money. Banks will also act as a safe deposit for valuables other than money.

2 Making payments

The cheque system

Each day more than eight million cheques are handled by banks in England and Wales. In order to make cheques more acceptable to sellers of goods and services, the banks provide cheque guarantee cards or bankers' cards. These cards guarantee that cheques for up to £50 will be honoured by the bank.

Standing orders

These enable depositors to instruct their banks to make regular payments of fixed amounts. They are very useful for paying for such items as rent, rates, insurance premiums, mortgage payments and so on.

Direct debits

Some bills are payable at regular intervals, but the amounts are variable. Obvious examples are the quarterly bills for the electricity, gas and telephone services. Direct debits are instructions to a banker to pay these bills, whatever their amounts, when they fall due.

Bank giro credits

This system enables depositors to use only one cheque to pay several bills. A form is filled in to show the names and bank account numbers of all the persons to be paid, and the amounts due to each of them. One cheque is then made out for the total amount.

The bills from the gas, electricity, telephone and water companies and other large enterprises usually have bank giro slips attached to them. These bills can be paid at any bank, either by cash or by cheque.

Credit cards

These plastic cards (e.g. Access and Barclaycard) are now widely used by bank depositors. They enable cardholders to buy goods and services from

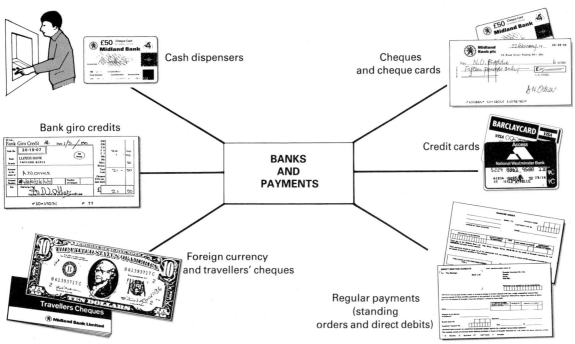

Figure 14.5

those shops, restaurants, garages, etc. which have joined the scheme, without paying in cash or by cheque. Each cardholder is given a limit to his or her total spending, and receives a monthly account which can be paid in full or by instalments. Interest is charged when the payment is made by instalments.

Cash dispensers

These machines are set into the outside walls of certain banks and provide bank customers with a 24-hour service for the supply of banknotes. Each bank customer is given a secret personal code number and a card. By inserting this card into the machine and tapping out the code number on a keyboard, a customer can obtain cash up to some agreed limit.

Travellers' cheques and foreign currency

For people travelling abroad, and for households and firms making payments to other countries, the banks provide travellers' cheques and foreign currencies.

3 Making loans

Lending is the most profitable activity of the banks – the interest they charge on loans is their most important source of income. Households, firms (of all sizes and in all industries), local authorities, the nationalised industries, and the government itself, all borrow from the banks. There are two methods by which banks provide money for customers who wish to borrow:

1 Bank loans

In this case, the bank lends a certain sum of money for a specified period of time. The amount of the loan is credited to the borrower's account, and interest is charged on the amount borrowed. Although banks tend to specialise in short-term loans, they also make loans for longer periods of time. In recent years they have begun to compete strongly with the building societies by providing long-term loans for house purchase.

2 Bank overdrafts

This type of lending allows a customer to over-draw his or her account by some agreed amount. If a firm is granted an overdraft of £5000, the bank will honour its cheques until its account is £5000 'in the red', that is, overdrawn. Interest is only charged on the amount overdrawn. Business firms use this form of borrowing because they can never be absolutely certain of the amount they might have to borrow.

Bank loans and security

A bank will probably ask a borrower to provide some kind of security, as evidence of his or her ability to repay the loan. A borrower may be asked to deposit some kind of asset with the bank so that, should he or she fail to repay the loan, the bank may recover its money by selling the asset. Insurance policies, shares in companies, and title deeds to property, are typical of the kinds of security which are acceptable to banks.

4 Other bank services

Banks will supply help and advice with the invest-ment of money (e.g. the purchase of government securities and company shares). They will also act as executors of wills (i.e. they will carry out the disposal of money and property left by a deceased person). Through their subsidiaries, banks also offer insurance services and operate unit trusts.

14.6
Markets for money

Just as there are markets for such things as wheat, copper, cars and cameras, so there are markets for money. Like these other commodities, money has a price. Borrowers are prepared to pay a price for the use of other people's money; this price is known as the rate of interest.

The aim of banks and other financial insti-tutions which operate in the money markets is to make sure that money does not lie idle. They are able to earn profits by putting money to work.

Savers and borrowers

Banks and other financial institutions such as building societies, insurance companies and pension funds collect savings from households and firms. These savings are lent to borrowers.

Households borrow in order to purchase houses, cars, furniture and so on. Firms borrow

SAVERS   **BANKS and other**   **BORROWERS**
                    financial institutions

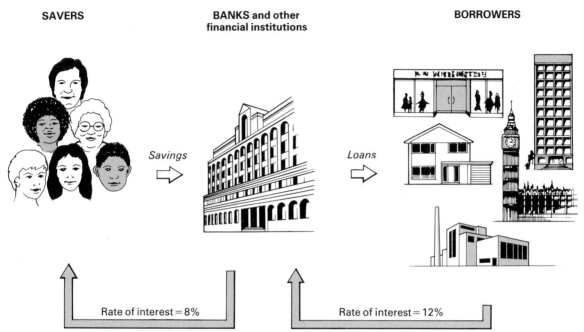

Savings   *Loans*

Rate of interest = 8%   Rate of interest = 12%

Figure 14.6
The difference between the two rates of interest is the
source of the financial institutions' profits. (Note that
these rates will depend on any changes in the supply
of and demand for loans.)

to buy machinery, transport equipment, materials
and so on. The government and local authorities
borrow when their expenditures are greater than
their incomes from taxes and local rates.

Banks and other financial institutions are able
to attract savings because they offer savers a
variety of services, such as
- security: the savers feel that their money is 'safe',
- the opportunity to earn an income in the form
  of interest,
- facilities for withdrawing cash when it is
  needed, and
- the convenience of many local branches.

Banks are able to earn profits because they
charge a higher rate of interest to borrowers than
the rate they pay to depositors (see Figure 14.6).

There are two main types of markets which
bring borrowers and savers together: *the money
market*, which tends to specialise in short-term
loans and is explained below, and *the capital
market*, which provides long-term loans and is
explained in Chapter 15.

The London money market

This is the market for loans whose periods range
from a few hours to several months. A variety of
banks trade in the London money market,
including the Bank of England, the discount
houses, the merchant banks, the commercial
banks and branches of foreign banks. These
different types of bank are described in Section
14.7.

It is important to have some understanding of
how money is transferred from lenders to
borrowers in this market. What happens is that
the lenders *buy* the IOUs or 'promises to pay' of
the borrowers. These IOUs are described as *securities* or *bills*. Several types of securities are traded
in the money market; two of them are described
below.

A bill of exchange

This is an important document which enables
traders in both home and overseas markets to
obtain *credit*, that is, to borrow money.

For example, suppose Firm A wishes to
purchase goods to the value of £100 000 from
Firm B but does not wish to pay for them immediately; it wants three months' credit. Firm B, on

the other hand, does not want to wait three months for its money. A bill of exchange can help overcome this problem.

Firm B will draw up a bill of exchange which sets out the value of the goods and carries a promise of payment for them in three months' time. It then sends this bill to Firm A (the buyer) which writes the word 'accepted' on the face of the bill, signs it and sends it back to Firm B. In the bill of exchange shown in Figure 14.7, ICI has accepted a bill for £100 000 which was sent to it by the British Gas Corporation.

Figure 14.7
A bill of exchange

Now the seller of the goods (Firm B) has a promise of payment in three months' time, but it does not have the money. It can, however, take the bill to a bank or a discount house, which will buy or *discount* the bill. To discount a bill means to buy it for less than its face value. For example, in this particular case, the bank or discount house might buy the bill for £97 000. When the bill comes due for payment, the bank or discount house will receive £100 000. In effect, it has charged an interest payment of £3000 for making a loan of £97 000 for three months.

This system enables the buyer of the goods to have three months' credit, while the seller does not have to wait three months for payment.

If Firm A is not well known in the banking world, a discount house or bank may not be willing to discount the bill. In this case, the bill can be taken to an accepting house (usually a well-known merchant bank) which, for a fee, will also write the word 'accepted' on the bill and sign it. In doing so it has guaranteed payment should Firm A default in its payment. There will now be no problem in getting the bill discounted.

Treasury bills

These are a type of bill of exchange issued by the British government. They have a life of 91 days (three months) and are the means by which the government borrows for a three-month period. They are issued in denominations ranging from £5000 to £1 000 000, and are sold to the highest bidders in weekly auctions. Discount houses and other financial institutions buy (i.e. discount) these bills.

When Treasury bills fall due for repayment, the government makes a payment equal to their full face value. When it sold them, however, it took the highest price it could obtain. For example, in the weekly auction, the highest bid for the £250 000 Treasury bill in Figure 14.8 might be £244 000. In three months' time, the Bank of England will pay the holder of this bill £250 000. The difference of £6000 is the amount of interest the government will have had to pay in order to borrow £244 000 for three months.

Figure 14.8
A Treasury bill

14.7
Different types of bank

The Bank of England

This is the central bank of the UK. It is a state-owned bank; other banks are privately owned. It has many important functions:

1. It is the government's bank. It receives the government's income from taxation and other

Figure 14.9
The Bank of England, which was founded in 1694

sources, and makes payments on its behalf.

2. It is the bankers' bank. Other banks keep accounts at the Bank of England and use them to settle debts between themselves. Thus, if Barclays makes a payment to Lloyds, it will do so by drawing a cheque on its account at the Bank of England. The central banks of other countries, and international organisations such as the International Monetary Fund, also keep accounts at the Bank of England.

3. It is responsible for managing the National Debt. The Bank of England carries out the borrowing of the central government, makes interest payments to those who hold the government's debt, and repays loans when they fall due.

4. The Bank of England is the sole note-issuing authority for England and Wales. It produces as many as eight million new notes per day. It checks and destroys worn notes.

5. It is the lender of last resort. This means that it will come to the aid of other banks if there is a shortage of cash in the banking system.

6. It is responsible for making sure that the banking system does not operate in ways which conflict with government policy. The Bank of England is able to influence the amount of bank lending and the rate of interest being charged on bank loans.

7. It holds the official stocks of foreign currency (e.g. dollars, francs, marks, yen, etc.) and the gold reserves. It operates in the foreign exchange market when it wishes to influence the exchange rate, that is, the price of pounds in terms of other currencies.

The discount houses

As their name indicates, these institutions specialise in discounting bills of exchange, Treasury bills and other short-term securities. In other words, they provide short-term loans. They borrow from the banks for very short periods and use this money to discount bills. Much of the money they borrow from the banks is 'at call'. This means that they undertake to repay these loans whenever the banks call upon them to do so.

Like other banking institutions, the discount houses make a profit by borrowing at rates of interest lower than those they charge for discounting bills (i.e. lending). When all the banks are asking for repayment of the money they have loaned 'at call', the discount houses may not have the money to repay these loans because they have used the money to buy bills of exchange and Treasury bills. In this case, they will be able to borrow from the Bank of England, although they may find themselves having to pay relatively high rates of interest on these loans from the central bank.

The merchant banks

These banks specialise in *wholesale* banking. They deal with large deposits of money and handle large loans to industry, both at home and abroad. They also do a lot of business in foreign currencies. They act as accepting houses (explained opposite), and they also organise and manage share issues for the larger firms. Merchant banks also deal with the financial problems involved in large-scale take-overs and mergers.

Foreign banks

There are branches of more than 250 foreign banks in the City of London. They are important in the financing of overseas trade – making payments and arranging loans. They are also important in the operations of the London money market as providers of short-term loans.

The commercial banks

These are the familiar high street banks and include the Big Four – Barclays, Lloyds, Midland and National Westminster. Commercial banks tend to be large national banks, with a large number of local branches.

They provide a wide range of banking services – all those services, in fact, which were described in Section 14.5. Since they are public limited companies, they are in business to earn profits for their shareholders. This means that they must arrange their assets (i.e. their loans) so as to earn the highest possible rates of interest. On the other hand, they must look after the interests of their depositors. The banks must make sure that they can always meet their depositors' demands for cash. The banks, therefore, have two main objectives, *profitability* and *liquidity*.

Liquidity

An asset is said to be liquid when it can easily and quickly be converted into cash. Notes, coins and bank deposits held in current accounts, therefore, are the most liquid of all assets. Time deposits in banks and building society deposits are not completely liquid, but they are still very liquid assets because they can be converted into cash fairly easily and with little delay. Houses and works of art, however, are illiquid assets. They could be converted into cash, but it could not be done quickly, and the selling of such assets can be a difficult and complicated process.

Although the banks have to hold some reserves of cash, they will tend to keep these reserves to a minimum because cash is an asset which earns no income. The banks' other assets, which are loans, do earn them an income. To protect themselves against any unexpectedly high demands for cash, therefore, the banks keep some assets which can easily and quickly be exchanged for cash. These assets consist of very-short-term loans. For example, some of their loans to the discount houses can be called back at any time. The banks also hold bills of exchange and Treasury bills

which can always be sold (discounted) in the London money market. Cash plus very-short-term loans make up the banks' liquid assets.

Profitability and liquidity

The need to have liquid assets *and* the desire to make as much profit as possible present the banks with a problem. The rates of interest on short-term loans tend to be lower than those on long-term loans. The banks are taking bigger risks when they lend money for long periods, and hence they charge higher rates of interest. Long-term loans, however, are illiquid assets. They cannot be 'called back' from the borrower, and the borrower's IOU cannot be discounted in the money market, which deals in short-term loans.

The problem for the banks, therefore, is that their liquid assets are much less profitable than their illiquid assets. The banks have to try and arrange their lending so that they have sufficient liquidity to meet any probable demands for cash, and sufficient profit to satisfy their shareholders.

The clearing of cheques

In a banking system with several different banks, it is very likely that many people making payments by cheque will have their accounts at different banks from the people receiving the payments.

For example, suppose that Mrs Jones, with an account at Lloyds, buys a second-hand car for £5000 from Mr Smith and pays for it by cheque. Mr Smith then pays this cheque into his own bank, say Barclays. Now Mr Smith cannot receive payment until £5000 has been transferred from Mrs Jones's account at Lloyds to his account at Barclays. Every day millions of such cheques are paid into the banks. It would be impossible to transfer money for each individual payment.

In order to deal with this problem, the banks have cooperated to set up a cheque clearing system. Cheques which are drawn on one bank and are payable to another bank are sent to a *clearing house* in London where, each day, the amounts which each bank owes to the other banks are totalled. For example, at the end of the day it may be found that the National Westminster owes £6000 million to the Midland, while the Midland owes £6500 million to the National West-

Figure 14.10

The clearing system. When cheques have passed through the clearing process they are sent to the bank branches on which they were drawn so that, after examination, payments can be made

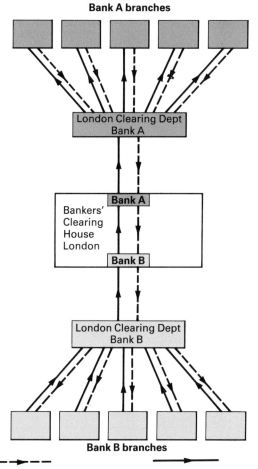

Bank A branches

London Clearing Dept
Bank A

Bankers' Clearing House London

Bank A

Bank B

London Clearing Dept
Bank B

Bank B branches

- - - - ▶   Route of cheques drawn on Bank B branches and paid into Bank A branches

──────▶   Route of cheques drawn on Bank A branches and paid into Bank B branches

Source: Banking Information Service

minster. Only the difference of £500 million needs to be transferred from the Midland to the National Westminster. These inter-bank settlements are carried out by using the accounts which the banks maintain at the Bank of England.

Considerable technical changes are taking place in the arrangements for clearing cheques. Increasing use is being made of computers and magnetic tapes to handle and record the transactions between banks.

The Trustee Savings Bank

In the nineteenth century, commercial banks were used mainly by the wealthy and by traders. This led to a number of savings banks being set up to accept the small savings of low-income households and to encourage the habit of saving. The Trustee Savings Banks have developed from these small beginnings and now have some 1600 branches. In more recent times, they have extended their operations and offer the full range of banking services. They are now owned and controlled by a holding company, the TSB Group plc.

The National Savings Bank

This bank was also set up to encourage the small saver. One of its advantages is that it operates through post offices, which gives it more 'branches' than any other bank. The funds accumulated in the NSB are loaned to the government.

The National Girobank

This was established in 1968 to provide a simple means of transferring money by using the facilities of the Post Office. Account holders can make and receive payments by means of giro cheques, and money can be withdrawn and paid in at post offices. The National Girobank has also gradually extended its range of banking services to include standing orders, travellers cheques and the provision of loans. As is the case with the NSB, its accumulated funds are loaned to the government.

Building societies

Building societies are not banks – they do not create deposits. Nevertheless, a large number of people use them as a form of savings bank.

They were established to help people to buy houses by providing them with loans. These loans take the form of mortgages because the building society holds the title deeds to the property as a security until the loan is repaid.

The societies attract savings by offering a variety of savings schemes, many of which allow cash to be withdrawn on demand.

They do not make a profit but they cover their costs by charging higher rates of interest to borrowers than those which they pay to savers. They can only continue to provide loans if they maintain a steady inward flow of savings. This is why they have to change their rates of interest from time to time: if the flow of savings begins to decline, building societies may have to offer higher rates of interest to savers, and this means that they would have to charge higher rates to borrowers.

In recent years, the building societies have begun to compete strongly with the banks. They now offer current accounts with cheque books, credit cards, travellers' cheques and other services similar to those offered by the banks.

14.8
The Bank of England and the control of the money supply

The government tries to control the money supply for several reasons. If prices are rising and the government fears an increase in the rate of inflation, it will try to reduce the money supply or slow down the rate at which it is increasing. If there is a serious slump, it might try to increase total spending by allowing the money supply to increase. The measures used for these purposes are described as *monetary policy*. The Bank of England is responsible for carrying out the government's monetary policy.

Since the greater part of the money supply consists of bank deposits, monetary policy must try to control the level of these deposits. The extent to which they are created depends upon
– *the bank customers' willingness and ability to borrow* (the demand for loans), and
– *the banks' ability to lend* (the supply of loans).

The Bank of England, therefore, must be able to influence the behaviour of both the banks and their customers.

Changes in the rate of interest

The price of a loan is the rate of interest one has to pay for it. Any changes in the rate of interest,

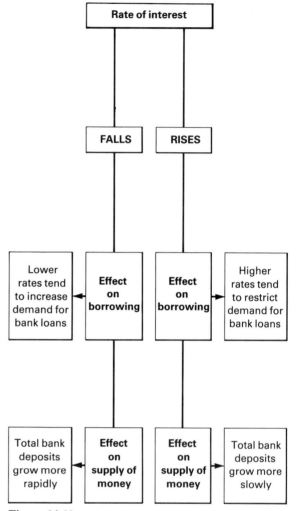

Figure 14.11

therefore, will affect people's willingness to borrow from the banks.

The Bank of England is able to operate in the money market as a major borrower and lender. It can, therefore, have a direct effect on the demand for and supply of loans. In other words, it can influence the price of loans – the rate of interest. A rise in the rate of interest raises the cost of borrowing. The demand for bank loans may fall or, more likely, grow more slowly. The rate at which total bank deposits are growing will slow down. A fall in the rate of interest will reduce the cost of borrowing and increase the demand for bank loans. Total bank deposits will tend to grow more rapidly.

Changes in the banks' reserves of cash

1 Open-market operations

The commercial banks hold deposits at the Bank of England in current accounts. These deposits are counted as part of the banks' cash reserves because cash can be withdrawn from them at any time. Any change in the level of these deposits at the Bank of England will change the level of the banks' cash reserves, and hence affect their ability to make loans and create bank deposits.

If the Bank of England sells securities in the open market to households and firms, the buyers will pay for them with cheques drawn on their accounts at the commercial banks. These banks, therefore, will now owe money to the Bank of England. This debt will be settled by taking money out of the commercial banks' deposits at the Bank of England. This will reduce the commercial banks' cash reserves, so their ability to create deposits will be reduced.

If the Bank of England buys securities in the open market, it will pay for them with cheques drawn on itself. The households and firms which sold these securities will pay these cheques into their accounts at the commercial banks. The Bank of England will now owe money to the commercial banks. The debt will be settled by paying money into the commercial banks' accounts at the Bank of England. This will increase the commercial banks' cash reserves, and enable them to increase their lending. The level of total bank deposits will tend to increase.

2 Special deposits

The Bank of England has the power to order the commercial banks to make payments into a special account at the Bank of England. These special deposits do not count as part of the banks' cash reserves. Payments into these special deposits reduce the banks' supply of liquid assets, which means that their ability to lend and create bank deposits is also reduced. If the Bank of England releases these special deposits, the commercial banks' cash reserves will be increased.

Directives

The Bank of England also has the right to issue instructions to the commercial banks regarding their lending activities. It can, if necessary, request them to restrict certain types of lending.

The Main Points

- Money is anything which is *generally acceptable* in exchange for goods and services.

- Money has four main functions:
  - as a medium of exchange,
  - as a measure of value,
  - as a store of value, and
  - as a standard for deferred payments.

- The money supply consists of
  - banknotes, which are supplied by the Bank of England,
  - coins, which are supplied by the Royal Mint, and
  - bank deposits, which are created by the banking system.

- Bank deposits can be converted into cash but, because of the widespread use of the cheque system, banks are able to create deposits to a much greater value than their holdings of cash.

- Bank deposits are created
  - when notes and coin are paid into a bank, and
  - when a bank makes a loan.

- The Bank of England is
  - the government's bank,
  - the bankers' bank,
  - the lender of last resort,
  - responsible for managing the National Debt,
  - responsible for carrying out the government's monetary policy,
  - the sole note-issuing authority in England and Wales, and
  - the holder of the official gold and foreign currency reserves.

- The London money market deals in short-term loans. Discount houses, banks and other financial institutions provide these loans by discounting (i.e. buying) short-term securities such as bills of exchange and Treasury bills.

- The commercial banks provide a range of banking services, including
  - safe deposit facilities,
  - a variety of ways of making money payments,
  - loans to households, firms and government,
  - travellers' cheques and foreign currencies, and
  - financial advice.

- The Bank of England aims to control the money supply by
  - bringing about changes in the rate of interest,
  - increasing or decreasing the commercial banks' holdings of liquid assets, and
  - if necessary, issuing instructions to the banks.

Test Your Understanding

Use the following terms to complete the sentences in questions 1 to 8:

liquid assets	*medium of exchange*
rate of interest	*lending money*
store of value	*Treasury bills*
current account deposits	*convertible*

1. In earlier times people only accepted bank notes as money because they were .... into gold.

2. By acting as a ...., money removes the main disadvantage of barter.

3. During periods of inflation, money is not a very satisfactory ....

4. The government borrows money for a period of three months by issuing ....

5. .... are transferable by cheque.

6. .... is the most profitable activity of the commercial banks.

7. The price of a loan is the ....

8. .... are those which can easily and quickly be converted into money.

9. Which TWO of the following are counted as part of the money supply?

   A postal orders
   B banknotes
   C cheques
   D bank deposits held on current account

10. Which TWO of the following would a bank count as part of its liquid assets?

    A banknotes
    B long-term loans to industry
    C Treasury bills
    D the buildings it owns

11. This question relates to the following banks:

    A the Bank of England
    B the National Girobank
    C a merchant bank
    D a commercial bank

    Which ONE of the above banks
    (a) operates through the Post Office?
    (b) has the right to issue banknotes?
    (c) is most likely to act as an accepting house?

12. Why do building societies often have to change the rate of interest which they charge on their loans to house buyers?

13. A banking system operates with a minimum cash ratio of 5 per cent. When its cash reserves amount to £100 million, what will be the upper limit to the value of bank deposits in this system?

BOX 14
Privileged treatment for students?

The advertisement below was aimed at students in full-time further education.

You won't pay normal account charges even when you're <u>overdrawn</u> – right up to the end of the December of the year you finish your studies. **If you need more money we can usually arrange <u>an overdraft</u>. Because we've found that you are unlikely to need more than £200 we can charge you a preferential <u>rate of interest</u> on an** *agreed overdraft.*

See our Personal Charges leaflet.

Your free Servicecard gives you access to your cash 24 hours a day 7 days a week, at over 1400 NatWest Servicetills. (As well as over 1300 cash machines at the Midland, Clydesdale and Northern banks). It's the largest 24 hour cash machine network in the country. You can use it at NatWest Servicetills to order a new cheque book or statement, or to check your Current Account balance 8am-6pm week days only.

If you are 18 and in receipt of an LEA award you also receive a free cheque card which will guarantee your cheques up to £50. (see terms and conditions of use).

To help you get started we will open your <u>Current Account</u> with a free deposit of £10 to spend as you like.

Questions
1. Which type of bank is most likely to run this kind of advertisement?
2. Explain the meaning of the underlined terms in the advertisement.
3. What is meant by 'normal account charges'? Why do banks make such charges?
4. For what purposes are students in full-time further education likely to borrow from a bank?

CHAPTER 15
Business finance

15.1 Why firms need finance
15.2 Short-term and long-term loans
15.3 Financial institutions
15.4 The Stock Exchange
15.5 Share prices, dividends and yields
15.6 Profits
15.7 How a company distributes its income

15.1
Why firms need finance

Firms need money to finance their operations because there is a time-lag between a firm's expenditure and its income. For example, a farmer may work himself and pay wages to those he employs for many months without any income to himself. Only when his crop is harvested and sold, will he be repaid for his own work and the wages he has paid out. A firm which pays for the building of a new factory will have to wait several years before the earnings from it will have equalled what the firm paid for the building.

This means that some person or persons must supply the money to pay for the costs of production until such time as a firm's earnings are sufficient to cover its costs and to repay its borrowings. In the case of the very small firm, the necessary money will be provided by the pro-prietor and his family and friends with, perhaps, a loan from the local bank. In the case of the larger firm, these sources cannot provide the much larger sums of money required.

Retained profits

For the well-established firm, the most obvious source of finance is its own profits. Instead of paying out all its profits to its shareholders, the firm can retain some within the business. Using retained profits in the business is described as 'ploughing back the profits'. It is an important

source of finance for the larger firm (see Table 15.1 on page 144).

15.2
Short-term and long-term loans

Short-term loans

A loan is usually regarded as short-term if it is repayable within three years. Many such loans are for periods of one year or less. Firms normally use short-term loans as *working capital* (see page 10).

In many cases, the things bought with the borrowed money will be changed in a matter of weeks or months into goods which can be sold. For example, a furniture manufacturer who obtains loans to buy timber will very soon convert it into tables, chairs, kitchen cabinets and so on. The sale of these goods will provide the means to repay the loan. Clearly, a loan for three or six months would be a suitable way of financing this kind of operation.

Long-term loans

Long-term loans are required for the purchase of fixed assets such as land, buildings and heavy machinery. It will be many years before the income from such assets covers the cost of purchasing them – they take a long time to pay for themselves. It is sensible, therefore, to use long-term loans to buy this kind of asset.

Sources of short-term loans

1 Banks

A bank overdraft is the most widely used type of short-term finance. As explained in Chapter 14, an overdraft is a flexible arrangement, and one of the cheaper forms of borrowing because interest is only charged on the amount outstanding each day.

2 Bills of exchange

In Chapter 14 we saw how a firm could obtain short-term loans by discounting bills of exchange. These bills are widely used to finance both exports and imports and to provide working capital.

3 Trade credit

It is quite normal for a firm which is supplying goods to another firm to allow a period of time, say three months, before payment becomes due. In effect, these firms are granting short-term loans to their customers. This system of trade credit is an important source of finance, especially for smaller firms. The firms do, however, have to pay a price for these loans, because they lose the discounts they would have received had they paid immediately on delivery.

4 Hire purchase

A firm may acquire capital equipment such as cars, lorries, office equipment and some types of machinery on hire-purchase terms. It makes a deposit and pays the outstanding amount by instalments over two or three years. Ownership passes to the buyer when the final instalment is paid.

5 Leasing

Whereas the user eventually becomes the owner under hire-purchase schemes, under leasing this is not the case. Banks and other financial institutions which run leasing schemes buy the equipment and retain the ownership of it. They offer it to other firms in return for regular rental payments.

Both hire-purchase and leasing schemes are a means of providing firms with working capital. If such schemes did not exist, firms would have to obtain loans and buy the equipment.

Sources of long-term loans – the capital market

Issuing shares and debentures

The different types of shares and debentures were described in Chapter 11. A private limited company might raise capital by issuing shares, but it would have to approach people privately; it cannot offer its shares to the public. A public limited company is able to offer its shares to the general public. In doing so it would probably enlist the services of an *issuing house*. Most of the issuing houses are well-known merchant banks. They make all the necessary arrangements for the issue of shares. There are a number of ways in which the newly-issued shares might be disposed of:

1 A public issue by prospectus

The share issue is widely advertised, the price of the shares is fixed and the public is invited to buy the shares.

2 Placing

The issuing house arranges for the shares to be sold in large blocks to financial institutions such as insurance companies, pensions funds and firms of stockbrokers.

3 Offer for sale

In this case, the issuing house buys the entire share issue. It then proceeds to sell the shares on its own behalf instead of acting as an agent for the company.

4 A rights issue

Instead of offering the shares to the general public, a company may offer them to its existing shareholders in proportion to the numbers of shares they already hold. For example, it might give its shareholders the right to buy one new share for every four shares already held.

5 Issue by tender

The public is invited to make bids for the shares, which are then sold to the highest bidder.

By similar procedures a company may raise money by making an issue of debentures.

15.3
Financial institutions

There are many important financial institutions which provide finance for companies. These institutions provide money in different ways. They may be prepared to buy shares and debentures in addition to making straightforward loans.

Banks

Although banks have tended to specialise in supplying short-term loans, they are prepared to make loans for longer periods – up to 20 years in certain circumstances.

Insurance companies

The activities of insurance companies can be divided into two main types, general business and long-term business. *General business* involves providing insurance against risks such as fire, theft and accident. *Long-term business* has two elements:
– life assurance, where a company agrees to pay an agreed sum of money in the event of the death of the person insured, and
– the provision of long-term savings schemes.

A typical life assurance scheme is the *endowment policy*, by which the company agrees to pay the holder an agreed sum of money at some future date (or when the insured person dies, if this is earlier).

The regular premiums paid by policyholders are invested in government securities, company shares and debentures, land, and property of all kinds. The income from these investments makes it possible for insurance companies to pay out benefits which are greater than the total payments made by policyholders.

Pension funds

Although in the UK there is a state pension scheme to which all workers contribute, a large number of employed and self-employed people also belong to private pension schemes. The money which accumulates in these pension funds is invested in a very similar manner to the funds of insurance companies. It is the income from these investments which enables pension funds to

Figure 15.1
Ownership of UK ordinary shares

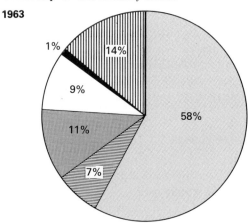
1963

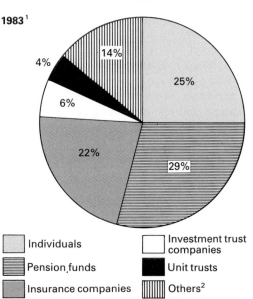
1983 [1]

Individuals
Pension funds
Insurance companies
Investment trust companies
Unit trusts
Others [2]

[1] The policy of privatisation in recent years has changed the situation: the number of shares held by individuals is now considerably more than it was in 1983 (see page 115)
[2] UK companies, overseas companies, charities, government
Sources: *Economics Brief: Savings and Investment*, Economist Books, 1986; *The Economist*, 14 July 1984

pay out pensions which exceed the value of the total contributions made by members of the funds.

In 1986, pension funds and insurance companies both invested more than £8 000 000 000 in the types of assets mentioned above. Figure 15.1 shows that pension funds and insurance companies now own more than half of the shares in UK companies, by value.

Investment trusts

These are limited companies, but the money they raise from selling their shares is not used to buy real assets such as factories, machines and materials; it is used to buy shares in other companies.

The managers of investment trusts use their shareholders' funds to buy shares in what they believe will be the most successful companies. People who buy shares in investment trusts are spreading their risks, because each of these shares represents a very small investment in a large number of companies.

The dividends paid out by an investment trust are obtained from the dividends it receives on the shares it holds in other companies.

Unit trusts

These operate in a very similar manner to investment trusts. The money invested in unit trusts is used to buy shares in many different companies. Like the person buying shares in an investment trust, a person buying units is spreading his or her risks.

Unlike investment trusts, unit trusts are not limited companies – they do not issue shares, they issue units. These units cannot be re-sold on the open market, but they can be sold back to the unit trust at any time. Every day, a unit trust publishes two prices: the higher price is the one at which it will sell units; the lower price is the one at which it will re-purchase units.

Finance houses

These institutions provide the loans which finance hire-purchase schemes and leasing arrangements. Firms which sell goods on hire purchase do not have to wait two or three years before their goods are fully paid for. They receive immediate payment from a finance house, and it is the

Figure 15.2
Money for business – a summary

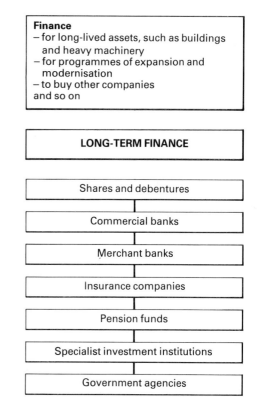

finance house which collects the regular instalments paid by the purchasers.

There are many other specialist financial institutions which provide finance for companies.

The government

The government is an important source of finance for privately-owned firms. It makes this aid available under several headings:

1 Technology

The government offers grants as a means of encouraging firms to introduce new methods of production, to make use of the latest technology and to introduce new products.

2 Regional aid

The financial assistance available to firms in assisted areas and enterprise zones was described in Chapter 13.

3 Employment subsidies

The government has a variety of subsidised schemes to provide people with temporary jobs, to encourage employers to take on more new workers and to offer training to young people (see pages 228–9).

4 Small firms

Grants, subsidies and tax incentives are made available to help people to set up in business for themselves and to encourage people to invest in small firms.

Table 15.1
Sources of funds for industrial and commercial companies, UK, 1986

	Percentage of total
Internal funds (retained profits)	64.3
Issues of ordinary shares	11.6
Issues of preference shares, debentures and other loans	1.5
Bank borrowing	11.4
Other sources	11.2
	100.0

Source: *Financial Statistics*, HMSO, July 1987

15.4
The Stock Exchange

The Stock Exchange is a market place for the buying and selling of shares, debentures and government securities. It is primarily a market in second-hand or existing shares, although some newly-issued shares are placed with dealers on the Stock Exchange. The main Stock Exchange in the UK is in London, although there are smaller exchanges in several other major cities.

Securities traded on the Stock Exchange

Only those public companies which have been approved by the Stock Exchange Council can have their shares traded on the Stock Exchange. These companies are described as *listed* or *quoted companies*.

The types of securities traded on the Stock Exchange include the following:
- gilt-edged securities (see below),
- securities issued by local authorities and other public authorities,
- debentures,
- preference shares,
- ordinary shares (these are commonly described as *equities*), and
- shares which are listed on Stock Exchanges in other countries.

Gilt-edged securities are fixed-interest securities issued by the British government. The government borrows by selling these securities to the general public and to financial institutions. They are described as 'gilt-edged' because there is no risk of the government defaulting on the payment of interest or on the repayment of the loan. Since the government is by far the largest borrower in the country, it is not surprising that the largest single market in the Stock Exchange is the gilt-edged market.

The functions of the Stock Exchange

1 It helps the government and companies to borrow on a long-term basis

Most shares carry no date for repayment – they represent permanent loans to companies. Debentures and long-term government securities may

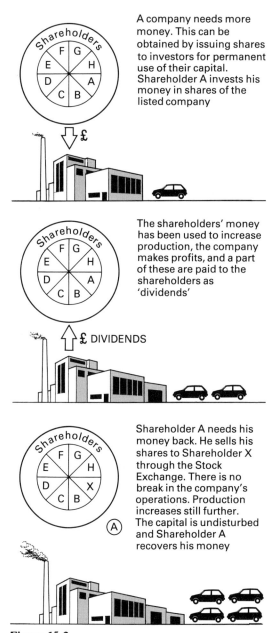

A company needs more money. This can be obtained by issuing shares to investors for permanent use of their capital. Shareholder A invests his money in shares of the listed company

The shareholders' money has been used to increase production, the company makes profits, and a part of these are paid to the shareholders as 'dividends'

Shareholder A needs his money back. He sells his shares to Shareholder X through the Stock Exchange. There is no break in the company's operations. Production increases still further. The capital is undisturbed and Shareholder A recovers his money

Figure 15.3
Investment through the Stock Exchange

not be repayable for many years. Very few people would be prepared to entrust their savings to the government or to companies on these terms. They are prepared to lend their savings because they want to earn interest and dividends, but they also want to be in a position to get their money back if it should become necessary.

The existence of a Stock Exchange solves this problem because it allows people to sell their shares and other securities at any time. Companies and the government are not affected directly by these sales. They keep the money which they have borrowed. People sell their shares and other securities to other investors (see Figure 15.3).

People who sell their shares may suffer a loss if the market price of the shares has fallen below the price they paid for them. If share prices have risen, they make a profit.

2 It influences the way in which savings are invested

The Stock Exchange is a free market, and share prices change frequently as the conditions of supply and demand change. The prices of shares in companies which are successful or which are believed to have good prospects will tend to rise as the demand for them increases. The opposite will happen to the prices of shares in companies which are performing badly. These movements in share prices will influence the way in which savings are invested. They will tend to flow to companies whose shares have been rising in price.

3 It provides a means of valuing financial assets

When wealth is held in forms other than money, it is often difficult to measure the value of that wealth. The price which was originally paid for a piece of land, a house, a work of art or a share in a company is not usually a good indication of its present value. In the case of shares, debentures and government securities which are sold on the Stock Exchange, however, this problem does not arise. The prices of these securities are published daily. It is always possible, therefore, to find their present value.

Speculation

The fact that prices of the shares and other securities being traded on the Stock Exchange change from day to day encourages some people to guess which way these prices will move in the immediate future. These people are speculators, and they hope to make a gain by guessing correctly. Speculators do not buy shares for the income they yield in the form of dividends; they buy them with the intention of selling them so as to make a *capital gain*.

If they expect prices to rise, they will buy shares and expect to sell them at higher prices. If they expect prices to fall, they will sell shares, hoping to re-purchase them later at lower prices.

Buying and selling on the Stock Exchange

In 1986 there were some important changes in the way business is carried out on the Stock Exchange. These changes drastically altered the older, traditional system of trading, which is explained briefly below.

The traditional system

Only members can trade on the Stock Exchange. These members grouped themselves into firms, which were mainly partnerships. Member firms were of two kinds, stockbrokers and jobbers.

Stockbrokers took orders from clients who wished to buy or sell shares. They carried out these orders on the Stock Exchange and charged a commission for their services. This commission would be equal to a percentage of the value of the shares bought or sold. The Stock Exchange fixed the minimum commission which stockbrokers could charge for their services.

Jobbers did not deal directly with the public. They operated within the Stock Exchange and were always prepared to buy shares from or sell shares to stockbrokers. Jobbers acted as wholesalers, buying and selling shares on their own account. They earned an income by adjusting their prices according to changes in supply and demand so that, on average, they sold shares at prices higher than those they paid for them.

A broker with an order to buy or sell some particular shares, say ICI, would approach a jobber and ask 'What is ICI?' The jobber would then quote two prices, say '398p to 400p'. This meant that he would buy ICI shares at a price of 398p or sell them at 400p. The broker would obtain quotations from several jobbers in order to get the best price for his client.

Recent changes on the Stock Exchange

1. By fixing the minimum commission which a stockbroker could charge for his services, the Stock Exchange restricted competition. It meant that the more efficient and larger firms of stockbrokers could not capture more business by charging lower fees for their services. Minimum commissions have now been abolished.
2. The arrangement whereby only jobbers could buy and sell shares on their own account, and brokers were restricted to acting as agents for people wanting to buy or sell shares, has also been abolished. Stock Exchange firms are now free to act as both jobbers and brokers.
3. The rules which restricted membership and ownership of Stock Exchange firms have been changed. This will allow larger institutions, such as banks (both British and foreign), to own Stock Exchange firms.

15.5
Share prices, dividends and yields

Nominal prices

Most shares have a nominal or face value; this is the value which is printed on the share certificate. It is sometimes referred to as the 'par value'.

Market prices

These prices are determined by supply and demand in the market for shares. The market price, therefore, may be higher or lower than the nominal price. If it is higher, the share is said to be at a *premium*; if it is lower, the share is said to be at a *discount*.

Dividends

The dividend on a share is expressed as a percentage of the nominal value. For example, if a company declares a dividend of 25 per cent on its £1 ordinary shares, then holders of these shares will receive 25p for each share they hold.

Yields

Suppose someone who is holding these £1 shares bought them when the market price was £1.25. This person would obviously like to know the actual return on the money he or she paid for the shares. This return is known as the *yield*, and is worked out by expressing the money value of the dividend as a percentage of the market price:

$$\text{Yield} = \frac{\text{Dividend per share}}{\text{Market price of share}} \times \frac{100}{1}$$

$$= \frac{25p}{125p} \times \frac{100}{1}$$

$$= 20 \text{ per cent}$$

15.6
Profits

Profit is a surplus. It is what remains from a firm's receipts after all the expenses of production have been met. Profit, therefore, can be negative, since a firm can make a loss.

Profit is often described as a reward for taking risks. It is the prospect of making profits which encourages people to set up in business. If there were no possibility of making a profit, there would be no incentive for people to use their own savings and borrow other people's in order to establish a business enterprise. Generally, people will only accept the risk of failure if there is a possibility of making profits.

There are several ways in which a firm's profit may be measured.

1 Profit margins

The profit margin measures the profit on each unit sold. It is the difference between the cost price and the selling price. This difference is expressed as a percentage of the cost price or of the selling price.

Example
Suppose the cost price was £8, and the selling price was £10. Then the profits per unit are £2.

Profit margin as a percentage of the cost price

$$= \frac{£2}{£8} \times \frac{100}{1} = 25 \text{ per cent}$$

Profit margin as a percentage of the selling price

$$= \frac{£2}{£10} \times \frac{100}{1} = 20 \text{ per cent}$$

2 Total profit

This is the difference between total revenue and total cost. It is this figure which is usually given in news items when companies publish their annual accounts. It can, however, give a misleading impression. For example, if Firm A declares an annual profit of £25 000 000 and Firm B declares an annual profit of £500 000, it does not follow that Firm A is a much more efficient and successful company than Firm B. This is explained in the following section.

3 Profit as a percentage of the capital employed

In order to say whether the amount of profit earned by a company represents a good performance or a poor performance, this profit has to be compared with the sacrifices which have been made to earn that profit. One way of doing this is to use the total value of the capital employed by the firm. This consists of the money invested by shareholders, debenture holders and various financial institutions who have made loans to the company. The total profit may now be expressed as a percentage of the capital employed.

Example
Firm A
Capital employed   £250 000 000
Profits   £25 000 000

Firm B
Capital employed   £2 500 000
Profits   £500 000

Profits as a percentage of capital employed:

Firm A
$$\frac{£25 000 000}{£250 000 000} \times \frac{100}{1} = 10 \text{ per cent}$$

Firm B
$$\frac{£500 000}{£2 500 000} \times \frac{100}{1} = 20 \text{ per cent}$$

We can see that the very much larger total profit figure for Firm A represents a much smaller return on the capital employed. Firm B is using its assets much more efficiently than Firm A.

15.7

How a company distributes its income

This chapter has been concerned mainly with the ways in which a company obtains the money it requires for fixed and working capital. But what happens to the income which a company earns?

In the annual accounts published by public limited companies, this income is described as *value added*. Income or value added is not the same thing as a firm's revenue. For example, if a firm bought shoes from a wholesaler at a price of £20 a pair and sold them at a price of £25, the income it earns from selling a pair of shoes is £5, not £25. Value added is equal to the total revenue from the company's sales *minus* the value of goods and services it has bought from other firms.

Figure 15.4
The distribution of ICI's income in 1986

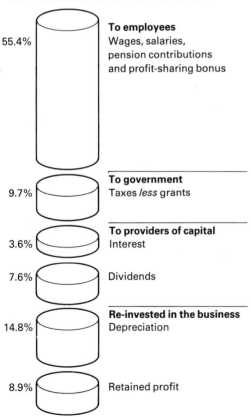

	To employees
55.4%	Wages, salaries, pension contributions and profit-sharing bonus

	To government
9.7%	Taxes *less* grants

	To providers of capital
3.6%	Interest
7.6%	Dividends

	Re-invested in the business
14.8%	Depreciation
8.9%	Retained profit

Source: *Annual Report, 1986*, ICI

Example

	£ million
Total sales revenue (= turnover)	100
Materials, fuel, power, transport and other goods and services bought from other firms	25
Income = value added	75

Value added, therefore, is the income earned from the company's own activities. Note that the word *turnover* is often used in company accounts to describe the total sales revenue.

Figure 15.4 shows how the income earned by one major UK company (ICI) was distributed in 1986.

The Main Points

- Firms need to borrow money
    - for short periods, because they need working capital to cover their variable costs until such time as their goods are ready for sale, and
    - for long periods, to cover expenditures on buildings, heavy machinery, ships, aircraft, etc. (things which take a long time to pay for themselves).

- Working capital (short-term finance) is provided by bank overdrafts, trade credit, hire-purchase and leasing schemes and the discounting of bills of exchange. Long-term finance is obtained by issuing shares and debentures, and in the form of loans from a variety of financial institutions.

- For larger companies, retained profits is the major source of finance.

- Insurance companies and pension funds are very important suppliers of finance to industry and commerce. Together they own more than half of the shares in UK public companies, by value.

- The government offers financial assistance in many different forms to both large and small firms.

- If there were no Stock Exchange, it would be difficult to persuade people to buy shares, debentures and long-term government securities. The Stock Exchange gives people an opportunity to 'get their money back'.

- The market price of a company's shares will be influenced by the company's present profitability and by people's views about its future prospects.

- There are several ways of looking at a company's profits:
  - Profit margins
    = Profit per unit as a percentage of either the cost price or the selling price
  - Total profit = Total revenue − Total cost
  - Total profit as a percentage of the capital employed (this gives some idea of how efficiently the company is using its assets).

Test Your Understanding

Use the following terms to complete the sentences in questions 1 to 7:

insurance companies	*retained profits*
equities	*pension funds*
trade credit	*investment trusts*
dividend	*working capital*
nominal value	

1. A company is receiving .... when it is given three or six months in which to pay for goods it has received.

2. The money which a company uses to pay for items of variable cost such as labour and materials is described as ....

3. Limited companies which use their shareholders' money to buy shares in many other companies are known as ....

4. For most large companies, ... is the main source of finance.

5. The .... is that part of a company's profit which is distributed to shareholders. It is expressed as a percentage of the .... of a share.

6. Two of the most important types of financial institution which supply long-term finance to UK public companies are .... and ....

7. Ordinary shares are often described as ....

8. What would be the likely effect on the market price of a company's shares if
   (a) the *Financial Times* described the company's prospects as 'very favourable'?
   (b) the company is affected by a serious and prolonged strike by its workers?
   (c) the government announces an increase in profits tax?

9. The figures below refer to a company's trading in a given year:

Total sales revenue	£500 000
Goods and services bought from other firms	£300 000
	£200 000

   (a) What term is used to describe the amount of £200 000?
   (b) How will this £200 000 be distributed?

10. A company declares a dividend of 20 per cent on its £5 shares.
    (a) How much will be received by someone holding 100 of these shares?
    (b) If the market price of these shares is £10, what is the present yield on them?

BOX 15
Profits and investment

R. SMITH & SON LTD.

Manufacturers of plastic toys

Capital employed:
Fixed capital	£110 000
Working capital	£40 000

This company's most recent accounts contained the following details:

Turnover	£75 000
Profit margin (as percentage of selling price)	
	20 per cent

Questions
1. Give examples of the kinds of item likely to be included in this firm's (a) fixed capital, and (b) working capital.
2. What was the total profit in this particular year?
3. What rate of return did the firm earn on the capital employed?
4. Would this firm be likely to borrow money for new machinery if the rate of interest were 12 per cent? Explain your answer.

CHAPTER 16

Incomes

16.1

Personal income

Money income and real income

Money income is the value of a person's income, expressed in terms of pounds and pence. Almost everyone receives income in the form of money payments. *Real income* refers to the quantity of goods and services which money income will buy.

An increase in money income may not make people better off. For example, a person who receives a wage increase of 10 per cent over a period during which prices rise by 15 per cent would suffer a fall in real wages.

Types of personal income

1 Income from employment

These are payments for the services of labour, and take the form of salaries and wages. Figure 16.1 shows that income from employment is the main source of personal income.

2 Income from self-employment

This is the income received by people who 'work for themselves', that is, who are in business as sole traders. Window cleaning, hairdressing, plumbing, painting and decorating, retailing, and farming are common examples of occupations where one finds

large numbers of self-employed people.

Sole traders often describe their income as 'profits' but, since they usually work full-time in the business, much of their income could be described as wages.

3 Income from the ownership of wealth

People have to pay a price for the use of other people's money and property. These prices are

Figure 16.1
Personal income before tax, UK, 1986 (percentages of total)

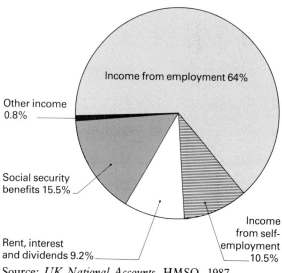

Income from employment 64%

Other income 0.8%

Social security benefits 15.5%

Rent, interest and dividends 9.2%

Income from self-employment 10.5%

Source: *UK National Accounts*, HMSO, 1987

incomes to the owners of wealth:
- Owners of land and buildings receive *rent* from their tenants.
- Lenders of money receive *interest* from borrowers.
- Owners of businesses receive income in the form of *profits*.

4 Social security benefits

For a large number of people, a part or all of their income consists of various social security benefits paid by the government. These payments include unemployment benefit, supplementary benefits, state retirement pensions, child benefit and many others.

The distribution of household income

Table 16.1 gives some details of the distribution of income among households in the UK. It considers two types of income:

1 Original income

This refers to the amounts of income paid to households in the form of wages, salaries, rent, interest, profits and occupational pensions.

2 Disposable income

This is the amount which a household has available for spending and saving. It is obtained by subtracting income tax and national insurance contributions from the original income, and then adding any income received in the form of cash benefits (these consist almost entirely of social security benefits), i.e.

Original income
- Income tax and national insurance contributions
+ Social security benefits
= Disposable income

It can be seen from Table 16.1 that original income is very unequally distributed. The 20 per cent of households with the lowest original incomes received only 0.3 per cent of the total original income. The top 20 per cent of households received 49.2 per cent of the total original income.

However, the payment of cash benefits and the imposition of taxes on income significantly reduces the inequality in the distribution of income. The effect of these measures is to increase the amount of income available to households with very low original incomes and to reduce the income available to the better-off households. Nevertheless, the top fifth of households still received more than 40 per cent of the total disposable income.

Table 16.1

Distribution of original and disposable income, UK, 1985

Fraction of all households, arranged according to size of income	Percentage of total original income received	Percentage of total disposable income received
Top fifth	49.2	41
Next fifth	27.3	24
Middle fifth	17.2	17
Next fifth	6.0	11
Bottom fifth	0.3	7
	100.0	100

Source: *Economic Trends*, HMSO, November 1986

Question on Table 16.1

Out of every £1 of original income, the bottom 40 per cent of households received .... pence. Out of every £1 of disposable income, they received .... pence. What are the missing figures?

Income and wealth

Quite apart from the incomes they receive from selling their services, people's incomes also depend upon the amount of wealth they own. Many of the households in the top fifth of the income distribution obtain an important part of their total income in the form of interest, rent and profits (i.e. from the ownership of wealth). An important reason for the inequality in the distribution of income is the fact that the ownership of wealth is very unequally distributed.

The distribution of wealth

Figure 16.2 shows that, in 1985, the most wealthy 10 per cent of the population owned 54 per cent of the total marketable wealth. There are several reasons why personal wealth in such forms as land, buildings, stocks and shares, jewellery, works of art and money is unequally distributed:

1. It can be inherited.
2. It can accumulate, because most forms of wealth earn an income. For example, if a sum of money is left in a deposit account earning interest at a rate of 8 per cent per annum, it will double in value in about nine years.
3. Older people own more wealth than younger people because they have had more years in which to accumulate wealth.
4. The distribution of income is very unequal, and those with higher incomes are able to save more.
5. Not only do people owning successful businesses receive an income from the business, but the value of the business itself also increases.

Figure 16.2 refers to *marketable* wealth. This consists of assets which can be bought and sold. Most of the working population, however, are accumulating rights to pensions as contributions are paid into pension funds by themselves and by their employers. These rights to pensions, of course, cannot by sold – they are not marketable. If these rights are included in personal wealth, the distribution is less unequal. In 1985, the most wealthy 10 per cent of the population owned 36 per cent of total personal wealth if pension rights are included.

16.2
Wages

Wage payments

Wages are normally paid weekly and in cash (notes and coins). Many people, however, are paid monthly by cheque, or sometimes the employer pays the money directly into the employee's bank account. Such monthly payments are normally described as *salaries*.

Gross wages

The gross wage is the total amount earned in a period of one week (or some longer period). It usually consists of a number of separate payments:

- *The basic wage.* This is the minimum payment for some agreed number of hours of work.
- *Bonuses.* These additional payments are usually linked to a worker's productivity. When a worker's output exceeds some target figure, he

Figure 16.2

In 1985 it was estimated that the most wealthy 10 per cent of the population owned 54 per cent of the total *marketable* wealth.

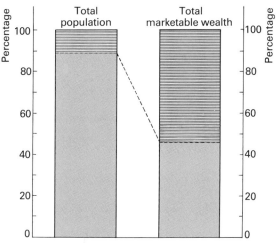

Source: *Social Trends*, HMSO, 1987

Figure 16.3

The basic wage is often supplemented by overtime, bonus payments and profit-sharing schemes

or she is paid a bonus that is related to the amount by which the target figure has been exceeded. Bonuses are also paid for night work, or when some difficult or disagreeable work has been undertaken.

– *Overtime.* Hours which are worked in excess of the standard working week are usually paid for at a higher rate. For example, if the hourly rate is £3 per hour, overtime may be paid for at 'time and a half', i.e. at £4.50 per hour.

Net wages

Net wages refer to the 'take-home pay'. This is the amount that remains from the gross wages after various deductions have been made. These deductions include

– income tax, and
– national insurance contributions,

which are payments to the government. Other deductions may consist of

– contributions to the firm's pension scheme, and
– savings, e.g. contributions to the 'Save-As-You-Earn' scheme.

These are payments into funds which belong to the employee.

Figure 16.4 shows a typical wages slip. Such slips are presented to workers with their wages, and show how the net wage has been calculated.

Piece-rates

Many workers are not paid a fixed amount per hour or per week. They are paid on a system described as 'piece-rate'; that is, they are paid according to the number of 'pieces of work' they produce. This system can only be used, of course, where it is possible to measure a worker's output. It is common, therefore, in manufacturing and in some jobs in the building industry. The system obviously encourages workers to work faster – the more they produce, the greater the earnings.

16.3
Wage differentials

There are large differences in the rates of pay received by people in different occupations. These differences are referred to as 'wage differentials'. Figure 16.5 gives some examples of these wage differentials.

Common sense tells us that these differences in rates of pay exist because different jobs require different levels of ability, education, training, experience, responsibility and risk-taking. These things do play an important part in determining wage rates, but they cannot fully explain the differences between them, because they mainly affect the supply of labour. Wages are prices and therefore must depend upon the demand for labour as well as on the supply.

Figure 16.4
A typical wages slip

WAGES DETAIL					
Code no. *379 H* Tax week no. *20*			Name *A.B. CARTER* Works/Dept no. *12*		
	£	p	Hours worked Normal *40* Overtime *4*		
Gross wages to date	*4600*	*00*		£	p
Tax deducted to date	*847*	*47*	Wages due Overtime	*200* *30*	*00* *00*
Deductions			------------------- -------------------		
Income tax	*42*	*37*	Bonus		
National insurance	*20*	*72*	Gross Non-taxable allowances	*230*	*00*
Savings			Total Less deductions	*230* *63*	*00* *09*
	63	*09*	Net £	*166*	*91*

Figure 16.5
Average gross weekly earnings of adult full-time employees in selected occupations, UK, 1987

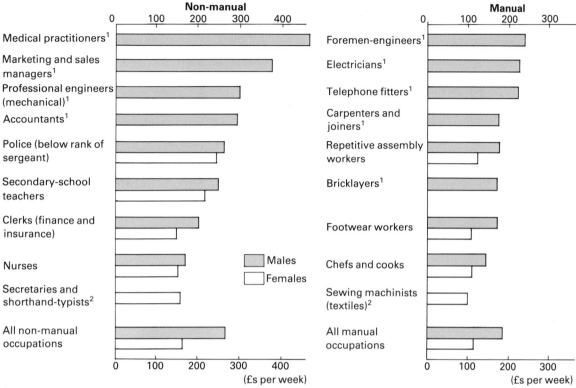

[1] No figures available for female employees
[2] No figures available for male employees
Source: *New Earnings Survey*, Department of
Employment, 1987

The demand for labour

1. The demand for labour is a *derived* demand –
   it is derived from the demand for the things
   which the labour produces. Highly trained and
   skilled workers are not employed simply
   because they have this training and skill. Their
   jobs depend upon there being a *demand* for the
   things they can produce. In a rapidly changing
   world, it may be necessary for a worker to learn
   several different skills during his or her
   working lifetime.
2. The number of workers demanded will depend
   upon the wage rate. Other things being equal,
   more workers will be demanded at lower wage
   rates. This is because higher wage rates often
   mean higher labour costs. But this is not always
   the case, as the following point demonstrates.

3. An increase in productivity may offset an
   increase in wage rates. In the following
   example, it can be seen that labour costs remain
   unchanged:

	Hourly wage rate	Output per worker-hour (units)	Labour cost per unit of output
Before increases in wage rate and productivity	£4	80	5p
After increases in wage rate and productivity	£5	100	5p

4. If low-cost labour-saving machinery is available, the demand for labour could be seriously
   affected if wage increases cause the costs of
   labour to rise. Higher labour costs might
   persuade employers to substitute machinery for
   labour.

The demand curve for labour

Demand curves are drawn on the assumption that other things remain equal. If we assume that other things do not change when wage rates change, the demand curves for different types of labour will be of the normal shape, sloping downwards from left to right, as in Figure 16.6. More labour will be demanded at lower wage rates.

As real wages increase, will workers choose

... more income?

... OR more leisure?

... OR more of both?

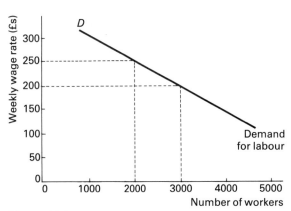

Figure 16.6
At lower wage rates, an industry will demand more labour

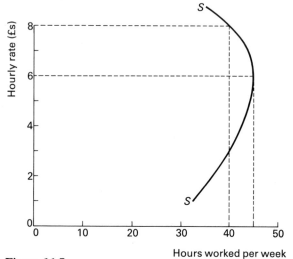

Figure 16.7

The supply of labour

An individual's supply of labour

The supply of labour means the number of hours of work supplied at any given wage rate. The supply curves used so far in this textbook have shown that more of a thing will be supplied at higher prices. Will this be true of the supply curve of an individual worker? Will he or she supply more labour at higher wage rates?

A worker may well do so when *real* wage rates are low. Experience seems to show, however, that as real income increases, leisure becomes more and more attractive. There comes a point where the satisfaction gained from an extra hour's leisure exceeds the satisfaction obtained from the income gained by working an extra hour. This idea is illustrated in Figure 16.7. Here, the individual's supply curve bends backwards; when the hourly wage rate exceeds £6, the worker chooses to work fewer hours.

When wage rates increase, the individual worker may prefer
- to work more hours and earn more income, but have less leisure, or
- to work fewer hours for the same income and have more leisure, or
- to have more income *and* more leisure.

Figure 16.7 shows a situation where a worker can have more income *and* more leisure.

Most workers, however, are not free to choose how many hours they work, because there is usually an agreed working week. However, over-time is normally voluntary, and self-employed workers can vary the number of hours they work. Employees can also press for a shorter working week through their unions.

The supply of labour to an occupation

The total supply curve of labour to an industry will be of the normal shape, sloping upwards from left to right, as in Figure 16.8. Even if the workers in an industry opt for a shorter working week, an increase in the wage rate will tend to attract more workers into the industry, and the supply of labour will increase.

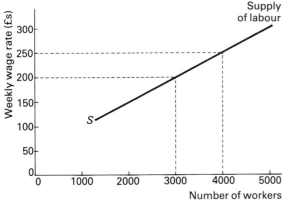

Figure 16.8
At higher wage rates, more workers are prepared to offer their services

The equilibrium wage rate

Like any other price, the equilibrium wage rate will be determined where the demand and supply curves intersect. At this wage rate, the amount of labour demanded is equal to the amount of labour supplied. This is shown in Figure 16.9.

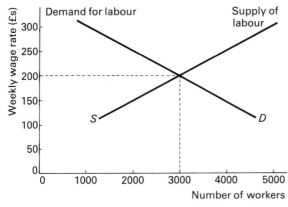

Figure 16.9
Only at the equilibrium wage rate (£200 per week) is the amount of labour demanded equal to the amount of labour supplied

Occupational mobility and wage differentials

The movement of labour from one occupation to another is described as occupational mobility. One of the main reasons for the large differences in wage rates is the fact that it is often very difficult for a worker to move from one occupation to another. In other words, *occupational immobility* is a major cause of wage differentials.

Suppose labour were occupationally mobile and it was very easy to move from one type of job to

Figure 16.10
If workers could move easily from one job to another, many of them would leave the lower-wage occupation and move to the higher-wage occupation. Hence, the wage differences would be greatly reduced

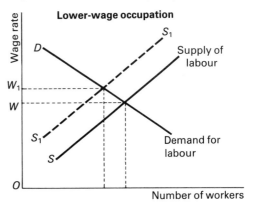

(a) The supply of labour to low-wage jobs would fall, and the wage rate would increase from W to W_1

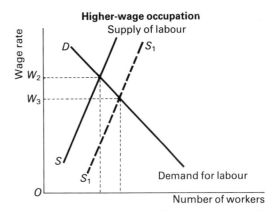

(b) The supply of labour to high-wage jobs would increase, and the wage rate would fall from W_2 to W_3

another. How would this affect wage rates? Figure 16.10 shows what would probably happen. There would be a movement of workers from lower-wage jobs to the higher-wage jobs, and this would have the effect of greatly reducing the differences in wage rates. The fact that, in the real world, this does not happen, shows that there must be some serious barriers to the movement of workers from one occupation to another.

Barriers to occupational mobility

1 Natural ability

Some occupations require a particular natural ability, which is only possessed by a small minority of the population. For this reason, the supplies of very talented mathematicians, scientists, surgeons, musicians, entertainers, sportsmen and sportswomen will always be very limited.

2 Education and training

Some occupations require long periods of education and special training. Medicine, architecture, accountancy and law are well-known examples. The long period required in order to obtain the necessary entry qualifications is a barrier to entry. It is only in the long run that the supply of such qualified people can be increased.

3 Finance

Persons wishing to set up in business for themselves can only do so if they are able to obtain the money necessary to cover the costs of premises, equipment, stocks, etc. Lack of finance, therefore, can be a barrier to someone wishing to be an entrepreneur.

The supply of labour may be elastic or inelastic

1. For occupations which are difficult to enter for the reasons set out above, supply will be inelastic. A large increase in wage rates will not have much effect on the supply of labour to these occupations. In the long run, however, the supply will be more elastic, because more people will try to obtain the necessary qualifications.
2. For occupations which require very little skill and for which few, if any, entry qualifications are required, the supply of labour will be

elastic. It will be easy for workers to move into and out of these jobs. If one of these occupations experiences an increase in wage rates, it will attract workers from other unskilled or semi-skilled jobs.

How technical progress might affect wages and employment

Figure 16.11 shows what might happen in the markets for labour when there is a change in the techniques of production in an industry. In this example, engineers have developed some very

Figure 16.11
The possible short-run effects of increased mechanisation

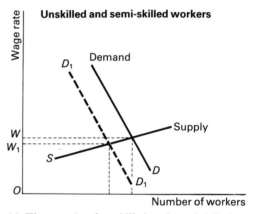

(a) The supply of unskilled and semi-skilled workers is elastic, so when the demand falls there is a relatively small fall in the wage rate and a relatively large fall in the numbers employed

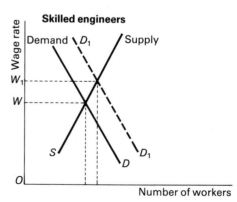

(b) The supply of skilled engineers is inelastic, so when the demand increases there is a relatively large increase in the wage rate and a relatively small increase in the numbers employed

efficient automated machinery, which is capable of doing most of the process and assembly work previously carried out by unskilled labour. Figure 16.11 shows that the effects of this development are likely to be
- a fall in demand for the unskilled workers, and
- an increase in demand for the skilled engineers who will be required to manufacture, install and maintain the new equipment.

Jobs have attractions other than the wage rate

The amount of labour supplied does not depend solely on the wage rate. Many people will accept a job which pays less than they could earn elsewhere because it offers them such things as
- good opportunities for promotion,
- a high degree of job security (that is, providing they are satisfactory workers, there is little risk of their becoming unemployed),
- varied and satisfying work,
- pleasant working conditions,
- various payments in kind, such as subsidised housing, a company car and so on.

16.5
Wage differences within an occupation

There can be quite large differences in the rates of pay received by different people working in the same occupation. Not all teachers receive the same salary, nor do all accountants, nor all engineers. There are several reasons for this state of affairs:

1 Piece-rates, bonus payments and overtime

These payments have already been described. They help to explain why workers doing similar jobs may have quite different weekly earnings.

2 Seniority

In some occupations, for example the civil service, local government and teaching, the salary scales are arranged so that, for several years, employees receive annual increases in their rates of pay. Those with more experience, therefore, will be paid higher salaries.

3 Profit sharing

In addition to their wages and salaries, employees in some companies receive a share of the firm's profits.

4 Regional differences

In some occupations, a supplementary allowance is paid to workers in the London area to compensate them for the relatively high cost of living there. If a region has a shortage of a particular skill, firms in that region may offer higher wages than those paid by firms in other areas.

5 Women's wages

In the past, one of the main reasons for different rates of pay within an occupation was the fact that female workers were often paid less than male workers doing the same job. The Equal Pay Act of 1976 made it illegal to pay women less than men for the same work. Nevertheless, as Figure 16.5 shows, the *average* rates of pay for women are still less than those for men. One reason for this is that many women take breaks in their careers (when they have children). This helps to explain why, in many occupations, the majority of the higher-paid positions are held by men. Another reason is that Figure 16.5 shows gross earnings, which include overtime payments and, in general, men work more overtime than women do.

16.6
Trade unions

Trade unions are associations of workers formed for the purposes of improving the pay and working conditions of their members. Over the years, trade unions have played an important part in achieving better working conditions for the workers, as well as protection from unfair dismissal, the right to compensation for injury at work, the right to redundancy pay and many other benefits. Many people, however, see the major role of the trade unions as representing the workers in wage negotiations.

Types of trade union

1 Craft unions

These unions have a long history. They tend to restrict their membership to workers possessing certain skills (e.g. electricians, printers, building craftsmen, etc.). It has been traditional for these unions to recruit only those workers who have served a recognised apprenticeship.

2 General unions

This type of union recruits mainly unskilled and semi-skilled workers, but membership is open to all types of worker. They recruit workers in all industries and, in the UK, they tend to be very large unions. The Transport and General Workers' Union (TGWU) has more than a million members.

3 Industrial unions

These unions aim to recruit all the workers in a particular industry, whatever their particular job. Industrial unions are common in the USA, Western Europe and Japan, but not in the UK. In this country, the National Union of Mineworkers and the National Union of Railwaymen are examples of industrial unions.

4 White-collar unions

The very large increase in the percentage of the population working in service industries has led to a rapid growth in the membership of what are commonly known as 'white-collar' unions. The unions representing health service workers, teachers, local government officers and managerial staff are now amongst the largest in the UK.

There are about 370 trade unions in the UK, with a total membership of about 11 million workers. The great majority of these unions are very small, and the movement is dominated by a few very large unions. Most of the unions are affiliated to the Trades Union Congress (TUC) which negotiates with the government on behalf of the whole trade union movement.

Collective bargaining

For the great majority of the labour force, wage rates and working conditions are decided by a process known as collective bargaining. In this process, individual workers do not bargain with individual employers. Instead, negotiations are carried out between trade union officials, who represent the workers, and members of employers' associations, who represent the different firms in an industry.

This does not mean that the forces of supply and demand play no part in wage bargaining. A trade union's power to influence wages depends very much on its ability to influence the supply of labour. By restricting, or threatening to restrict, the supply of labour to an industry, a trade union may be able to achieve an increase in wage rates.

Trade unions and the supply of labour

A trade union can influence the supply of labour in several ways:
– by restricting entry to those who have served a recognised apprenticeship,
– by insisting that certain types of work can only be carried out by members of that union,

Table 16.2
Membership of selected trade unions, 1985

	thousands
Transport and General Workers' Union	1434
Amalgamated Union of Engineering Workers	975
General Municipal, Boilermakers and Allied Trades Union	827
National and Local Government Officers' Association	752
National Union of Public Employees	664
Association of Scientific, Technical and Managerial Staffs	390
Union of Shop, Distributive and Allied Workers	385
Electrical, Electronic, Telecommunications and Plumbing Union	384
National Union of Mineworkers	370
National Union of Teachers	253
Confederation of Health Service Employees	213

Source:
Social Trends, HMSO, 1987

- by operating a *closed shop* (where the employer agrees to employ only those workers who are members of that union),
- by calling a strike (at the present time, this can only be done after the union has held a ballot and obtained a majority for strike action).

The power of the threat to strike varies from industry to industry. Certain unions, such as those representing workers in power stations, transport and communications, are in a strong bargaining position because a strike by these workers could disrupt the whole economy. Similarly, a firm which is heavily dependent on exports and has to meet promised delivery dates is very vulnerable to the strike weapon.

But both employers and unions will be very much aware of the effect of any wage increase on the demand for labour. They know that any wage increase which raises labour costs will raise the price of the product and reduce the amount demanded. This could lead to some members of the union becoming unemployed.

Claims for higher wages

Trade unions will base their claims for higher wages on one or more of the following grounds:

1 An increase in the cost of living

Unions are anxious to maintain the real wages of their members, and will ask for wage increases to cover any increase in prices.

2 An increase in productivity

Where the productivity of labour has increased, trade unions will press for some of the benefits to go to the workers, in the form of higher wages.

3 An increase in profits

If the profitability of an industry is increasing, the unions will try to ensure that the workers obtain a share of the increased profits.

4 Comparability

Trade unions will not want the wages of their members to fall out of line with the wages of workers in other industries. A pay rise to one group of workers will probably lead to demands for pay increases by other groups of workers who do not want 'to be left behind'.

If there is no increase in productivity, wage increases based on the arguments in points 1 and 4 could well lead to rising prices and a further round of wage claims.

Trade unions, wages and employment

Figure 16.12 shows what might happen when a trade union in a competitive industry is able to enforce a minimum wage which is higher than the free market wage. (We assume that there is no increase in productivity.) It shows that if there were no trade union, the free market wage would be £5 per hour and that 6000 workers would be employed at this wage rate. If, however, most of the workers belong to a trade union, and the union instructs its members not to work for less than £6 per hour, the effects would be as follows:
- The supply curve for labour will become the dotted line, because no labour will be supplied at a wage rate of less than £6 per hour.
- The amount of labour demanded will fall from 6000 workers to 5000 workers.
- The higher wage rate will benefit those who keep their jobs, but this will be at the cost of other workers who lose their jobs.

The demand for labour, however, may not fall if
- the productivity of labour increases, or
- the union is able to obtain the wage increase at the expense of the firms' profits, or

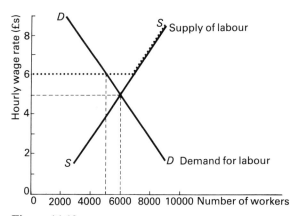

Figure 16.12
In this industry, the free market wage rate is £5 per hour. If a trade union negotiates a minimum wage rate of £6 per hour, union members will not work for less than this wage rate. The supply curve will change from *SS* to the dotted line

– there is an increase in the demand for the product, which raises its price.

16.7
The government and wages

By affecting costs and prices, movements in wages can have a serious effect on an industry's ability to compete in world markets. If UK prices rise faster than those in the countries with which it competes, it will be difficult to sell UK goods in foreign markets. For this reason, governments have tried by various means to influence the rate at which wages are increasing. The subject of wage-inflation is discussed in Chapter 21.

Early this century, the government established what are now known as *wages councils* for those industries and occupations where trade union organisation was very weak. There are now some 26 wages councils, covering about 2.75 million workers in such trades as retailing, catering and farming. These councils make proposals on such matters as minimum wages, length of the working week and annual holidays for workers in their particular industries. These conditions of work become legally enforceable when the government approves the proposals of the wages councils.

The government has also provided machinery to help settle wage disputes. The Advisory, Conciliation and Arbitration Service (ACAS) can supply the services of qualified staff to help find a solution when negotiations between unions and employers are in deadlock. The government also has a direct influence on wages because it is the largest employer in the country: it has about one million employees in the health service alone.

16.8
The rate of interest

The rate of interest is the price of a loan and, like other prices, it is determined by supply and demand – in this case, the supply of and demand for loans.

The demand for loans

Loans are demanded by

– firms wishing to buy capital goods,
– firms wishing to buy other firms,
– households, for the purchase of houses (both old and new),
– households wishing to buy durable consumer goods such as cars, furniture and other household goods,
– governments, to finance that part of their spending which is not covered by taxation, and
– firms and households which have run into financial difficulty.

The demand curve for loans will be of the normal shape – the lower the rate of interest, the greater the demand for loans. To the borrower, the rate of interest is a cost, and the lower the cost, the greater the willingness to borrow. An investment project which appeared unprofitable when the rate of interest was 15 per cent might appear very attractive if money could be borrowed at 10 per cent.

The supply of loans

The supply of loans comes from
– savings (explained in Chapter 4), and
– new money created by the banking system (explained in Chapter 14).

The supply curve for loans will also be of the normal shape, sloping upwards from left to right. People are more willing to lend when interest rates are high.

The market rate of interest

Figure 16.13 shows that the market rate of interest, *OR*, is determined at the point where the demand for loans is equal to the supply of loans. Thus, other things being equal,
– an increase in the demand for loans will raise the rate of interest, while a fall in the demand for loans will lower the rate of interest;
– an increase in the supply of loans will lower the rate of interest, while a fall in the supply of loans will raise the rate of interest.

There are many rates of interest

Newspaper advertisements by banks, building societies and other financial institutions show that many different rates of interest are offered to lenders and charged to borrowers (see Figure 16.14).

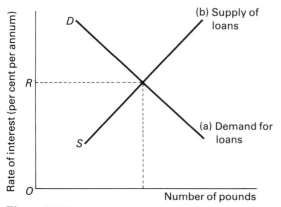

Figure 16.13
Borrowing and lending
(a) The demand for loans: at lower rates of interest, people are more willing to borrow
(b) The supply of loans: at higher rates of interest, people are more willing to lend

For borrowers, the rate of interest charged on a loan will depend on the following factors:

1. *The duration of the loan*: long-term loans are more risky for the lender than short-term loans – the longer the period of the loan, the greater the risk of 'things going wrong'. Therefore interest rates tend to be higher on long-term loans.
2. *The credit-worthiness of the borrower*: some borrowers can offer greater security than other borrowers. For this reason, large well-known companies can obtain loans at lower interest rates than small newly-established companies.

For savers, the rates of interest paid on their deposits will depend upon the following factors:

1. *The minimum amount kept in the deposit*: a person who maintains a minimum balance of £5000 will receive a higher interest rate than someone whose average deposit is £50.
2. *The amount of notice required for withdrawal*: a deposit requiring six months' notice of withdrawal will earn a higher rate of interest than a deposit from which withdrawals can be made on demand.

Strictly speaking, interest is not paid for saving; money saved at home in a tin box or a piggy bank will earn no interest. It is only when the money

CURRENT INTEREST Rates ■

From 6th April 1988

	Net rates of interest	Gross equivalent to income tax payers
■ **Platinum Key Account**		
Balances £25,000 and above		
*Instant access penalty free	7.50%	10.00%
Monthly Income *Instant access penalty free	7.25%	9.67%
Balances £10,000 and above *Instant access penalty free	7.25%	9.67%
Monthly Income *Instant access penalty free	7.00%	9.33%
Balances £500 and above Withdrawals at 60 days' notice or loss of interest	7.00%	9.33%
Monthly Income Withdrawals at 60 days' notice	6.75%	9.00%
■ **Golden Key Account** Instant access penalty free		
Balances £25,000 and above	7.05%	9.40%
Balances £10,000 and above	6.80%	9.07%
Balances £5,000 and above	6.55%	8.73%
Balances £1,000 and above	6.05%	8.07%

Figure 16.14
Banks offer different rates of interest on different types of account.
Can you explain the difference between *net* rates and *gross* rates?

is deposited in some kind of financial institution that it begins to earn interest. When a saver puts money into a bank or building society or similar institution, he or she is, in fact, making a loan to that institution. Interest is paid for lending, not for saving.

Although there are many different rates of interest, they all tend to move in the same direction. Changes in the supply of and demand for loans will tend to influence all interest rates – they will all move up or down.

16.9
Economic rent and transfer earnings

In everyday usage, the word 'rent' describes payment which is made for the hire of land, property, machinery, motor cars, office equipment, television sets and so on. These rents, however, include payments made to all the factors of production. The revenues received by the firms renting various types of property and equipment will be paid out as wages to employees, interest on loans, rents to landlords, and profits to the owners of the firms.

In economics, the word 'rent' has a special meaning, and for this reason the term *economic rent* is used. A factor of production may earn more than is strictly necessary to keep it in its present employment. The difference between what it is earning in its present employment and what it could earn in its next-best-paid occupation is known as economic rent.

Transfer earnings describe the minimum reward which would prevent a factor of production transferring to another employment, and *economic rent* is the amount which a factor earns over and above its transfer earnings:

Actual earnings − Transfer earnings
                                    = Economic rent

For example, if a lorry driver is earning £250 per week and his next-best-paid alternative job is that of a bus driver earning £225 per week, his present wage consists of £225 in the form of transfer earnings and £25 in the form of economic rent.

Economic rent arises when the demand for a factor of production increases but it is difficult to increase the supply of that factor. The increase in demand will cause the earnings of the factor to increase. Economic rent can be earned by land, labour and capital. It is best illustrated by using labour as an example and working through the following changes (see Figure 16.15).

1. A firm commences business with five workers, which it is able to attract with a weekly wage of £180.
2. When it wishes to expand, it seeks a further five workers, but it has to pay a wage of £200 per week in order to attract them.
3. Since all the workers are doing the same job, the original five workers will also be paid £200 per week. These employees are now receiving economic rent equal to £20 per week.
4. Further expansion of the firm causes it to increase its labour force by another five workers, but these can only be obtained by raising wages to £220 per week, which must then be paid to all the firm's workers.

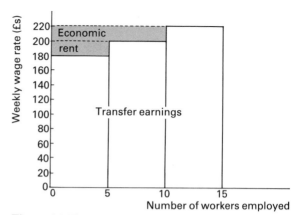

Figure 16.15

5. The original five workers will now be receiving economic rent equal to £40 per week, and the second group of workers will now receive £20 per week in the form of economic rent. Only the last five workers engaged will receive no economic rent, since £220 per week is equal to their transfer earnings.

16.10
Profits

Profits are the rewards to people who put their money at risk by investing it in privately-owned businesses. Profits were described in Chapter 15.

The Main Points

- Wages, rent, interest and profits are the price paid for the services of the factors of production.

- Personal incomes may take the forms of income from employment, income from self-employment, income from the ownership of wealth, and various social security benefits.

- There are great inequalities in the distributions of income and of wealth. The imposition of income taxes and the payment of social security benefits reduce the inequality in the distribution of income.

- The demand for labour is a derived demand: it depends on the demand for whatever the labour is producing.

- Wage differences arise because there are different conditions of supply and demand in the markets for the different types of labour.

- Occupational mobility is restricted by many factors, including the need for educational qualifications and long periods of training.

- Trade unions can raise money wages when they can control the supply of labour. Real wages, however, may not increase if the rise in money wages causes prices to rise.

- The rate of interest is the price of a loan. The supply of loans depends on the rate of saving and on the amount of new money created by the banking system. Loans are demanded by households, firms and government.

- Transfer earnings describe what a factor of production could earn in its next-best-paid employment. Economic rent is any payment over and above a factor's transfer earnings.

Test Your Understanding

Use the following terms to complete the sentences in questions 1 to 6:

occupational mobility   collective bargaining
closed shop   marketable wealth
disposable income

1. The income which is available for spending or saving is described as ....

2. .... consists of those assets which can be bought and sold.

3. Wages and working conditions for the great majority of the working population are decided by a process known as ....

4. A .... exists when an employer agrees to employ only workers who belong to a union.

5. When it is difficult for workers to move from one type of job to another .... is said to be restricted.

6. To which type of trade union does each of the following belong?
   (a) The Amalgamated Union of Engineering Workers (AUEW)
   (b) The National Union of Seamen (NUS)
   (c) The National and Local Government Officers' Association (NALGO)

7. Will an increase in money wages always cause costs of production to increase? Explain.

8. Why is the rate of interest charged on a loan for house purchase less than the rate charged on a loan for setting up a new business?

9. The table shows the percentage changes in retail prices and average wages in a country.

Year	Change in retail prices	Change in average wages
1984	+10 per cent	+20 per cent
1985	+5 per cent	+6 per cent
1986	−3 per cent	0 per cent

In which years did real wages increase?

10. In a particular industry, skilled workers are paid £4.50 per hour, and unskilled workers are paid £3 per hour. Assume that every year, for a period of five years, both skilled and unskilled workers receive flat-rate increases of 30p per hour.
    (a) What would happen to the *money difference* in the wage rates of skilled and unskilled workers?
    (b) What would happen to the *percentage difference* in their wage rates?

11. When a woman earns more than the wage necessary to keep her in her job, the extra payment is known as

    A opportunity cost   **B** transfer earnings
    C economic rent   **D** real wages

12. A businessman employs 20 workers at a wage rate of £5 per hour. In order to attract one more worker, he has to raise the wage rate to £5.50 per hour. By how much does the total hourly wage bill increase?

    A 50p   **B** £5.50   **C** £10   **D** £15.50

13. 'Paying wages and salaries by crossed cheques offers much more security than payments made in cash.' Explain why this is so.

BOX 16
Miners, lawyers and airline pilots

Miners are towards the top of the hourly earnings league largely because the demand for British coal is inelastic, given the technology of our power stations and our reluctance to import cheaper coal from abroad.

We must expect jobs which cannot be mechanised or automated, such as lawyers, to be able to raise their wages well above the competitive level.

Airline pilots receive very high pay relative to their qualifications partly because the total cost of labour amounts to less than 3 per cent of the operating costs of a modern airliner.
Source: Extracts taken from D. Metcalf, 'Unions and pay' *Economic Review*, vol. 2, no. 1

Questions
1. If labour costs are such a small percentage of the total costs of operating an airliner, what are the major costs?
2. Why is it not possible to mechanise the work done by lawyers?
3. What would be the likely effect on the price of airline tickets of a large increase in the pay received by airline pilots?
4. Explain why the 'technology of our power stations' helps to make the demands for British coal and for coalminers inelastic.

CHAPTER 17

The income and expenditure of government

17.1 Public expenditure
17.2 Taxation
17.3 The British system of taxation
17.4 The Budget
17.5 Income and expenditure of local authorities

17.1

Public expenditure

This chapter deals with the ways in which the government sector obtains its income and with the ways in which that income is spent.

The government sector includes the central government and local authorities. The revenues and expenditures of the nationalised industries are not included. Only the money which these industries borrow from the government is included in public spending.

In the UK, the total spending of the government sector is a very large figure: it was estimated to be about £173 billion in 1987–88. This is approximately £3100 for every man, woman and child.

Public spending and private spending

Most of the goods and services we want or need are obtained through the market. They are supplied by privately-owned firms and we obtain them by paying market prices.

There is, however, a wide range of goods and services which are not allocated in this way – these are listed in Figure 17.1, and are supplied by the government. Most of these goods and services are 'free', in the sense that they do not have market prices. We do not pay market prices for state education and health services or for the services of law and order and defence.

These things, of course, are not free – they have to be paid for. The difference is that they are paid for publicly, not privately. As Figure 17.1 shows, the costs of the goods and services supplied by the government sector are financed mainly by taxation (national insurance contributions and local authority rates are forms of taxation).

The difference between these two systems of allocating goods and services is very important. It is a source of great political argument. Many people think that more goods and services should be provided by the state and paid for by means of taxation. Many others think that public expenditure and taxation should be reduced, so that people can keep more of their income and spend it as they wish.

Real spending and transfer payments

There two very different kinds of public expenditure, real spending and transfer payments.

Real spending

This takes place when goods and services are bought by the central government and local authorities. The payments for the services of civil servants, teachers, policemen and nurses represent real spending. This type of spending also includes such things as the purchase of the food and medicines used in the hospitals and the textbooks and equipment used in schools.

Transfer payments

As the name suggests, these consist of transfers of money in the form of grants from the government to households and firms. They are not payments for goods or for work done. Unemployment benefit, child benefit and investment grants are examples of transfer payments. Although transfer payments are counted as part of government expenditure, the actual spending of the money is done by the households and firms which receive these payments. About half of total public expenditure consists of transfer payments.

Where the money comes from

Figure 17.1 shows that 84 per cent of the income of the government sector was obtained from taxation in 1987–88. This figure is obtained by including national insurance contributions and local rates as forms of taxation. This is reasonable, since they are both compulsory payments. National insurance contributions have to be paid by employers, employees and the self-employed. Local rates are a tax on the owners of property.

The government sector also obtains some income from its ownership of company shares (dividends) and from its ownership of land and buildings (rent). The Conservative government elected in 1979 also obtained large sums of money by selling off state-owned industries. This procedure, known as privatisation, was explained in Chapter 12.

Any additional income which the central government and local authorities may need must be obtained by borrowing.

Some arguments for public expenditure

1 Public goods

There are some things which people would like to have and which many people regard as necessities, but which would not be supplied by a market

Figure 17.1
Public money, UK, 1987–88

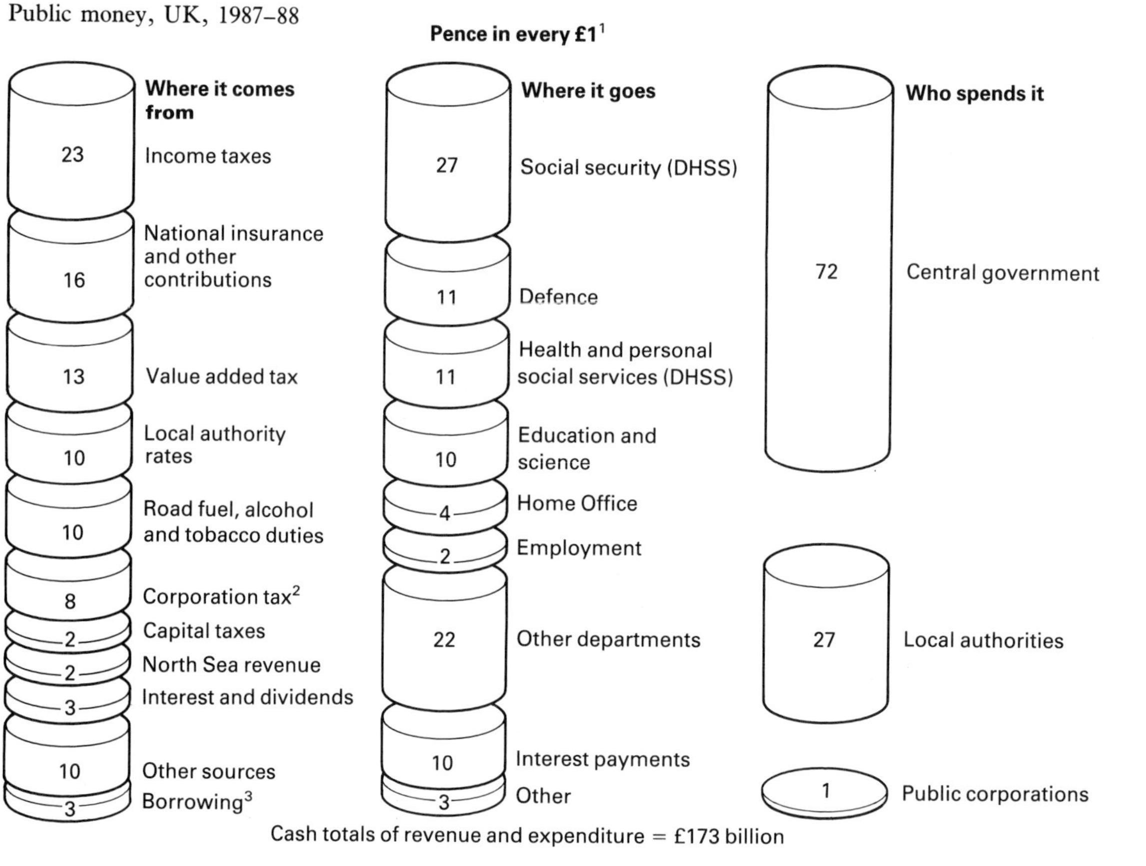

Pence in every £1[1]

Where it comes from		Where it goes		Who spends it	
23	Income taxes	27	Social security (DHSS)		
16	National insurance and other contributions	11	Defence	72	Central government
13	Value added tax	11	Health and personal social services (DHSS)		
10	Local authority rates	10	Education and science		
10	Road fuel, alcohol and tobacco duties	4	Home Office		
		2	Employment		
8	Corporation tax[2]	22	Other departments	27	Local authorities
2	Capital taxes				
2	North Sea revenue				
3	Interest and dividends				
10	Other sources	10	Interest payments		
3	Borrowing[3]	3	Other	1	Public corporations

Cash totals of revenue and expenditure = £173 billion

[1] Rounded to the nearest penny
[2] Excluding North Sea
[3] By central and local government

Sources: *Economic Progress Report Supplement*, HMSO, March–April 1987; *Government's Expenditure Plans, 1987–88 to 1988–89*, HMSO

economy. These things are known as *public goods*. Examples of public goods are defence, law and order, street lighting, street cleaning, lighthouses, and barriers to prevent flooding.

The reason why such goods and services would not be supplied in a market economy is the fact that the consumption of such goods and services cannot be restricted to those who are prepared to pay for them. For example, if some people agreed to pay for street lighting or street cleaning, or defence, everyone else, whether they had paid for them or not, would get the benefit. In these circumstances few, if any, people will volunteer to pay for such things as improving the pavements, or for the services of the police.

The only practical way of providing the citizens with public goods is for the state to supply them and to recover the costs from taxation.

2 Merit goods

Merit goods are goods which provide great benefits both to individuals and to society as a whole. The most obvious examples are the education and health services. It is widely believed that people ought to have more of these services than most of them would buy, or could buy, if they were sold at market prices.

Although we have private education and private health care in the UK, there seems general agreement that the supply of these services should not be left entirely to the private sector, i.e. sold at market prices, for the following reasons:

– Many people would not be able to afford adequate health services and a reasonable education.
– Those who could not afford these services would find their opportunities for living a healthy life and making the most of their abilities greatly restricted.
– Even when people could afford to pay, some of them might not act in their own best interests. They might not fully appreciate the long-term benefits of spending on health and education.
– Quite apart from the benefits to the individual, we all benefit from living in a healthy and well-educated society.

For these reasons, the government makes health and education services freely available to all citizens. Figure 17.2 shows how this is done.

Figure 17.2

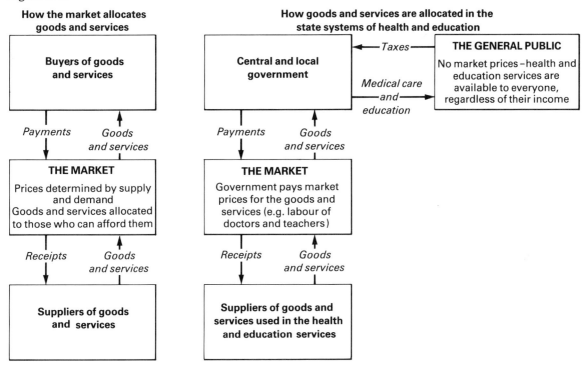

3 Helping those in need

A major reason for the great increase in public spending since the Second World War has been the attempt by various governments to create a welfare state. This is a state in which
- everyone is guaranteed some minimum level of income,
- people are protected from unnecessary hardship when they suffer misfortunes such as sickness and unemployment, and
- certain social services, such as education, health, help for the aged, etc., are made available to all regardless of their income.

Social security payments of various kinds now account for more than a quarter of total public expenditure.

4 Supporting industry and employment

Large sums of public money are spent on schemes to improve industrial efficiency and to create more jobs. There is a wide variety of such schemes; some examples are:
- investment grants to encourage firms to expand and modernise,
- grants to help firms in assisted areas (see page 120),
- grants to help with the costs of research and development,
- organising and financing schemes of industrial training and re-training,
- subsidies to encourage firms to take on unemployed workers (see page 228), and
- financing improvements in the road and rail networks.

5 Managing the economy

Spending by the government sector is a large percentage of total spending in the economy. This means that any changes in public spending will have important effects on the demand for goods and services and the level of employment. For this reason, the government may deliberately change the amount it spends so as to increase or decrease the total demand for goods and services. This subject is discussed in Section 17.4, which deals with the Budget.

Taxation

Taxes may be levied on
- *income*, i.e. taxes on wages, salaries, interest, rent and profits,
- *expenditure*, i.e. taxes on the goods and services people buy, and
- *wealth*, i.e. taxes which transfer part of the value of a person's assets to the government.

Why does a government impose taxes?

The government may use taxation for various purposes:

1. The main purpose of taxation is to provide the government with the money it needs to pay for the many services it provides.
2. Taxes may be used to control the amount of spending in an economy. This is most likely when excess demand is causing prices to rise. An increase in income tax will reduce people's ability to spend.
3. An important purpose of taxation is to reduce the inequalities in the distribution of income. The higher-income groups can be made to pay higher rates of tax.
4. Taxes may also be used to protect industry from foreign competition. Tariffs are a form of taxation.
5. If the government wishes to discourage the consumption of some commodity, for example tobacco, it may place a heavy tax on the commodity.

Types of taxation

Direct and indirect taxation

Taxes are usually classified as direct or indirect.

Direct taxes

These are those taxes which are placed on income and wealth; the most obvious example is personal income tax. These taxes are described as 'direct' because the person who is responsible for paying the tax has to bear the burden of the tax.

Indirect taxes

These are those taxes which are levied on spending. The best-known example is VAT, but the excise duties on petrol, tobacco and alcoholic drinks are also important. These taxes are described as 'indirect' because the person responsible for paying the tax may pass on all or part of the burden of the tax in the form of higher prices.

Proportional taxes

A tax is proportional when all taxpayers pay the *same percentage* of their income (or wealth or expenditure) in tax. Corporation tax – the tax on company profits – is a proportional tax.

Progressive taxes

A tax is progressive when those with higher incomes pay a *larger percentage* of their income in tax. Taxable income is arranged in bands, and the higher bands are subject to higher rates of tax. This is illustrated in the example below.

Example of a progressive tax

Taxable income (£s)	Rate of tax
0–10 000	30 per cent
10 001–20 000	40 per cent
20 001–30 000	50 per cent

A person with a *taxable* income of £8000 will pay tax equal to

30 per cent of £8000 = £2400

A person with a *taxable* income of £14 000 will pay tax equal to

30 per cent of £10 000 *plus* 40 per cent of £4000
    = £3000 *plus* £1600
    = £4600

Question

How much tax will be paid by a person with a taxable income of £25 000?

Regressive taxes

These taxes work in exactly the opposite way to progressive taxes: as income increases, a smaller and smaller percentage is taken in taxation. People with higher incomes pay a smaller percentage of their income in tax than people with lower incomes do.

Some of the British excise duties act in a regressive manner. Everyone pays the same amount of tax when they buy a gallon of petrol, a pint of beer or a packet of cigarettes. But the amount of tax paid on these purchases represents a larger burden for the low-income groups than it does for the higher-income groups.

Economic effects of taxation

1 Taxes on income

A progressive tax on income reduces the inequality in the distribution of income. This is because those with higher incomes pay a larger proportion of their income in taxation. It is widely believed that this is the fairest way of sharing out the burden of taxation.

Progressive income taxes, however, are sometimes criticised because they may affect people's incentive to work harder, or to take more responsible jobs, or to invest in risky enterprises. This is because any extra income is taxed at higher and higher rates.

2 Taxes on expenditure

VAT and the excise duties on petrol, tobacco and alcoholic drinks raise vast sums of money for the government. The demands for these commodities are inelastic, so an increase in the rate of tax does not have much effect on the amounts purchased.

A major problem with expenditure taxes, however, is the fact that an increase in the rate of tax raises prices. This could have the effect of increasing wage demands and might, therefore, lead to an increase in the rate of inflation. As mentioned earlier, a further disadvantage of taxes on spending is that they take a larger percentage of the incomes of the less well off.

3 Taxes on wealth and capital

These taxes are intended to reduce the inequality in the ownership of wealth. In the UK, the major tax on wealth is an inheritance tax which taxes the wealth which is passed on when a person dies.

Taxing wealth causes problems when the wealth is held in the forms of land, buildings, works of art and jewellery. If these things have been in a family's possession for many years, it may be difficult to estimate their market value for tax purposes.

Taxing wealth may, perhaps, encourage some people to spend rather than save.

17.3
The British system of taxation

The taxes levied by the central government are collected by two separate government departments. Taxes on income, wealth and capital (direct taxes) are collected by the *Inland Revenue Department*. Taxes on expenditure (indirect taxes) are collected by the *Customs and Excise Department*.

Figure 17.3

HM CUSTOMS
AND EXCISE

The Inland Revenue collects *direct taxes*

HM Customs and Excise collects *indirect taxes*

1 Direct taxes – taxes on income, wealth and capital

Income tax

This tax raises more revenue than any other tax. Details of its structure are given in Box 17.

Corporation tax

This is levied on the profits of companies. It is a proportional tax.

Petroleum revenue tax

This is levied on the income of oil companies working in the North Sea and other offshore oilfields.

Capital gains tax

When assets are sold at higher prices than those at which they were bought, the difference between the prices is described as a capital gain. This capital gain is subject to tax. The most obvious example of a capital gain is when shares are sold at higher prices than the prices at which they were bought.

Inheritance tax

As the name suggests, this tax is levied on wealth which is inherited. It is a proportional tax.

Stamp duties

Documents which transfer the ownership of property have to bear stamps, the value of which is related to the value of the property.

2 Indirect taxes – taxes on expenditure

Value Added Tax (VAT)

This is the most important of the expenditure taxes. It is levied at a rate of 15 per cent (1987 rate) on a wide range of goods and services. Some goods and services, however, are not subject to VAT. These include food (except meals out), children's clothing and footwear, books, newspapers, passenger transport, and prescribed medicines.

Excise duties

These are levied on certain home-produced products and imported goods. The most important of these duties are those on petrol, tobacco, alcoholic drinks, and betting and gaming.

Customs duties

These are the duties levied on imports. They are paid over to the EEC.

Car tax

This is a special tax levied on new cars in addition to VAT.

3 Other taxes and duties

Vehicle excise duties

All motor vehicles in use in the UK have to be registered and licensed.

Figure 17.4
Sources of revenue, UK, 1987–88

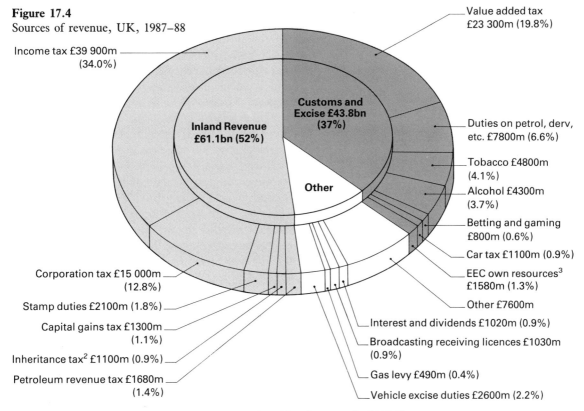

Income tax £39 900m (34.0%)

Value added tax £23 300m (19.8%)

Customs and Excise £43.8bn (37%)

Inland Revenue £61.1bn (52%)

Other

Duties on petrol, derv, etc. £7800m (6.6%)

Tobacco £4800m (4.1%)

Alcohol £4300m (3.7%)

Betting and gaming £800m (0.6%)

Car tax £1100m (0.9%)

EEC own resources[3] £1580m (1.3%)

Other £7600m

Corporation tax £15 000m (12.8%)

Stamp duties £2100m (1.8%)

Capital gains tax £1300m (1.1%)

Inheritance tax[2] £1100m (0.9%)

Petroleum revenue tax £1680m (1.4%)

Interest and dividends £1020m (0.9%)

Broadcasting receiving licences £1030m (0.9%)

Gas levy £490m (0.4%)

Vehicle excise duties £2600m (2.2%)

Total Consolidated Fund revenue[1] = £117.5bn

[1] National insurance contributions are paid into a separate fund, and are estimated at £28.5bn.
[2] Includes estate duty and capital transfer tax
[3] Taxes raised for the EEC, including customs duties
Source: *The Independent*, 18 March 1987

Miscellaneous licences

Some central government revenue is obtained from various licences, of which the television licence is the most important.

Figure 17.4 shows the planned revenues for 1987–88 from the various taxes listed above. It contains a relatively large item (£7600 million) labelled 'other'. This includes the expected receipts from the sale of state-owned enterprises to the private sector (i.e. privatisation).

The percentages shown in Figure 17.4 differ from those in Figure 17.1. This is because Figure 17.4 contains only those items of revenue which appear in the Budget account and which are paid

into the Consolidated Fund. There are three other sources of income to the government which are not included in the Budget account. These were included in Figure 17.1, and are:

National insurance contributions

These contributions from both employers and employees are paid into the National Insurance Fund, and are used to help pay for national insurance benefits, such as unemployment benefit.

Local authority rates

These are a form of local taxation and are levied on the owners of property. They are collected by city and county councils.

Borrowing

The various forms of government borrowing are explained later.

The Budget

On Budget Day, the Chancellor of the Exchequer presents a statement which gives details of the central government's income and expenditure for the financial year which has just ended. He also presents a forecast of the same items for the year ahead. His statement contains details of the planned spending of the various government departments. The Budget statement also contains details of the proposed changes in the system and rates of taxation for the coming year.

The Budget, however, is more than a simple balance sheet showing how the government spends its income and how it intends to obtain that income: it is a very important instrument of economic policy.

For example, if the government wishes to reduce unemployment by increasing the demand for goods and services, it will deliberately spend more than its income from taxation. In other words, it will aim for a *Budget deficit*. By this means, it can put more purchasing power into the economy than it takes out in taxation. The deficit will have to be financed by borrowing.

On the other hand, if it wishes to reduce the total demand for goods and services because of fears of inflation, it will aim for a *Budget surplus*. It will spend less than its income from taxation. This will reduce the amount of purchasing power in the economy.

Using the Budget in this way is described as *fiscal policy*.

Borrowing and the National Debt

In 1987–88, 3 per cent of total public spending was financed by borrowing (see Figure 17.1). Both central and local governments borrow in order to pay for some of their activities. The central government borrows in a variety of ways:
- by selling long-term securities (described as *gilt-edged* securities),
- by selling short-term securities, such as Treasury bills,
- by selling Premium Bonds and National Savings Certificates,
- by obtaining loans from the banks, and
- by obtaining loans from overseas.

Local authorities borrow by selling longer-term and short-term securities, by borrowing from the central government, and by borrowing from the banks.

The National Debt is the debt of the central government. Much of this debt is due to the borrowings which were made to help pay for the First and Second World Wars. It has, however, continued to grow steadily over the years since the Second World War. In 1986 it amounted to £171 591 million. Figure 17.1 shows that the annual interest payments on the debts of the central government and local authorities accounted for 10 per cent of total public spending in 1987–88.

Income and expenditure of local authorities

Local authorities – city and county councils – are responsible for about a quarter of total public expenditure. The main items of expenditure and the sources of income are shown in Figure 17.5. Note that
- education is by far the largest item of expenditure, and
- a large part of the revenue of local authorities consists of grants from the central government.

Local rates

Each house, shop, office, factory, etc. is given a rateable value, which is expressed in pounds. This rateable value usually represents an estimate of what the property would earn in one year if it were rented in a free market. The rate is then fixed at 'so many pence in the pound'.

For example, if a house has a rateable value of £300 and the annual rate is fixed at 120p in the pound, the owner of the house will be obliged to pay annual rates equal to

$$300 \times 120p = £360$$

Figure 17.5
The income and expenditure of one local authority

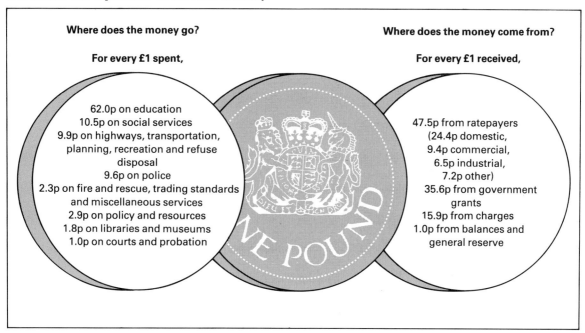

Where does the money go?

For every £1 spent,

62.0p on education
10.5p on social services
9.9p on highways, transportation,
planning, recreation and refuse
disposal
9.6p on police
2.3p on fire and rescue, trading standards
and miscellaneous services
2.9p on policy and resources
1.8p on libraries and museums
1.0p on courts and probation

Where does the money come from?

For every £1 received,

47.5p from ratepayers
(24.4p domestic,
9.4p commercial,
6.5p industrial,
7.2p other)
35.6p from government
grants
15.9p from charges
1.0p from balances and
general reserve

Source: Leicestershire County Council

The Main Points

- Public spending in the UK is a very large figure: in 1987–88 it amounted to about £3000 for every man, woman and child.

- Public expenditure is paid for almost entirely by taxation. This enables the government to supply many public goods and merit goods to all citizens without charge.

- About half of public spending consists of transfer payments.

- The main reason for the growth in public spending has been the development of the welfare state. Social security payments and the provision of social services such as health and education account for a very large part of total public spending.

- Taxes are imposed on income, expenditure and wealth. They may be progressive, proportional, regressive or flat-rate.

- The taxes which raise the most revenue are income tax, corporation tax, VAT, and the excise duties on petrol, tobacco and alcoholic drinks. National insurance contributions and local rates are also very important sources of revenue for the government sector.

- The Budget is a statement which shows
  - the central government's income and expenditure for the year just ended, and
  - its planned expenditure and income for the year ahead.

- The government may deliberately aim for a Budget deficit or surplus. A deficit must be financed by borrowing. A Budget deficit, therefore, will lead to an increase in the National Debt.

- Local authorities are responsible for about a quarter of total public spending. They are financed by local rates and by grants from the central government.

- The income and expenditure of central and local government are summarised in Figure 17.6 (over the page).

Figure 17.6
Income and expenditure of the government sector

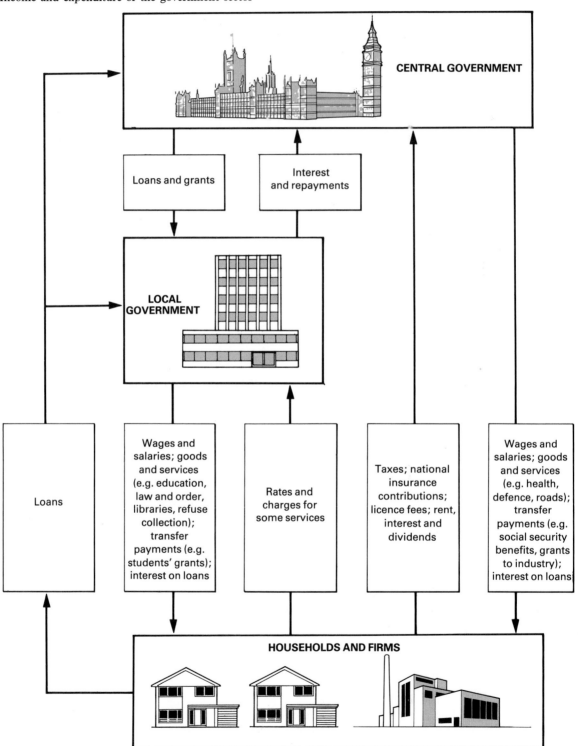

Test Your Understanding

1. Which ONE of the following is a transfer payment?

   A teachers' salaries
   B purchases of medicine for use in hospitals
   C child benefit
   D rental payments on photocopiers used in schools

2. Which ONE of the following is a direct tax?

   A VAT
   B inheritance tax
   C the tax on petrol
   D the tax on betting and gaming

3. What is the missing item in the following list of the five largest items of public expenditure?

   ....
   defence
   interest on borrowings
   health
   education

4. Which major item of public expenditure consists mainly of transfer payments?

5. Figure 17.7 shows how different types of taxation affect the percentage of income paid in tax. Which of the lines A, B and C represents
   (a) a regressive tax?
   (b) a progressive tax?
   (c) a proportional tax?

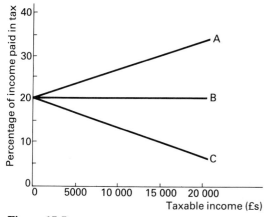

Figure 17.7

6. Why are lighthouses described as public goods?

7. A government reduces income tax and corporation tax and, at the same time, increases VAT. These changes will shift some of the burden of taxation from (a) taxes to (b) taxes. Which of the following words should be inserted at (a), and which at (b)?

   indirect   direct

8. A local authority has a total rateable value of £50 million. It needs to raise £40 million from the rates. What rate in the pound should it set?

9. The revenue and expenditure of the government sector of a particular country are set out in the tables below.

Central government

Revenue (£m)		Expenditure (£m)	
Taxes	95	Spending on goods and services	50
Borrowing	5	Transfer payments	40
		Grants to local authorities	10
	100		100

Local authorities

Revenue (£m)		Expenditure (£m)	
Rates	20	Spending on goods and services	25
Grants from central government	10	Transfer payments	5
	30		30

(a) What is the total of *real* spending?
(b) What is the total public expenditure? (Note: the answer is not £130 m.)

BOX 17
Personal income tax in the UK

Income tax is not charged on a person's gross income: there are various allowances which are not subject to tax, for example
- the single person's allowance,
- the married allowance,
- allowances for dependent relatives, for people over 65, and for certain expenses associated with a person's job.

This means that people on very low incomes do not pay income tax, because their incomes will be less than their allowances. Thus,

Taxable income = Gross income − Allowances

   The diagram shows the rates of income tax which were applied in 1987–88. The first £17 900 of *taxable* income was taxed at a rate of 27 per cent, the next £6500 of taxable income at a rate of 40 per cent, and so on.

Income tax in the UK, 1987–88

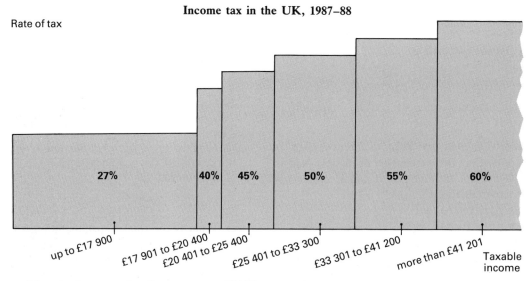

Rate of tax

27%   40%   45%   50%   55%   60%

up to £17 900   £17 901 to £20 400   £20 401 to £25 400   £25 401 to £33 300   £33 301 to £41 200   more than £41 201   Taxable income

■ The single person's allowance was £2425.   ■ The married allowance was £3795.

In the questions, assume that these were the only allowances that could be claimed.

Questions
1. (a) What was the *taxable income* of a single woman whose gross earnings were £15 000 per annum?
   (b) What *rate of tax* would have been charged on her taxable income?
2. (a) What was the *taxable income* of a married man whose gross earnings were £25 000 per annum?
   (b) What *rates of tax* would have been charged on his taxable income?
3. How much tax would the single woman have paid?

CHAPTER 18

International trade

18.1 International trade and specialisation
18.2 Why countries gain from trade
18.3 Restrictions on trade – protection
18.4 Free trade areas and customs unions
18.5 The European Economic Community (EEC)

Figure 18.1

18.1

International trade and specialisation

The fact that human beings have different abilities, aptitudes, interests and personalities helps to explain why workers specialise – the 'jack of all trades' is a very rare person in modern societies.

Similarly, the fact that different countries have different 'abilities to produce' explains why they tend to specialise and trade with one another. Countries differ in their supplies of fertile land and mineral deposits, in the skills of their workers, in their geographical location and climate, and in the size of their populations. These differences mean that one country may have an advantage over another country in the production of wheat, or the manufacture of motor cars, or the production of coal, and so on.

International trade gives countries the opportunities to specialise in the things they do best.

Why countries gain from trade

1 Countries can import goods which they cannot produce for themselves

This is the oldest form of international trade, and it is still an important part of present-day trade. For example, Britain can only obtain products such as rice, natural rubber, tropical fruits and certain types of minerals by means of international trade. Trading with other countries enables people to enjoy a much wider range of goods than they can produce for themselves.

2 More specialisation means larger outputs and lower costs

The major part of world trade takes place between countries which could produce for themselves many of the goods they import. Britain, for example, imports cars, motor cycles, footwear, electrical appliances and many other goods which she is quite capable of producing. The reason for this state of affairs is that countries are much better at producing some things than they are at producing others. International trade makes it possible for them to specialise in producing those goods in which they have some kind of advantage over other countries.

Therefore, countries specialise, and exchange their goods for those produced by other countries. Specialisation increases total world output. Goods are produced on a larger scale and at lower cost. International trade enables countries to have more goods than they could obtain by trying to be self-sufficient, i.e. producing only for themselves.

A simple model of international trade

The way in which a country might gain from international trade can be explained by assuming that there are only two countries (A and B), each of which is capable of producing two particular products (video recorders and cameras).

If each country is more efficient than the other in one of the industries

In this case, we assume that Country A is more efficient than Country B in the production of cameras, and that Country B is more efficient in the production of video recorders. It is usual to describe this situation by saying that each country has an *absolute advantage* in the production of one of the goods. Figure 18.2 illustrates this particular situation.

Figure 18.2

Each country has an *absolute* advantage

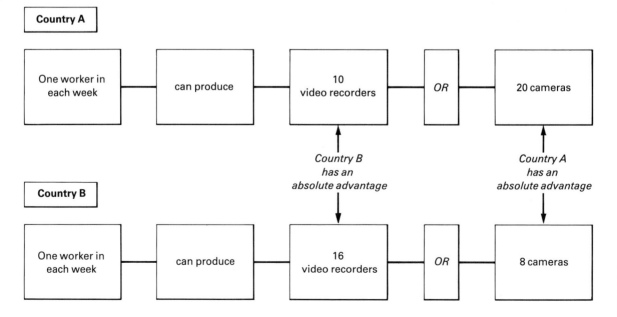

Questions on Figure 18.2

1. Assume that each country has 1000 people available for work in these industries, and that the countries do not specialise and trade – they both employ 500 workers in each industry.
   (a) What are the total outputs of (i) video recorders and (ii) cameras *in each country?*
   (b) What are the *combined outputs* of (i) video recorders and (ii) cameras?
2. Now assume that each country decides to specialise in the production of the good in which it has an absolute advantage. It puts all the 1000 workers into this industry.
   (a) What are the total outputs of (i) video recorders and (ii) cameras now?
   (b) By how much has specialisation increased total output?
3. Now assume that, after specialising, the countries trade with one another. Using an exchange rate of 'one video recorder for one camera', show that both countries can have more video recorders *and* more cameras than they had before they decided to specialise and trade with one another.

If one country is more efficient than the other in both industries

Even if one country is more efficient than the other in producing both video recorders and cameras, it may still benefit both countries to specialise and trade.

Figure 18.3 shows a situation where Country A can produce both goods more efficiently than Country B. It has an absolute advantage in both industries. Whether both countries can benefit from specialising and trading depends upon the *opportunity costs* of producing video recorders and cameras in each country. The opportunity costs are also set out in Figure 18.3. It shows what has to be given up in order to produce a video recorder and a camera in each country. It can be seen that

– the opportunity cost of producing video recorders is lower in Country B than in Country A, and
– the opportunity cost of producing cameras is lower in Country A than in Country B.

This situation is described as follows:
– Country B has a *comparative advantage* in the production of video recorders, and
– Country A has a *comparative advantage* in the production of cameras.

Figure 18.3
Each country has a *comparative* advantage

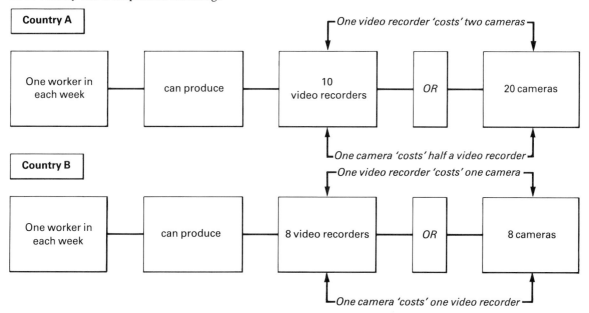

Where the opportunity costs are different in the two countries, specialisation will lead to a greater total output of both goods, and both countries can obtain benefits from trading with one another. Trade, therefore, is beneficial if each country has a *comparative advantage*.

This is illustrated in the following example.

Example	Effect on total weekly output	
	of video recorders	*of cameras*
Country A moves five workers from making videos to making cameras	−50	+100
Country B moves ten workers from making cameras to making videos	+80	−80
Change in total output	+30	+20

These simple examples help us to explain why countries import things they could make for themselves. A country is able to obtain more goods and services by specialising and trading than by trying to produce all the things it is capable of producing.

Some disadvantages of free trade

Although there are clear advantages of free trade between countries, it can cause some problems.

Dangers of over-specialisation

A country may build up a large industry by specialising and developing a large export market. But we live in a world of change, and it might happen that this export market is lost, perhaps for one of the following reasons:

1. Another country may become more efficient in that industry. This happened in the industry making motor cycles: Japan's superiority led to a serious decline in the European motor cycle industry.
2. Technical progress may develop a highly competitive substitute. For example, the introduction of synthetic rubber affected countries which specialised in the production of natural rubber for export.

Immobilities

When a country loses an important export market, it will find itself in difficulties. Factories and machinery which have been specially designed to produce one good cannot be easily transferred to another industry. This also applies to workers who have been trained to work in that industry.

For these and several other reasons, which are explained in Section 18.3, countries do not engage in completely free trade. In the real world, international trade is subject to restrictions.

18.3
Restrictions on trade – protection

Most countries put some restrictions on foreign trade, mainly to protect their own industries.

Methods of restricting imports

1 Tariffs

These are taxes placed on imports. They protect home producers by increasing the prices of foreign goods in the home market. They also raise revenue for the government.

2 Quotas

These are the most serious barriers to trade, because they place an upper limit on the quantity of foreign goods entering a country. For example, a country may limit the imports of foreign cars to 500 000 each year, or the import of footwear to 5 million pairs of shoes each year.

3 Exchange control

Imports can only be purchased with foreign currency. The government can limit imports, therefore, by restricting the amount of foreign currency available to firms wishing to import goods.

4 Subsidies

A tariff raises the price of a foreign good in the home market. By subsidising home producers, a government can reduce the prices of goods made by domestic firms. Subsidies, therefore, help to protect home producers from foreign competition.

Why countries place restrictions on international trade

In addition to the reasons given earlier, there are several other problems which might cause countries to limit imports.

1 Balance of payments problems

If a country is persistently spending more on imports than it is earning from exports, it is getting into debt with the rest of the world. If it finds difficulty in increasing its exports, it may be forced to remedy the situation by placing limits on its imports.

2 To protect an infant industry

A newly-established industry will be operating on a small scale, and its average costs will be relatively high. It will not be able to compete with imports from large-scale foreign producers. To enable such an industry to grow and achieve large-scale production, a government may protect it from foreign competition by restricting imports.

3 'Unfair' competition from low-wage countries

The argument here is that imports from low-wage countries represent unfair competition for home industries which are paying much higher wages than producers in countries where wages are relatively low. If exports from such countries are restricted, however, the effect would be to increase unemployment in those countries and drive wages even lower. (This argument might, in fact, be used against Britain: several countries to which she exports goods have higher wage levels than those paid in Britain.)

Nevertheless, in countries with rising levels of unemployment, governments will be under great pressure to protect jobs by restricting imports.

4 Strategic arguments

Some industries may be regarded as essential to secure a country's survival in time of war. Obvious examples are agriculture, steel, chemicals and several types of engineering. It may be necessary to protect some of these industries by tariffs and quotas to prevent firms in them from being driven out of business by foreign competition.

5 To prevent dumping

A country may restrict its imports when it believes they are being dumped, i.e. sold below cost by a country which is trying to get rid of a surplus. Dumping may also be carried out by a country which is deliberately cutting prices to drive out competitors so that it can establish a monopoly.

Some arguments against protection

1. Tariffs, quotas and exchange controls restrict the supply of goods available to home consumers, and prices will be higher than they would be under free trade.
2. When a country restricts its imports, it is restricting other countries' exports. These countries might well retaliate by restricting their own imports. This would lead to a general lowering of world trade. Countries which decided to restrict their imports would find their own exports being restricted.
3. Protecting a home industry from foreign competition may cause it to become less efficient.

The General Agreement on Tariffs and Trade (GATT)

This organisation was set up in 1948 and now has more than 90 member countries. Its aim is to

Figure 18.4
The growth in world trade, 1960–85

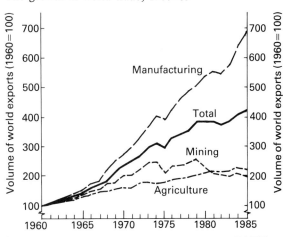

Sources: *The Economist*, 13 September 1986; GATT

encourage the growth of world trade by persuading member countries to remove or reduce the various restrictions on international trade.

Representatives from member countries meet at regular intervals and negotiate agreements for the reduction of tariffs, quotas and other barriers to trade. The great expansion of world trade since the Second World War owes much to the work of GATT.

18.4
Free trade areas and customs unions

In several parts of the world, groups of nations have joined together to form regional trading blocs. The countries in these blocs make agreements to remove restrictions on trade between themselves. In other words, there is free trade between the members of a trading bloc. The great

attraction of forming such a regional organisation is that it gives each member country a much larger 'home' market. It is able to sell its goods in the home markets of the other member countries without facing restrictions such as tariffs and quotas.

These trading groups are of two kinds, free trade areas and customs unions. The main differences between them are illustrated in Figure 18.5.

Free trade areas

The member countries of a free trade area remove all tariffs, quotas and other restrictions on imports from other member countries. As far as trade with the rest of the world is concerned, each country is free to set its own tariffs and other trade barriers. This can be seen in Figure 18.5(a). An example is the European Free Trade Area (EFTA), the members of which are Norway, Sweden, Austria, Iceland, Finland and Switzerland.

Customs unions

The countries which form a customs union also agree to remove the restrictions on trade between themselves but, in addition, they also agree to erect a common external tariff on imports from the rest of the world. This means that goods entering a customs union meet the same tariff barriers whichever country they enter. This arrangement is illustrated in Figure 18.5(b). The European Economic Community (EEC) is an example of a customs union.

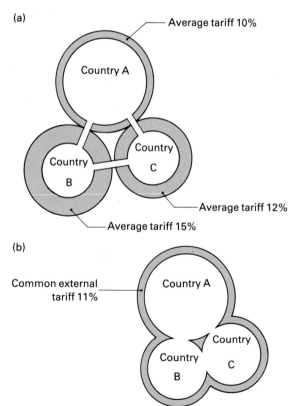

Figure 18.5
(a) A free trade area   (b) A customs union

18.5
The European Economic Community (EEC)

The EEC was established in 1957 when six countries – Belgium, France, Italy, Luxembourg, the Netherlands and West Germany – signed the Treaty of Rome. Denmark, Eire and the United Kingdom joined in 1973, Greece in 1981 and Spain and Portugal in 1986. There are now twelve member countries.

The EEC has a total population of 320 million and is the world's largest exporter and importer. About half of Britain's overseas trade is with the EEC.

Figure 18.6
How the EEC has grown

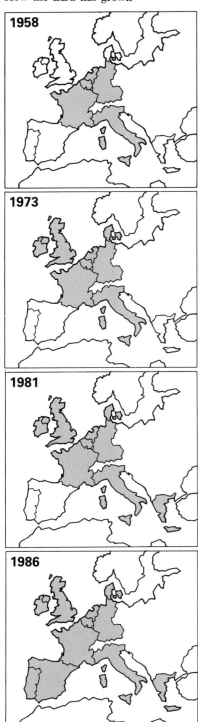

Source: *Finance and Development*, IMF and the World Bank, September 1986

Aims of the EEC

1. Free trade between member countries – tariffs and all other restrictions to be removed.
2. A common external tariff – all members to apply the same tariff on goods entering the EEC.
3. The free movement of labour, services and capital within the EEC. For example, workers in one member country should be free to seek jobs in any other member country.
4. Common policies on agriculture and transport.
5. Freedom to compete – all member countries to be subject to laws forbidding practices which restrict competition in trade between member states.

The EEC has gone a long way towards achieving these aims. Tariffs and quotas have been abolished, a common external tariff has been adopted, there is a common policy on agriculture, and machinery for dealing with restrictions on competition has been established. Much remains to be done, however, before the EEC becomes a true common market with no restrictions on the movement of goods, services, workers and capital.

Financial assistance from the EEC

The EEC has created several institutions to provide financial assistance to member states:

1. *The European Investment Bank* supplies loans to help with the costs of investment projects in member countries. It has made loans which have helped finance the modernisation of railways, the construction of hydroelectric stations and water supplies, and many other projects.
2. *The European Social Fund* makes grants to help create jobs and to cover costs of training and re-training redundant workers and unemployed young people.
3. *The European Regional Development Fund* provides grants to help areas suffering from higher-than-average unemployment. These grants are intended to help finance the construction of such things as roads, and gas, electricity and water supplies, as well as factories.
4. *The European Agricultural Guidance and Guarantee Fund* accounts for most of the expenditure of the EEC. It finances the Common Agricultural Policy of the EEC (see below).

The Common Agricultural Policy (CAP)

A small part of the spending on the CAP takes the form of grants to help EEC farmers cover some of the costs of improving their land, buildings and machinery. But more than 90 per cent of the spending goes on schemes which guarantee that the prices of farm products will be high enough to give farmers a reasonable income. In other words, the farmers are subsidised.

EEC farmers are given this assistance because their costs of production are higher than those of farmers in many other parts of the world. The agricultural producers in Europe would not be able to compete with imports from the rest of the world if there were free markets in farm products.

The main purposes of the CAP are
– to increase the efficiency of farming,
– to stabilise markets in farm products, i.e. to prevent large fluctuations in prices,
– to maintain farmers' incomes at a satisfactory level, which compares favourably with incomes earned in industry, and
– to protect consumers, by making sure that adequate supplies of foodstuffs are always available at reasonable prices.

Guaranteed prices

Under the CAP, prices for the main agricultural products are set annually by the authorities. The CAP supports farm prices within a guaranteed price range. It fixes *a minimum price*, to protect farmers' incomes, and *a maximum price*, to protect consumers' interests. The price is free to fluctuate between these limits. The prices of farm products are held between these limits by various means.

1. If there is a *surplus* of a commodity (which will tend to push the price below the guaranteed price), the authorities can take the following actions:
   – Enter the market as a buyer and purchase the surplus for stockpiling. Increasing the demand in this way will prevent the market price falling below the guaranteed minimum.
   – Reduce supplies of the commodity by increasing the taxes on imports of the commodity.
   – Reduce supplies in the EEC by granting subsidies on exports of the commodity.

2. If there is a *shortage* of a commodity (which will tend to raise its market price above the upper limit), the authorities may take the following actions:
   – Increase supplies in the market by taking goods out of stocks.
   – Increase supplies in the EEC by lowering the taxes on imports of the commodity.

'Food mountains' and 'wine lakes'

The CAP has been severely criticised for creating large stockpiles of foodstuffs and wine which are costly to store and costly to dispose of. Figure 18.7 gives some indication of the problem.

These stocks have arisen because the CAP has set minimum guaranteed prices, which has encouraged farmers to produce more than consumers are prepared to buy at these prices. The authorities have been obliged to buy up the surpluses and store them.

In addition to the high cost of buying these surpluses, the stocks are costly to dispose of. World prices are lower than EEC prices for most of the products in store, so these stocks can only

Figure 18.7
Mountainous Europe: EEC farm surpluses as at 1 April each year

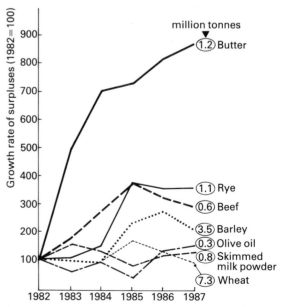

Sources: *The Economist*, 11 July 1987; EEC Commission

be sold on world markets at prices well below those at which they were bought.

To try and reduce the surpluses of farm products, the EEC has started to introduce a system of quotas, whereby farmers will only be able to obtain guaranteed prices for some fixed amount of output.

The CAP has succeeded in increasing the outputs of agricultural products – the EEC is now self-sufficient in all the farm products it can grow itself. It has also held up farmers' incomes and prevented large swings in the prices of food. The prices of many foodstuffs in the EEC, however, are substantially higher than world prices and the cost, to consumers and taxpayers, of supporting the CAP has been high.

Financing the EEC

The expenditure of the EEC – most of which goes on the CAP – is financed by contributions from member governments. Each member country pays to the EEC

- the income it receives from taxes levied on food imports from countries outside the EEC,
- the revenue it obtains from customs duties on goods imported from outside the EEC, and
- a contribution equal in value to the maximum revenue from a VAT rate of $1\frac{1}{4}$ per cent (*not* $1\frac{1}{4}$ per cent of the country's VAT revenue).

Membership of the EEC – some arguments for and against

1 Greater specialisation and economies of scale

The EEC offers the firms and industries in each member country a 'home' market containing more than 300 million people. This should enable the more efficient firms to expand, produce on a larger scale and achieve lower average costs.

2 More competition

The removal of trade barriers greatly increases competition in a member country's home market. Home producers are no longer protected by tariffs and quotas. This increased competition should cause firms to produce more efficiently. Weaker firms, however, may be driven out of business.

3 Helping poorer regions

An organisation such as the EEC can operate schemes which transfer financial assistance from the wealthier regions of the community to the poorer regions. This is done through the various funds mentioned earlier.

4 Cooperation

The EEC encourages cooperation between European countries, and this has made it very unlikely that there will be any repetition of the wars which ravaged Europe for centuries.

5 More expensive food

EEC citizens pay relatively high prices for the food produced within the EEC. The UK, for example, could obtain its food much more cheaply by buying it in world markets. It must be pointed out, however, that before the UK entered the EEC it spent very large sums of public money on subsidies to its farmers.

6 Loss of sovereignty

Many of the laws which affect the daily lives of people in the member countries are now made in the headquarters of the EEC rather than in the individual capital cities. The UK, for example, can no longer fix its own tariffs on imports. Many people regard this loss of sovereignty as a disadvantage of membership of the EEC.

The Main Points

- Like people, different countries have different abilities to produce. International trade enables countries to specialise in the things they do best.

- If a country can produce a commodity at a lower cost than another country, it is said to have an *absolute advantage* over that country.

- If a country can produce a commodity at a lower *opportunity cost* than another country, it is said to have a *comparative advantage* over that country.

- If each of two countries has a comparative advantage over the other, specialisation can increase total output, and both countries can benefit from trading with one another.

- In the real world, international trade is restricted by tariffs, quotas, exchange control and subsidies.

- These restrictions are imposed when a country
  - has a serious balance of payments problem,
  - wishes to protect an infant industry,
  - regards imports from low-wage countries as unfair competition,
  - wishes to protect strategic industries, or
  - believes that other countries are guilty of dumping.

- Barriers to trade
  - produce higher prices for consumers,
  - cause other countries to retaliate,
  - reduce the volume of world trade, and
  - might cause protected industries to become less efficient.

- The General Agreement on Tariffs and Trade (GATT) is an international organisation which tries to reduce the restrictions on international trade.

- The EEC is a customs union. Its aim is to create a true common market where there are no obstacles to the movement of goods, services, labour and capital between member countries.

- Most of the spending of the EEC is devoted to the Common Agricultural Policy (CAP). Offering guaranteed minimum prices to farmers has led to large stockpiles of farm products. About half of the UK's overseas trade is with the EEC countries (see Figure 19.7 on page 200).

Test Your Understanding

1. Use the following words to complete the passage below:

   quotas   subsidies   tariffs

   Home producers may be protected from foreign competition by
   - ...., which are taxes on imports,
   - ...., which place an upper limit on the quantities of foreign goods allowed into the country,
   - ...., which lower the costs of home producers.

2. Which of the following organisations is (a) a free trade area, (b) a customs union, (c) an organisation working for a reduction in the restrictions on world trade?

   A GATT
   B EFTA
   C EEC

3. What is the main cause of the food surpluses in the European Economic Community?

4. Why do people in the richer countries often describe imports from poorer countries as unfair competition?

Questions 5 to 8 are based on the table below, which shows the costs of producing two different goods in two different countries.

	Cost of producing	
	one pair of ladies' fashion shoes	*one pocket calculator*
Country A	$20	$5
Country B	$16	$8

5. Which country is the more efficient at producing (a) ladies' footwear, and (b) pocket calculators?

6. How many pocket calculators have to be given up to produce one pair of ladies' shoes (a) in Country A, and (b) in Country B?

7. Which country has the lower opportunity cost in the production of pocket calculators?

8. If these two countries decide to specialise and trade with one another, in which good should (a) Country A specialise, and (b) Country B specialise?

BOX 18
The EEC's dairy surplus – too much of a good thing?

The visionaries who saw the EEC as a way to a Europe of milk and honey were right – at least as far as the milk is concerned. The Community has been producing so much of the stuff that, unless something is done soon, the cost of supporting surplus output could bust the budget.

Surplus butter is being crammed into cold stores at the rate of 100 000 tonnes a month.

The biggest mistake was that when the Community introduced quotas two years ago in an attempt to limit production, they were set too high. The EEC's cows still produce about 8 million tonnes of milk more than its citizens can swallow in any form, be it as liquid or as butter, cheese or milk powder.

Ideas for knocking a bit off the butter mountain include simply destroying the oldest stocks – now more than five years old – at a cost of $3000 per tonne, or using it as cattle feed. A first lot of several-years-old butter was offered for sale on 21 August at a derisory price of $90 a tonne – 3 per cent of what it cost the EEC budget to buy in the first place.

Source: Adapted from an article in *The Economist*, 30 August 1986

Questions
1. If large quantities of dairy produce had not been purchased for stockpiling,
    (a) what would have happened to the market price?
    (b) would there have been a surplus? Explain your answers.
2. Apart from the difference between the buying and selling prices, what other costs are incurred in stockpiling dairy products?
3. (a) What is a quota?
    (b) What is meant by the statement that 'the quotas were set too high'?
4. What would be the likely effects on EEC dairy farming of
    (a) a substantial reduction in the quotas?
    (b) a substantial reduction in the guaranteed minimum price?

CHAPTER 19

The balance of payments and the rate of exchange

19.1 The balance of payments
19.2 The rate of exchange
19.3 The International Monetary Fund (IMF)
19.4 Britain's overseas trade

The balance of payments

The flows of money payments between countries

The payments for goods and services which cross international boundaries are quite different from payments made within a country. This is because every country has its own currency which circulates quite freely within that country, but which cannot be used to buy goods and services in other countries. For example, if a British firm wishes to buy goods from the USA, it must first obtain dollars; if it wishes to buy Italian goods and services, it will have to acquire lire. In other words, our imports cause us to *spend foreign currency*.

On the other hand, residents in other countries who wish to buy British goods and services will have to exchange their own currencies for sterling. British exports, therefore, bring foreign currency into Britain; they cause an *inflow of foreign currency*.

The balance of payments is an account of a country's payments to and receipts from the rest of the world. Although it shows the values of the transactions in that country's own currency, it must be remembered that the transactions which actually took place were foreign currency transactions.

Why payments flow from country to country

There are many different types of transaction which cause the residents of one country to make payments to residents of another country. (The word 'residents' includes households, firms and government.)

Visible trade

This refers to the trade in physical goods – those things which we can see being loaded and unloaded at docks and airports. Foodstuffs, machinery, motor cars, oil and raw materials are important items in the UK's visible trade.

The difference between the values of exports and imports of physical goods is known as the *balance of trade*, or the *visible balance*.

Invisible trade

Invisible trade consists of three main types of transaction:

1 Services

The buying and selling of services accounts for a large part of the UK's trade with other countries. It includes the income earned by UK firms from selling transport, insurance, banking, hotel, catering and other services to residents of other countries; these items are *invisible exports*. It also includes the payments made by UK residents for similar services provided by foreign firms; these items are *invisible imports*.

Figure 19.1

Visible trade

Invisible trade (tourism)

2 Interest, profits and dividends

UK firms own land, mines, factories, offices and shops in many overseas countries. Profits earned on these investments bring foreign currency into the UK. Similarly, interest payments on loans made to overseas borrowers will also earn foreign currency for UK residents. There is, of course, an outflow of foreign currency when profits earned by foreign-owned firms are taken out of the UK, and when UK residents pay interest on loans from overseas.

3 Transfer payments

These are not payments for goods and services – they are gifts or grants. They consist of such

payments and receipts as
- the UK's payments to the EEC budget, and any grants received from the EEC,
- gifts of money sent back to their home countries by immigrants to the UK, and by emigrants from the UK, and
- grants to developing countries and international organisations.

Invisible 'exports' and 'imports'

While it is easy to see the difference between visible exports and imports, it is not so easy to identify invisible exports and imports. The way to do this is to ask yourself, 'Does the transaction cause UK residents to receive foreign currency or to spend it?'

If the transaction leads to UK residents receiving foreign currency, it is a *credit item* or export, and is entered in the balance of payments with a *plus* sign. If the transaction causes UK residents to make payments in a foreign currency, it is a *debit item* or import, and is entered in the balance of payments with a *minus* sign.

Figure 19.2 gives a number of examples which should help to make the distinction between invisible exports and imports quite clear.

The current account

When the balance of visible trade is added to the balance of invisible trade, the result is known as the balance of payments on current account. Table 19.1 shows how the balance on current account is calculated (the figures do not apply to any particular country).

Table 19.1

The current account (£ million)

Visible trade			
Exports	+70 000		
Imports	−80 000	Visible balance	−10 000
Invisible trade			
Exports	+50 000		
Imports	−35 000	Invisibles balance	+15 000
		Current balance	+5 000

'EXPORTS' Britain *earns* foreign currency when	'IMPORTS' Britain *spends* foreign currency when
British airlines and British ships carry foreign passengers, or carry cargo for foreign firms	British firms and British citizens make use of foreign-owned airlines and ships
People from other countries come to Britain as tourists	British citizens take holidays abroad
British entertainers (e.g. pop groups) make overseas tours	Foreign entertainers perform in Britain
British-owned companies located abroad bring profits back to Britain	Foreign-owned companies located in Britain take profits back to their home countries
Overseas residents pay interest on loans made to them by British banks	British citizens pay interest on loans made to them by foreign banks
British insurance companies insure people and property in foreign countries	British citizens and British firms buy insurance from foreign-owned companies
Foreign governments buy services in Britain to maintain their London embassies and to meet the needs of their armed forces stationed in Britain	The British government makes payments abroad for the upkeep of its embassies in foreign countries and to meet the local costs of British troops stationed overseas

Figure 19.2
Some examples of invisible trade

The balance on current account is very important, because it tells us whether a country is paying its way in the world as a trading nation. When the value of exports is greater than the value of imports, the account is said to be *in surplus*. When the value of imports is greater than the value of exports, the account is said to be *in deficit*.

A deficit on visible trade may not be a problem if it is offset by a surplus on invisible trade. This has very often been the case with the UK's balance of payments, but in 1986 there was a substantial deficit on current account (see Table 19.2 on page 195).

Figure 19.3 (over the page) shows recent trends in the UK's visible and invisible trade, and the way in which these trends have affected the balance of payments on current account.

Surpluses and deficits

If a country has a persistent deficit on its balance of payments, it will be getting into debt with the rest of the world. When a family's expenditure is greater than its income, it will have to borrow money or reduce its savings, and a country is in very much the same situation.

A *deficit* must be covered by either
− borrowing from overseas central banks or from organisations such as the International Monetary Fund (see page 199), or
− taking money from the official reserves of foreign currency.

There are, however, limits to how much a country can borrow and to the amount of foreign currency reserves it holds. If the deficit persists, therefore, it must take steps to correct the situation.

A *surplus* may be used to
− increase the nation's foreign currency reserves,
− make loans to residents of other countries or to repay loans which have been obtained from overseas, or
− make investments overseas, e.g. buying land and property in other countries and buying shares in foreign companies.

Question
What steps might a country take in order to cure a persistent deficit on its balance of payments?

Figure 19.3
UK external trade, 1980–87

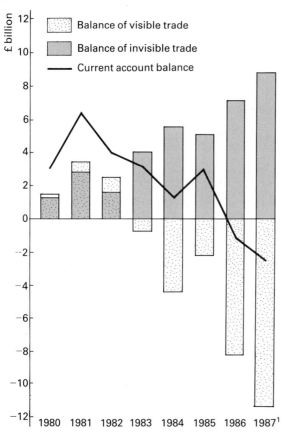

¹ Forecast
Sources: *Economic Trends*, HMSO, March 1987;
Barclays Review, May 1987

Question on Figure 19.3
How would you explain the fact that, during the years 1983 to 1985, the visible trade was in deficit but the current account was in surplus?

Capital transactions

The trade in goods and services is not the only reason why money flows from one country to another. Payments between countries also take place because residents in one country might wish to lend to or borrow from people in other countries, and to purchase assets from or sell assets to residents in other countries. These are described as capital transactions, or investment transactions.

Examples
1. A British citizen buys shares in a German company.
2. A Japanese company builds a factory in Britain.
3. The British government makes a loan to India.
4. An American company deposits money in a London bank.

In examples 1 and 3, foreign currency will flow out of the UK. In examples 2 and 4, foreign currency will flow into the UK.

Capital transactions bring about changes in a country's *external assets and liabilities*. Borrowing from overseas increases our stock of foreign currency, but increases our external liabilities. Buying property overseas increases our external assets but reduces our stock of foreign currency.

Examples
1. *Marks and Spencer buys a department store in Paris:*

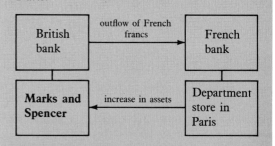

2. *British Petroleum borrows money from a New York bank:*

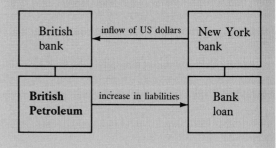

In the British balance of payments account, capital transactions are recorded under the heading 'transactions in external assets and liabilities'.

The balance of payments always balances

The balance of payments account is a balance sheet and, like all balance sheets, it must balance. The total of the credit items (those with a *plus* sign) must be equal to the total of the debit items (those with a *minus* sign). This does not mean that there can be no surpluses or deficits. It simply means that the account contains items which show how the money to pay for a deficit has been obtained, or how any surplus has been distributed.

The idea of a balanced account can be illustrated by using two simple balance sheets showing a family's weekly income and expenditure:

1. *The family has a deficit.*

Income received		Disposal of income	
Wages	£160	Household expenses	£180
Withdrawals from savings (or borrowing)	£20		
	£180		£180

2. *The family has a surplus.*

Income received		Disposal of income	
Wages	£200	Household expenses	£170
		Additions to savings (or lending)	£30
	£200		£200

It can be seen that although the family has a deficit in example 1 and a surplus in example 2, both accounts are balanced. This is because the accounts show how the deficit was financed and how the surplus was disposed of.

The same kinds of procedures are followed in the balance of payments account. Deficits are balanced by entries which show withdrawals from the foreign currency reserves or borrowing overseas. Surpluses are balanced by entries which show additions to the foreign currency reserves or the purchase of overseas assets.

In the balance of payments account, receipts and expenditures are not shown in two separate columns as in the balance sheets above. They are arranged in one vertical column. Receipts of foreign currency are given plus signs, and outflows are given minus signs. Since the account balances, the total of the various transactions must be equal to zero. The transactions which bring about the balance in the account are entered under the heading 'transactions in external assets and liabilities'.

The UK balance of payments

In 1986, changes were made in the way in which the balance of payments account is presented. Table 19.2 is a summary of the new form of presentation.

Table 19.2
The UK balance of payments, 1986 (£ million)

Current account			
Visible trade			
Exports	+72 843		
Imports	−81 306	Visible balance	−8 463
Invisible trade			
Exports	+76 202		
Imports	−68 719	Invisibles balance	+7 483
		Current balance	−980
Transactions in external assets and liabilities			
Private investment	−20 634		
Transactions by UK banks	+10 494		
Changes in foreign currency reserves	−2 891	Net transactions in external assets and liabilities	−10 747
Other capital transactions	+2 284		
Balancing item			+11 727

Source: *UK Balance of Payments 1987*, CSO, HMSO

Notes on Table 19.2

The current account

In 1986, the UK had a large deficit on visible trade. An important reason for this deficit was the fact that a fall in the world price of oil had drastically reduced export earnings. There was also an increased deficit on the trade in manufactured goods.

Invisible trade yielded a large surplus. Much of this was accounted for by the foreign currency earnings of British banks and insurance companies and by the substantial income (in the form of interest and profits) on British investments overseas.

The surplus on invisibles, however, was not sufficient to offset the deficit on visible trade.

External assets and liabilities

The figures under this heading are *net* figures. They represent the difference between the total inflow of foreign currency and the total outflow for each type of transaction.

For example, it is clear that, in 1986, UK residents invested far more in other countries than overseas residents invested in Britain. It can also be seen that UK banks borrowed far more from other countries than overseas residents borrowed from UK banks.

The balancing item

In any one year, there are millions of transactions between the residents of the UK and the residents of other countries. It is impossible to get a complete and accurate record of all these transactions – there are bound to be errors and omissions. Part of the problem arises from the fact that the payments for exports and imports often take place some considerable time after the goods have been delivered or the services have been rendered. The balancing item is the sum of all these errors and omissions.

19.2
The rate of exchange

The foreign currency market

The fact that different countries have different currencies means that people and firms who trade with other countries must have some means of changing one currency into another. British firms wishing to buy goods from Switzerland will have to change pounds into Swiss francs. British firms selling goods to Switzerland may wish to change the Swiss francs they have earned into American dollars.

The foreign exchange market exists so that these kinds of exchange can take place. It consists of dealing rooms in banks and other financial institutions located in the world's major banking centres, such as New York, London, Frankfurt, Zurich and Tokyo. The dealers in these different cities use systems of telecommunications which enable them to do business with one another just as effectively as if they were in the same room. These dealers buy and sell billions of pounds worth of foreign currency every day.

The rate of exchange is a price

The rate of exchange is the price of one currency in terms of another. For example, if the rate of exchange were £1 = $2.0, then the price of a pound would be $2.0 and the price of a dollar would be 50p.

Like other prices, the rate of exchange is determined by demand and supply. The rate at which the pound exchanges for other currencies depends upon the demand for and the supply of pounds in the foreign exchange market.

The demand for pounds in the foreign exchange market

Pounds will be demanded by households and firms in other countries when
– they want to buy British goods and services, or
– they wish to invest in Britain; that is, they wish to buy property in the UK, buy shares in British companies, or make loans to British residents.

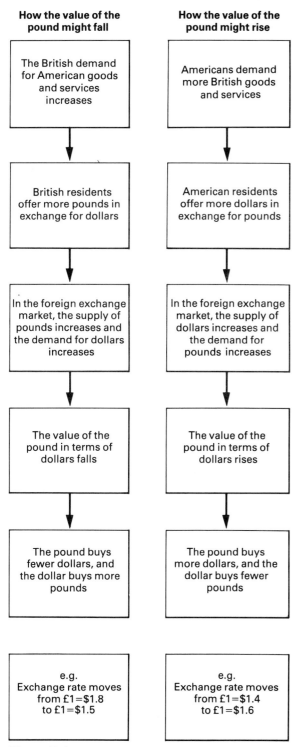

How the value of the pound might fall

The British demand for American goods and services increases

↓

British residents offer more pounds in exchange for dollars

↓

In the foreign exchange market, the supply of pounds increases and the demand for dollars increases

↓

The value of the pound in terms of dollars falls

↓

The pound buys fewer dollars, and the dollar buys more pounds

↓

e.g.
Exchange rate moves from £1=$1.8 to £1=$1.5

How the value of the pound might rise

Americans demand more British goods and services

↓

American residents offer more dollars in exchange for pounds

↓

In the foreign exchange market, the supply of dollars increases and the demand for pounds increases

↓

The value of the pound in terms of dollars rises

↓

The pound buys more dollars, and the dollar buys fewer pounds

↓

e.g.
Exchange rate moves from £1=$1.4 to £1=$1.6

Figure 19.4
Some examples of causes of changes in the exchange rate

For these purposes, overseas residents will need pounds, and they will demand these pounds by offering their own currencies in exchange for them.

The supply of pounds in the foreign exchange market

Pounds will be supplied by British residents when they wish
- to buy goods and services supplied by overseas firms, or
- to make investments overseas.

For these purposes, UK residents will need foreign currencies, which they will demand by offering pounds in exchange for them.

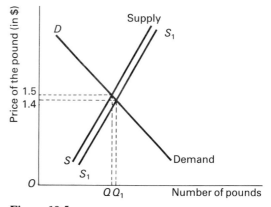

Figure 19.5
An increased demand for imports increases the supply of pounds in the foreign exchange market, and the external value of the pound falls

Figure 19.5 shows how the rate of exchange is determined and how it might be affected by an increased demand for imports. Initially, the exchange value of the pound is $1.5 – this is the price at which the demand for pounds equals the supply of pounds. An increased demand for imports increases the supply of pounds. The supply curve moves to S_1S_1, causing the value of the pound to fall to £1 = $1.4.

Question on Figure 19.5
How might Figure 19.5 be used to show the effect of a large increase in the number of American tourists visiting Britain?

THE INDEPENDENT

▓ TOURIST RATES ▓
£1 buys

Australian dollars	2.445
Austrian schillings	21.70
Belgian francs	65.10
Canadian dollars	2.265
Cyprus pounds	0.82
Danish kroner	11.96
Dutch guilders	3.47
Finnish marka	7.44
French francs	10.52
German marks	3.09
Greek drachmas	244.00
Hong Kong dollars	14.30
Irish punts	1.164
Italian lire	2300.00
Japanese yen	233.00
Maltese pounds	0.58
New Zealand dollars	2.76
Norwegian kroner	11.45
Portuguese escudos	249.00
Spanish pesetas	203.00
Swedish kronor	10.90
Swiss francs	2.555
Turkish lire	2185.00
US dollars	1.86
Yugoslav dinars	2650.00

Figure 19.6
Tables like this, showing the different exchange values
of the pound, are published in the newspapers

There are many rates of exchange for the pound

Although we have been discussing *the* rate of
exchange, there is no single exchange rate for the
pound or for any other currency. The rate of
exchange for the pound may be expressed in terms
of dollars, marks, francs, lire, yen and many other
currencies (see Figure 19.6). It is usually
expressed in dollars, because the US dollar is by
far the most important currency internationally.

Speculation

The foreign exchange market is a free market
where the rates of exchange are always changing.
For this reason it tends to attract speculators.
These are people who hope to make a profit by
correctly guessing which way a particular rate of
exchange will move in the immediate future.

Example
Suppose that when the rate of exchange was
£1 = $1.4, a speculator thought that the value
of the pound would fall in the near future. He
exchanged £10 000 for $14 000.

It turned out that he had guessed correctly:
the value of the pound fell to £1 = $1.25. He
then changed his $14 000 back into pounds
and received £11 200. He had made a profit of
£1200.

If his expectations had proved wrong and the
value of the pound had increased, he would
have made a loss when changing his dollars
back into pounds.

The rate of exchange and the prices of exports and imports

When the exchange value of a currency falls, it is
said to *depreciate*. When the exchange value of a
currency rises, it is said to *appreciate*. Thus, a fall
in the value of the pound from £1 = $1.8 to
£1 = $1.6 would be described as a *depreciation* of
the pound. An increase in its value would be
described as an *appreciation*.

Changes such as these are very important
because they affect a country's exports and
imports. When the currency of a country depre-
ciates, the overseas prices of its exports fall and
the home prices of its imports increase. When the
currency of a country appreciates, the overseas
prices of its exports rise and the home prices of
its imports fall.

Worked example
Suppose that
– the UK exports motor cars priced at £20 000
  to the USA, and
– the USA exports machines priced at $36 000
  to the UK.

1. *When the rate of exchange is £1 = $2.0:*
   The price of the British
   motor car in the USA   = $40 000
   The price of the American
   machine in the UK   = £18 000
   (continued)

2. *If the rate of exchange changes to £1 = $1.8:*
    The price of the British
    motor car in the USA   = $36 000
    The price of the American
    machine in the UK   = £20 000

British exports have become cheaper in overseas markets, and imports have become dearer in the home market.

Question
Calculate the effects on the prices of these particular exports and imports of a rise in the value of the pound from £1 = $2.0 to £1 = $2.25.

19.3

The International Monetary Fund (IMF)

This important organisation was set up during the Second World War with the aim of encouraging economic cooperation between the nations of the world once the war had ended. There are now more than 140 member countries.

It is described as a 'fund' because it holds a stock of national currencies. Each member country is obliged to contribute a certain amount – a quota – of its own currency to the fund. Rich countries contribute more than poor countries. Member countries may borrow foreign currencies from this fund.

Among the more important aims of the IMF are the following.

1 Helping countries with balance of payments problems

A country with a serious balance of payments deficit may be forced to restrict its imports. However, this could lead to retaliation by other countries. The result would be a fall in world trade. To prevent this happening, the IMF can provide the country with short-term loans of foreign currency, but the country would be expected to take some action to deal with the cause of its deficit.

2 Encouraging countries to make their currencies convertible

The idea here is that anyone holding a particular currency should be able to change it into any other currency, that is, to convert it. If this cannot be done, international trade would be restricted. For example, a firm selling goods to the USA earns dollars. Suppose that it does not want to spend these dollars in the USA. In this case, it will only be interested in selling to the USA if it can change the dollars it earns there into some other currency.

3 Encouraging countries to keep their exchange rates stable

We have seen that changes in the exchange rate cause changes in the prices of exports and imports. Frequent changes in the exchange rates, therefore, would add a great deal of uncertainty to trading with other countries. Exporters would be uncertain about the prices they were likely to get and importers would be uncertain about the prices they were likely to pay. The IMF believes that stable exchange rates will encourage a faster growth in world trade.

19.4

Britain's overseas trade

Britain's major trading partners

Over the past 30 years there has been a great change in the geographical pattern of Britain's overseas trade. In 1955, a large proportion of Britain's trade was with the countries of the Commonwealth and with developing countries.

This pattern of trade has changed, and about 80 per cent of Britain's trade is now with developed industrialised countries. About 60 per cent of the overseas trade is with Western Europe, most of it with the other members of the EEC. There has also been a significant increase in the importance of Japan as a source of imports.

Not only has UK trade shifted towards Western Europe, it has also become increasingly concentrated in fewer markets. The top ten export markets now account for 60 per cent of total exports. These markets include West Germany, the USA, the Netherlands, France, Switzerland, Eire and Belgium.

Figure 19.7
UK visible trade by area, 1986 (percentages of totals)

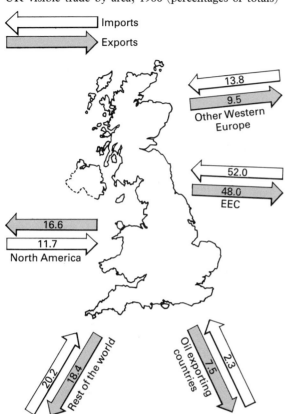

Source: *Monthly Digest of Statistics*, HMSO, May 1987

Figure 19.8
UK visible trade by commodity, 1986 (percentages of totals)

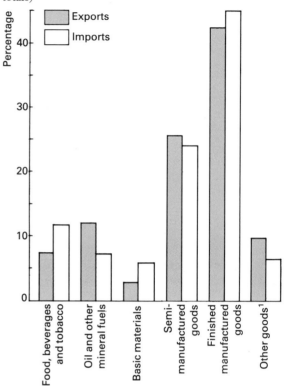

[1] Includes ships, aircraft and precious stones
Source: *Monthly Digest of Statistics*, HMSO, May 1987

Commodity trade

The older pattern of UK trade was one in which exports of manufactured goods were exchanged for foodstuffs and raw materials. This pattern too has changed. The overseas trade of the UK is increasingly dominated by an exchange of manufactured goods with other industrialised countries. The countries mentioned in the previous section, together with Japan, are also major suppliers of imports. Figure 19.8 shows that the UK is now a net importer of manufactured goods.

The development of North Sea oil has had an important effect on the commodity trade of the UK. Oil is now a major item in Britain's total exports. Oil is still imported because industry requires several different grades of oil, some of which are not found in the North Sea.

The Main Points

- The UK balance of payments shows
  - the receipts of foreign currency from selling goods and services to overseas residents, and from foreign loans to and investments in the UK, and
  - the outflow of foreign currency caused by spending on foreign goods and services, and by lending and investing overseas.

- Exports, or credit items, are those items which increase the amounts of foreign currency held by UK residents. Imports, or debit items, are those items which reduce the amounts of foreign currency held by UK residents.

- The balance on current account is equal to (visible + invisible exports) *minus* (visible + invisible imports).

- A nation is in deficit when, as a result of all the current and capital transactions, the outflow of foreign currency is greater than the inflow. A surplus means that there has been a net inflow of foreign currency.

- A deficit may be covered by drawing on the official foreign currency reserves or by borrowing abroad. These, however, can only be temporary measures.

- A surplus may be added to the foreign currency reserves or used to acquire investments overseas, or to repay previous overseas borrowings.

- The rate of exchange is the price of one currency in terms of another. It is determined by the supply of and demand for the currency in the foreign exchange market.

- In the foreign exchange market, an increase in exports will increase the demand for that country's currency. An increase in imports will increase the supply of the currency.

- Changes in the rate of exchange will bring about changes in
  - the foreign prices of a country's exports, and
  - the home prices of its imports.

- The IMF is an international organisation which aims to promote the growth of world trade by
  - helping countries with balance of payment problems, and
  - encouraging member countries to maintain stable exchange rates and convertible currencies.

- Britain's major trading links are with Western Europe, especially the EEC countries. The major items in both imports and exports are manufactured goods. The development of the North Sea oilfields has made Britain a major exporter of oil.

Test Your Understanding

1. In which sections of the balance of payments would the following items appear?
   (a) A British firm buys a factory in West Germany.
   (b) A British citizen buys an Italian car.
   (c) A French orchestra carries out a tour of the UK.
   (d) The British government employs local residents to work in its Paris embassy.

2. The following items are taken from a country's balance of payments account:

	$ million
Balance on visible trade	−500
....	....
Balance on current account	+200

   What is the missing item, and what is its money value?

3. British companies supply engineers and technical experts to help with the construction of a dam in a country in the Middle East. The foreign currency earned from this employment will be recorded as an .... export. What is the missing word?

4. If the surplus on invisible items does *not* cover the deficit on visible items, the country is said to have ONE of the following. Which is the correct answer?

   A a surplus on current account
   B a deficit on capital account
   C a deficit on the balance of payments
   D a deficit on current account

5. The following details are taken from a country's balance of payments:

	$ million
Balance on current account	−2000
Balance on capital transactions	+1500
Borrowing from the IMF and other sources	+1000

   Which ONE of the following statements is correct? During this particular year, the country's foreign currency reserves

   A fell by $500 million
   B increased by $500 million
   C increased by $1000 million
   D remained unchanged

6. This question is based on the following information.

   In January, the pound had the following exchange values:
   £1 = 200 Spanish pesetas
   £1 = 10 French francs
   In the summer of the same year, the rates of exchange were
   £1 = 180 Spanish pesetas
   £1 = 12 French francs

   Choose words from the following list to complete the passage below:

   more   less   pesetas   francs   loss   profit

   After the change in the exchange rates, British citizens would find that
   – the pound would buy more .... but fewer ....,
   – a holiday in France had become .... expensive,
   – a holiday in Spain had become .... expensive, and
   – if they had bought francs in January and sold them in the summer, they would have made a ....

BOX 19

Britain experiences a large trade gap

Britain's trade remained firmly in deficit last month (September), pushing the cumulative gap so far this year to more than £6 billion.

In September, invisible transactions such as tourism and insurance are estimated to have yielded a £600 million surplus, leaving a shortfall of £277 million on the current account.

News of the trade deficit, which was higher than most City expectations, unsettled sterling, which lost ground against a generally stronger dollar.

Mr Nigel Lawson, Chancellor of the Exchequer, has indicated that he believes the sharp depreciation of sterling this year will lead to a recovery in non-oil exports.

Source: Adapted from an article in *The Financial Times*, 24 October 1986

Questions

1. What was the extent of Britain's deficit on foreign trade for the period January to September 1986?
2. What was the visible trade deficit for the month of September?
3. What is meant by the statement that 'sterling lost ground against a generally stronger dollar'?
4. What is the 'City' referred to in the quotation?
5. Why should a depreciation of sterling be expected to lead to a recovery in exports?

CHAPTER 20

The government and the national economy

20.1 The national output – some important terms
20.2 Measuring the national income
20.3 The circular flow of income
20.4 Economic policy

Like most other governments, the UK government has the job of managing the economy. The people hold the government responsible for the way the economy is working. Whether they think it is working well or not depends upon such things as the level of unemployment, the rate at which prices are rising, the rate at which real wages are increasing and so on.

In order to manage the economy, the government requires a great deal of information about the present state of the economy and the ways in which it has been changing. For example, it needs to have facts and figures on such matters as

- the way in which the total output of goods and services has been changing,
- recent changes in the numbers of people employed and unemployed,
- the extent to which the prices of goods and services have been increasing,
- whether exports have been increasing more slowly or more quickly than imports,
- recent changes in money incomes and real incomes,
- which industries have been expanding and which have been declining, and
- the rate at which firms have been investing in new capital goods.

Each year, the government publishes a book entitled *National Income and Expenditure*, which is generally known as the Blue Book. It contains a great deal of information on all the topics outlined above and on many other features of the economy.

20.1
The national output – some important terms

It is necessary to know what is happening to the total output of goods and services because it has an important influence on the standard of living and on the numbers of people employed. There are three different measures of the UK's annual output of goods and services.

1 Gross Domestic Product (GDP)

This term describes the total output produced by the factors of production located in the UK. Some of these factors (e.g. capital) will be owned by foreign firms.

2 Gross National Product (GNP)

This is the total output produced by British-owned factors of production wherever they happen to be located, whether at home or abroad.

Some part of the value of what is produced in the UK will be taken out of the country in the form of profits by foreign-owned firms which have businesses in this country. On the other hand, British-owned firms located abroad will bring profits back to the UK. The national accounts show the difference between these two flows as follows:

Property income *earned* abroad
    – Property income *paid* abroad
    = Net property income from abroad

Therefore,

Gross National Product
   = Gross Domestic Product
      + Net property income from abroad

3 Net National Product (the national income)

During the course of a year, the nation's stock of capital will depreciate. Some of the buildings and machines will become worn out or out of date. Each year, therefore, some part of the GNP is required to replace this worn-out and obsolete capital. The value of the goods required to make good the depreciation of capital is deducted from the GNP in order to obtain the Net National Product, which is usually referred to as the national income:

Gross National Product − Depreciation
                           = National income

The national income, therefore, tells us how much of the annual output is available for consumption and for adding to the national stock of assets.

Measuring the national income

In measuring the national income, we are *not* measuring a *stock* of goods. Goods and services are being produced and used up continuously. The national income is a measure of the total *flow* of goods and services over a period of one year. There are three methods of measuring the national income.

1 The output method

This method attempts to measure the value of the outputs of all the different industries. This is not so straightforward as it seems. One serious problem is that of *double counting*. For example, if the value of the total output of the steel industry is added to the value of the total output of the car industry, the value of the steel in the motor cars will be counted twice.

This problem is overcome by counting only the *value added* by each firm. For example, suppose a firm buys materials for £20 000 and uses them to make goods which it sells for £30 000. It has actually produced £10 000 worth of output, not

£30 000 worth. The value of its output is measured by the value it has added to the materials it purchased.

The subject of value added was discussed on page 148.

2 The income method

The money value of the goods and services produced will be equal to their costs of production plus profits. But all these costs of production represent incomes to the owners of the factors of production. They are payments for the services of labour, capital and land, and take the form of wages, interest and rent. Profits too are income payments to entrepreneurs and shareholders.

The value of what is produced, therefore, must be equal to the payments made to the factors of production which have produced the goods and services. It is possible, therefore, to measure the value of the national output by adding up all the *factor incomes* (including profits) which have been paid out during the course of production.

Note that only the incomes *earned* in producing goods and services are counted in the national income. Transfer payments such as pensions and social security benefits do not represent payments for factor services, and are not included in the national income.

3 The expenditure method

Whatever is produced must be either sold or added to stocks. When a firm adds some of its output to stocks, it has already paid out the costs of producing those goods. In effect, therefore, it has 'bought' the goods it puts into stock. If we count the additions to stocks as part of total expenditure on the national output, we can say that national expenditure equals national output.

Only that spending which creates income in the UK can be counted in the national income. Spending on imports must be excluded because it creates income overseas, and not in the UK. However, expenditure on exports must be included, because these payments create income in the UK.

Another problem is that the market prices of many goods and services include taxes such as VAT, and some of them include subsidies. Taxes on goods and services must be deducted from total spending if we are to get a figure which represents the costs of production plus profits. Subsidies should be added on to market prices in order to obtain the costs of production including profits.

All three methods are measuring the same thing: the value of the national income. They should, therefore, all yield the same total:

$$\underset{\text{total output}}{\text{Value of}} = \underset{\substack{\text{of production}}}{\underset{\substack{\text{the factors}}}{\underset{\substack{\text{received by}}}{\underset{\substack{\text{incomes}}}{\text{Sum of the}}}}} = \underset{\substack{\text{stocks}}}{\underset{\substack{\text{plus additions to}}}{\underset{\substack{\text{national outputs}}}{\text{Spending on the}}}}$$

OUTPUT = INCOME = EXPENDITURE

Figure 20.1 gives some details of the shares of total spending and of total factor incomes in the UK national income.

> **Question on Figure 20.1**
> Which of the factors of production received the largest share of the national income?

Money national income and real national income

National income is measured using the prices of the goods and services in the year in which they were produced. In other words, the national income records the *money values* of total output, total factor incomes and total expenditure.

Real national income refers to the actual quantities of goods and services produced. It is important to know what is happening to real national income because the standard of living depends very much on the *quantities* of goods and services produced.

Changes in money national income, therefore, can be very misleading: they can be due to changes in prices, rather than changes in the amounts produced. If money national income increases by 10 per cent in a year when prices rise by 12 per cent, the real national income is falling. In order to find out how real national income is changing, it is necessary to remove the effects of any price changes from the figures for money national income. This can be done by using an index of prices, as in the following example. (The construction of an index of prices is described in Chapter 21.)

Figure 20.1
UK national income, 1986

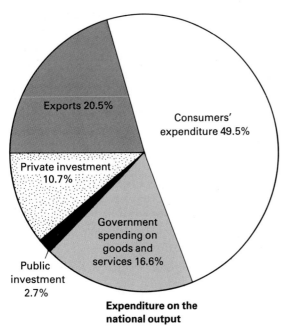

Expenditure on the national output

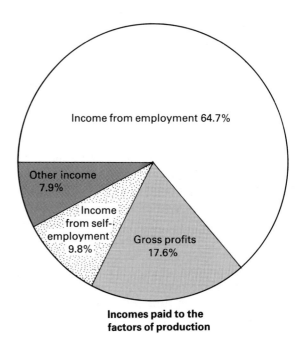

Incomes paid to the factors of production

Source: *Economic Trends*, HMSO, February 1988

Example

	Year 1	Year 4
Money national income	£10 000 million	£15 000 million
Index of prices	100	120

Over the period Year 1 to Year 4, money national income increased by 50 per cent. Over the same period, prices rose by 20 per cent. In other words, prices rose in the ratio 100 : 120. The value of £1 in Year 4, therefore, was only $\frac{100}{120}$ or $\frac{5}{6}$ of the value of £1 in Year 1.

We can use this information to find out how much real national income has changed:

$$\frac{£15\ 000\ \text{million}}{1} \times \frac{100}{120} = £12\ 500\ \text{million}$$

This means that £15 000 million in Year 4 would only buy the same amount of goods and services as £12 500 million would have bought in Year 1. Real national income, therefore, has increased by 25 per cent.

Reasons for measuring the national income

1 To provide the government with essential information

When the government is making plans for the economy, it must have reasonably accurate and up-to-date information on which to base its decisions. The national income accounts provide much of the information which the government requires.

2 To indicate changes in the standard of living

Changes in the standard of living are usually estimated by looking at the change in real income per head – the real value of total output divided by the total population. This figure tells us, *on average*, how the amount of goods and services available to each person has changed. It is, however, only an average figure and, like all averages, it can be misleading:

– It does not tell us how the national income is distributed – are there a few rich people and

many poor people, or is the national income fairly evenly distributed?

– It does not tell us anything about the types of goods and services produced. For example, a large increase in the output of defence equipment or capital goods would increase the national income per head, but the standard of living depends mainly on the output of consumer goods and services.

– An increase in production will raise the national income but, at the same time, it may also lead to an increase in social costs, in the form of more pollution, more traffic congestion and more noise. The standard of living would not have risen by as much as the increase in national income per head would indicate.

3 To compare the standards of living in different countries

Figures for national income per head are used as a means of comparing living standards in different countries. Since each country will value its national income in its own currency, international comparisons can only be made if national incomes are expressed in a common currency; this is invariably the US dollar. These comparisons, however, can also be misleading:

– People in different countries have different tastes, different ways of life, different climates and so on. For example, people in a North European country will have to spend far more on heating than people in a tropical country. This expenditure on heating will increase the national income in the country with the cold climate, but it does not follow that, *in this respect*, the people in that country are better off than those in the tropical country.

– Two countries may have the same income per head, but their standards of living will not be the same if people in one country have to work much longer hours than those in the other country, or if one country spends a greater percentage of its income on defence than the other country, or if income is much more unequally distributed in one country than in the other.

20.3
The circular flow of income

Economic activity is continuous and consists of a series of flows. The production of goods and services can be seen as a flow of output. In the opposite direction is a flow of spending on these goods and services. These flows can be illustrated by using a simple model of the economy.

1 An economy with only households and firms

Figure 20.2 represents the most simple model of an economy. It has only two sectors, households and firms. It does, however, help us to understand how income *circulates* from firms to households and back again to firms:
- Members of households own labour, land and capital. They supply the services of these factors of production to firms. In return, they receive payments in the form of wages, rent, interest and profits. These two flows are shown in the upper 'pipes' in Figure 20.2.
- Firms employ the factors of production to produce goods and services, and households use their incomes to buy these goods and services.

These two flows are shown in the lower 'pipes' in Figure 20.2.

Figure 20.2 can also be used to illustrate the three different methods of measuring the national income:
- The total annual flow through pipe A will be equal to the national *income*.
- The total annual flow through pipe B will be equal to the national *output*.
- The total annual flow through pipe C will be equal to the national *expenditure*.

Figure 20.2 represents a *closed* system – the same amount of income keeps flowing round the system. In the real world this is not the case.

2 A more realistic model

A real-world economy is not a closed system like the one shown in Figure 20.2, because
- in various ways, income is both withdrawn from and injected into the system, and
- it does not consist solely of households and firms – there is also a government sector and a foreign trade sector.

A more realistic model of the circular flow of income is shown in Figure 20.3. This diagram shows only the flows of money payments; the flows of goods and services are not included.

Figure 20.2
A highly simplified diagram of the flow of income

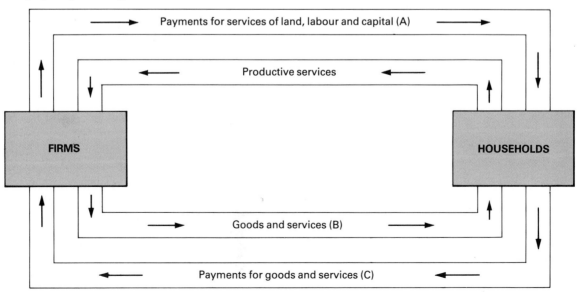

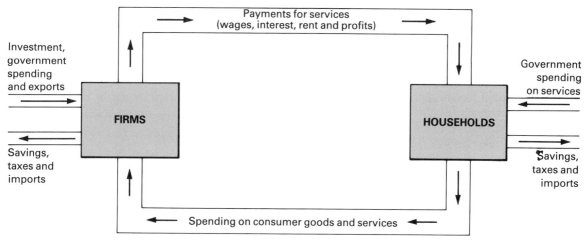

Figure 20.3
A diagram of the circular flow of income, showing the main leakages and injections

Savings and investment

Savings

Households do not spend all their income – some of it is saved. Savings, therefore, can be seen as a kind of leakage from the circular flow. They are part of the income paid out by firms which does not come back to them in the form of household spending.

Investment

In addition to the demands from households for consumer goods and services, firms also receive demands for capital goods (i.e. investment). These demands come from other firms. In this way some of the savings of households flow back into the system. Savings are placed in banks and other financial institutions which lend the money to firms so that they can buy capital goods. Investment is an addition to or injection into the circular flow.

The government sector

Taxation

When the government levies taxes on income and spending, it takes money out of the circular flow. Taxes, therefore, are a withdrawal or leakage from the circular flow of income.

Government spending

When the government buys goods and services, it adds income to the circular flow. It creates income when it buys goods and services from firms. As a very large employer of labour, the wages and salaries it pays to its employees add directly to the incomes of households. Government spending is an injection into the circular flow of income.

The foreign trade sector

Imports

When British residents buy foreign goods and services, income is withdrawn from the circular flow. This spending creates income overseas, and not in the UK. Imports are a leakage from the circular flow.

Exports

When British goods and services are purchased by overseas residents, income is added to the circular flow of income in the UK. Exports act as an injection into the circular flow of income.

Question on Figure 20.3
Which TWO of the following types of government spending represent payments for the services of factors of production and would, therefore, be injections into the circular flow of income?

A teachers' salaries
B state retirement pensions
C students' grants
D payments for hospital equipment

The government and the circular flow of income

The model of the circular flow of income helps us to understand how the government might influence the spending, income and employment in the economy. For much of the post-war period, governments adopted the policies advocated by Lord Keynes. He argued that the government should take steps to reduce unemployment by increasing the total demand for goods and services. For this purpose, he believed that fiscal and monetary policies should be used to
- increase government spending and investment (injections), or
- reduce savings and taxation (leakages).

If, on the other hand, total demand is excessive and causing inflationary problems, fiscal and monetary policies should be used to
- reduce one or more of the injections, or
- increase one or more of the leakages.

More recently, however, Keynesian policies to reduce unemployment have tended to lead to problems with inflation and the balance of payments.

20.4
Economic policy

Economic policy refers to the economic objectives of the government and the ways in which it tries to achieve those objectives.

The different political parties disagree with each other quite strongly on questions of economic policy. Nevertheless, there is a wide measure of agreement on the *objectives* or *aims* of economic policy. The main disagreements between the parties seem to be on the amount of importance they would give to the different aims and especially on the ways in which they would go about achieving these aims.

The aims of economic policy

1 A high and stable level of employment

This does not mean zero unemployment. We shall see later that this cannot be achieved. The objective is to create a situation where people who are willing to work are able to find jobs within a reasonable period of time. In a rapidly changing world, this objective may be difficult to achieve.

2 A relatively stable price level

This means that inflation should be brought under control and kept under control. Inflation can have several harmful effects on the economy. This is discussed in Chapter 21.

3 A satisfactory balance of payments position

A country which is persistently spending more on foreign goods and services than it is earning from its exports will be getting deeper and deeper into debt with the rest of the world. One aim of economic policy is to prevent this from happening. This does not mean that the balance of payments should never be in deficit. It means that the deficits of some years should be offset by surpluses in other years.

4 A rising standard of living

People have come to expect that, as the years go by, they will be able to enjoy such things as higher real wages, better housing, more modern hospitals, improvements in the education system, more leisure facilities and so on. These things are possible when real income per head is increasing, that is, when there is steady economic growth.

5 A more equal distribution of income and wealth

Earlier in this book we saw that income and wealth are very unequally distributed. There is a widely-held view that it should be an aim of economic policy to reduce these inequalities.

Instruments of economic policy

The methods or techniques which the government uses to try and achieve its economic aims are described as instruments of economic policy.

1 Fiscal policy

A government is using fiscal policy when it deliberately changes the rates of taxation and the amount of its own spending in order to bring about changes in the economy. This subject was explained on page 174. The main instrument of fiscal policy is the Budget.

2 Monetary policy

When using monetary policy, the government tries to influence the economy by changing the rate of interest and by controlling the banks' ability to make loans. Monetary policy was explained on pages 136–7.

3 Direct controls

The government has the power to place legal controls on such things as wages, prices, rents and dividends. It can also use its power to grant planning permission to control the number, type and location of all kinds of buildings. Rationing is another form of direct control which the government can use if it wishes.

4 Public ownership

Many people believe that if the government owns several major industries (nationalised industries), it will be able to control the economy much more effectively. It can create more jobs by investing heavily in these industries. It could also affect the costs of production in other industries by controlling the prices charged by the nationalised industries (e.g. electricity).

One policy may conflict with another

One of the greatest problems facing a government is that a policy designed to achieve one economic objective might conflict with a policy designed to achieve another objective. For example, unemployment might be reduced by a large increase in public spending without any increase in taxation. This increased public spending would increase incomes, so the demands for goods and services would increase, output would increase and unemployment would fall. But a large increase in public spending may have undesirable effects too:
– it might lead to inflation, and
– there would almost certainly be an increase in imports which could, in turn, cause a balance of payments deficit.

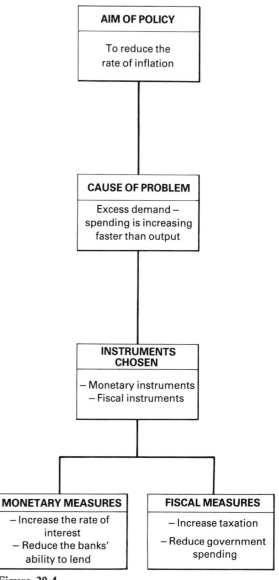

Figure 20.4
Economic policy – an example

Question on Figure 20.4
Can you think of another policy measure which might be used to reduce the rate of inflation?

The Main Points

- Gross Domestic Product
  = Total output of goods and services produced within the UK
  Gross National Product
  = Total output produced by British-owned factors of production wherever they happen to be located
  National income
  = Gross national product − Depreciation

- The national income may be measured as
  - the total output of goods and services, or
  - total factor incomes, or
  - total expenditure on the national output (including additions to stocks).

- In an economy there is a circular flow of income. Households receive income from firms for services rendered, and firms receive income from households as payments for their goods and services.

- There are leakages from the circular flow of income and injections into it. The leakages are savings, taxes and imports. The injections are investment, government spending on goods and services, and exports.

- The broad aims of government economic policy are a high level of employment, stable prices, a satisfactory balance of payments position, a steady rate of economic growth, and a more equal distribution of income and wealth.

- There is a wide measure of agreement on these aims, but much disagreement on which of the aims are the most important and on the ways of achieving them.

- To carry out its policies, the government can use fiscal policy, monetary policy, direct controls and nationalisation.

- A major problem of economic management is the fact that one aim of economic policy may conflict with another aim.

Test Your Understanding

1. The national accounts of a country contain the following information:

   Gross Domestic Product   £50 000 million
   Depreciation   £5 000 million
   Net property income from
       abroad   £2 000 million

   (a) What is the Gross National Product?
   (b) What is the national income?

2. Which THREE of the following are payments for the services of factors of production?

   A the salaries of policemen and policewomen
   B winnings on the football pools
   C the profits made by a furniture manufacturer
   D government grants to firms in assisted areas
   E interest payments on a bank loan which has been used to buy machinery

3. In measuring the national income, why would it be misleading to add the total value of the outputs of flour mills to the total value of the outputs of bakeries?

4. When a government wishes to reduce the total demand for goods and services, it will tend to increase the rates of taxation. However, an increase in taxation will not have much effect on demand if people decide to reduce their .... rather than their spending. What is the missing word?

5. This question is based on Figure 20.5, which shows *some of* the flows of money payments in an economy.
   Which of the flows represent
   (a) payments of taxes?
   (b) payments for exports?
   (c) consumers' spending on goods and services?
   (d) payments for imports?
   (e) the government's payments of wages and salaries to its own employees?

Figure 20.5
Some of the main flows of money payments

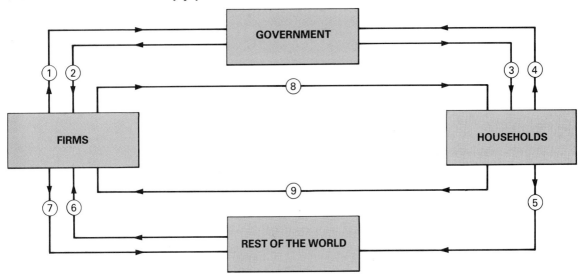

Value added

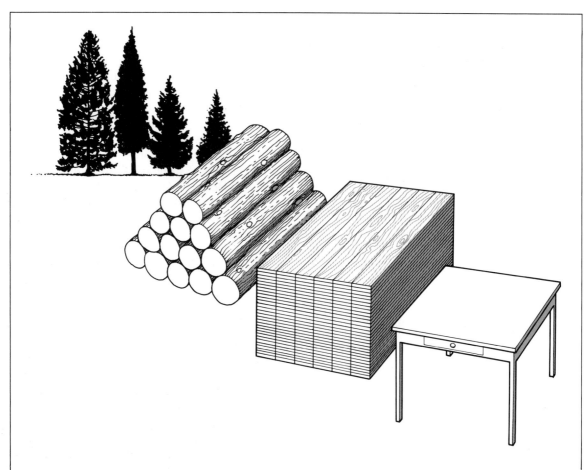

- Firm A owns woodland and cuts down trees. It sells timber for £2000 to Firm B, which operates a saw mill.
- Firm B saws the timber into various lengths and sections, and sells them for £4000 to Firm C, which manufactures furniture.
- Firm C uses the timber to make furniture, which it sells for £7000 to Firm D, which owns several furniture shops.
- Firm D sells the furniture to the general public for £9000.

Questions
1. What was the total value of the *sales* of these four firms?
2. The outputs of these firms will be included in the Gross National Product. What will be the *total value of output* recorded in the GNP?
3. Assume that this industry is subject to a value added tax at a rate of 10 per cent. What would be the total amount of VAT payable on the transactions described above?

CHAPTER 21

Inflation

21.1

The meaning of inflation

Inflation describes a situation where prices are persistently rising. It does not mean that all prices are moving to the same extent, or even in the same direction. Some prices may be rising very sharply, others may be rising very little, and a few may even be falling. Inflation is taking place when prices, *on average*, are rising.

Inflation may also be described as a situation where the value of money is falling. When prices are rising, the purchasing power of the pound is falling; it will buy fewer and fewer goods and services.

Figure 21.1 provides a striking illustration of the cumulative effects of inflation. It shows that, in 1987, £1 would only buy the same amount of goods and services as $7\frac{1}{2}$p would have bought in 1945. In other words, the purchasing power of £1 fell by $92\frac{1}{2}$ per cent between 1945 and 1987.

Inflation has been a world-wide problem in the post-war period, but different countries have experienced very different rates of inflation. Some countries, such as Switzerland and Japan, have had relatively low rates of inflation. On the other hand, Brazil experienced inflation at a rate of 200 per cent per annum in 1984, and in 1985 Bolivia had an inflation rate of more than 20 000 per cent per annum. Extremely high rates of inflation such as these are described as *hyperinflation*.

Inflation in the UK

Figure 21.2 (over the page) shows the annual rates of inflation in the UK over recent years. After reaching a peak of about 25 per cent per annum in 1975, the rate of inflation fell to less than 4 per cent per annum in 1986.

Figure 21.1
Purchasing power of the pound, 1945–87

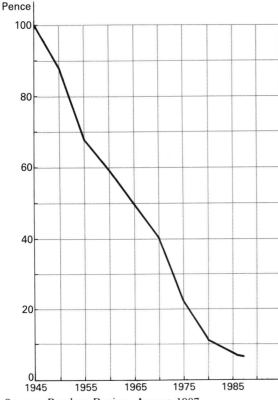

Source: *Barclays Review*, August 1987

Figure 21.2
Inflation in the UK, 1970–87

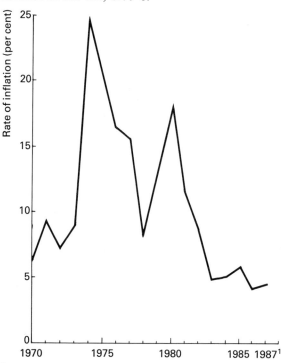

¹ Forecast
Source: *Economic Progress Report Supplement*, HMSO,
March–April 1987

Question on Figure 21.2
Like the UK, many other countries experienced large increases in the rate of inflation in 1975 and 1980. Can you think of one possible reason why this happened?

21.2
Measuring inflation – index numbers

In order to measure the rate of inflation, it is necessary to measure the rate at which prices are changing. This is done by means of an index of prices. An index number deals with percentage changes. An index of prices is an average of the percentage changes in the prices of a number of different goods and services. The following example shows how such an index number is calculated.

Example 1

Year 1

Commodity	Price	Index
A	10p	100
B	£1.00	100
C	£5.00	100
	3)	300

Index = 100

Year 2

Commodity	Price	Index
A	12p	120
B	£1.50	150
C	£4.50	90
	3)	360

Index = 120

1. The year in which the index begins is known as the *base year*.
2. In the base year, each price is given the index value of 100.
3. Prices in the following years are expressed as changes on this base of 100. For example, the price of Commodity A has risen from 10p to 12p, so its index has risen from 100 to 120.
4. The price indexes for the different commodities are added together and divided by the number of commodities.
5. The index of prices for the base year, therefore, will always be 100.
6. In this example, the index number for Year 2 is 120. This means that, on average, prices have increased from 100 to 120, that is, by 20 per cent.

Weighting

Example 1 does not take account of the fact that some prices are more important than others. The average family spends far more of its income on some items than it does on others. The prices of meat, vegetables, fruit, electricity, gas and the costs of housing are far more important to most people than the prices of luxury cars or high-fashion clothing.

This problem is solved by giving each item a weight to represent its share in the total spending of the average family.

In Example 2 we use the same commodities and prices as in Example 1. In this case, however, each commodity is given a weight, which is based on the percentage of household expenditure devoted to that commodity. In this example, households clearly spend far more of their income on Commodity C than on Commodity A.

Example 2

Year 1

Commodity	Weight	Price	Index	Weighted index
A	1	10p	100	100
B	2	£1.00	100	200
C	3	£5.00	100	300
	6			6) 600

Index = 100

Year 2

Commodity	Weight	Price	Index	Weighted index
A	1	12p	120	120
B	2	£1.50	150	300
C	3	£4.50	90	270
	6			6) 690

Index = 115

1. In each year, the price index for each commodity is multiplied by its weight.
2. These weighted indices are added together and divided by the total of the weights.
3. As in Example 1, the index in the base year will always be equal to 100.
4. As a result of the weighting, the average increase in prices has been reduced from 20 per cent to 15 per cent. The index increases from 100 to 115, instead of 120 as in Example 1.
5. This result is due to the fact that the most heavily weighted commodity is the one which fell in price.

21.3
The Index of Retail Prices (RPI)

This is an official index published monthly by the Department of Employment. It is the index which is normally used to measure the rate of inflation.

It includes a wide range of goods and services, and aims to show what is happening to the value of the money spent by the average household. The main features of this index are summarised below.

1. A sample of about 7000 households is selected each year. Every fortnight, about 270 of them are asked to keep a careful record of their expenditures over a two-week period.
2. The information in these household budgets is used to decide which goods and services should be included in the index and what weights should be given to them. An item which accounts for 20 per cent of household spending will be given a weight twice as large as one which accounts for 10 per cent of household spending.
3. A date is chosen as a base date, and prices on this date are given the value 100.
4. Around the middle of each month, some 130 000 price quotations for 600 different items are obtained from retail outlets throughout the country. From these quotations, the changes in the prices of different goods and services are estimated.
5. The index for each month is then calculated in a manner similar to that used in Example 2.

As time goes by, the pattern of consumer spending changes, and new consumer goods come on to the market. This means that the range of goods and services included in the index and the weights attached to them must be revised at regular intervals. A new index, with the weights shown in Table 21.1 (over the page), was introduced on 13 January 1987. Prices on this date were given the value 100. The previous index, introduced on 15 January 1974, had reached a value of 394.5 by January 1987. This means that prices had almost quadrupled between January 1974 and January 1987.

The Index of Retail Prices tells us what is happening to the value of the money spent by the *average family*. There will, however, be very few (if any) households which spend their money in exactly the same way as this 'average family'. For example, increases in the prices of alcoholic drinks and tobacco will increase the index of prices. But the value of the money spent by someone who did not smoke or drink would not be affected.

Table 21.1
The Index of Retail Prices

	Weights used in 1987	Weights as a percentage
Food	167	16.7
Catering	46	4.6
Alcoholic drink	76	7.6
Tobacco	38	3.8
Housing	157	15.7
Fuel and lighting	61	6.1
Household goods	73	7.3
Household services	44	4.4
Clothing and footwear	74	7.4
Personal goods and services	38	3.8
Motoring expenditure	127	12.7
Fares and travel costs	22	2.2
Leisure goods	47	4.7
Leisure services	30	3.0
	1000	100.0

Source: *Department of Employment Gazette*, April 1987

Question on Table 21.1
Over the years, the weight given to food has gradually fallen (it was 253 in 1974). Does this mean that people are spending less money on food?

21.4
The effects of inflation

1 It tends to accelerate

When inflation has been experienced for some time, people will begin to anticipate future price increases. Workers will base their wage claims on past price increases *and* on expected future price increases. Similarly, firms will tend to raise prices to cover both past *and* expected future increases in costs. These actions will tend to speed up the rate of inflation.

2 It affects the distribution of income

When inflation is taking place, people naturally try to obtain increases in their incomes to compensate them for the increase in prices. Some of them will be more successful than others. Some trade unions are in a strong bargaining position, and will be able to protect their real wages. Other worker organisations, with less bargaining power, may find that their wages do not keep up with the rising prices.

Some workers get automatic wage increases because their earnings are linked to the Index of Retail Prices. Some groups, for example those receiving private pensions or those who obtain an income from fixed-interest securities, will not be able to avoid a fall in real income.

3 Borrowers gain at the expense of lenders

Suppose someone borrows £1000 for one year and, during the course of that year, prices increase by 10 per cent. When the £1000 is repaid, it will buy less than the £1000 which was borrowed. It is true that the borrower will have to pay interest on the loan, but if the rate of interest is less than 10 per cent, the purchasing power of the money repaid will still be less than that of the money borrowed.

As the largest borrower in the country, the government benefits from inflation. It is able to repay its debts with money which has a lower value than the money it borrowed.

4 It affects the balance of payments

If the prices of goods produced in the UK are rising faster than prices in competing countries, there will be harmful effects on the balance of payments. The UK's exports will become relatively more expensive in overseas markets, and hence more difficult to sell. Imports into the UK will become relatively cheaper when compared with UK products. The balance of payments will tend to move into deficit.

Inflation can get out of control

The best-known example of runaway inflation, or hyperinflation, occurred in Germany in 1923, when prices rose at an astronomical rate. At the end of 1923, prices were one billion times higher than they had been at the beginning of the year. Towards the end of 1923 it cost 20 000 000 000 marks to post a letter (see Figure 21.3). Before the inflationary trend began, a postage stamp had cost much less than one mark!

Figure 21.3
This postage stamp vividly illustrates what hyperinflation means: in 1923 it cost 20 000 million marks to post a letter, but before the inflation began, the cost had been much less than one mark!

21.5
The causes of inflation

There is still much disagreement among economists on the causes of inflation. Some of them believe that prices are *pulled upwards* by excess demand. Others maintain that prices are *pushed upwards* by rising costs. Many economists now believe that inflation takes place when the money supply is allowed to rise at a faster rate than total output.

1 Demand-pull inflation

People who support this explanation say that prices will rise when the total demand for goods and services persistently exceeds the total supply of goods and services at current prices.

This theory helps to explain inflation when the economy is fully employed. In these circumstances it will be very difficult to increase supply to meet an increase in demand. However, if there is a great deal of unemployed labour and capital, an increase in demand should not have any great effect on prices. More goods and services could be produced by putting the unemployed resources to work. There could be a problem, though, if the increased demand called for labour skills which were in short supply even though large numbers of workers were unemployed. These unemployed workers could not fill the vacant jobs.

2 Cost-push inflation

Costs represent the payments made for the services of the factors of production. Experience has shown that the prices of materials, labour and capital may rise even when there is no excess demand in the economy.

If the world prices of raw materials increase, then costs of production in the UK will rise, whatever the state of demand in the UK economy. The massive increases in the price of oil in the 1970s showed how prices in the UK can be pushed upwards by cost increases which are beyond the control of the government.

Costs and prices may also be pushed upwards by increases in indirect taxes such as VAT and by increases in import prices due to higher tariffs or to a fall in the exchange rate of the pound.

Those who support the cost-push theory usually argue that the main cause of rising prices is an increase in labour costs. Wages are the largest single element in total costs. When wages rise faster than productivity, labour costs will increase and so will prices. Trade unions have shown that they can push up wages even when there is a fairly high level of unemployment.

3 Inflation and the money supply

It is a common mistake to confuse the amount of *spending* in the economy with the amount of *money* in the economy. It is a mistake because, during a period of time, a unit of money can change hands several times. In other words, it can be *spent* several times.

If a £1 coin changes hands four times, the amount of spending will be £4, but the amount of money is only £1. It is the amount of spending which is likely to affect prices, and this depends upon
- the total supply of money, and
- the rate at which money changes hands (i.e. its velocity of circulation).

Example

In a particular year, the total supply of money in an economy is £1000 million. On average, each unit of money changes hands five times each year. Therefore, in this particular year,

Total supply of money = £1000 million
Total spending   = £5000 million

If, in the following year, the money supply increases to £1500 million, total spending would increase to

5 × £1500 million = £7500 million

This example shows that, if the rate at which money changes hands remains constant, an increase in the money supply would cause an increase in total spending.

Many economists – they are known as Monetarists – argue that an increase in the money supply *does* cause total spending to increase, because the rate at which money changes hands *is* fairly constant. They believe that inflation takes place when the government allows the money supply to increase at a faster rate than the supply of goods and services. In other words, they are saying that inflation is due to excess demand which is caused by allowing the money supply to grow too quickly.

21.6
Policies to deal with inflation

1 Reducing demand

When the government believes that inflation is being caused by excess demand, it will probably use one or more of the following measures:
- *fiscal policy*: increasing taxes and reducing government spending,
- *monetary policy*: putting restrictions on bank lending and raising the rate of interest – these measures will slow down the growth of the money supply,
- *hire-purchase restrictions*: raising the minimum deposit and reducing the time allowed for repayment.

These measures will reduce demand by reducing people's incomes, reducing their ability to borrow, and making borrowing more expensive.

2 Increasing supply

One way of overcoming the problem of excess demand would be to increase the supply of goods and services. This may be difficult in the short run, but the government could help to increase the efficiency of industry in several ways:
- by improving the training and re-training of labour to make workers more mobile,
- by providing grants to encourage investment in more up-to-date equipment,
- by promoting horizontal integration where it would lead to economies of scale, and
- by carrying out improvements in the road and rail networks.

3 Incomes policies

An incomes policy is an attempt to deal with inflation by slowing down the rate at which costs of production are rising. These costs, remember, are incomes to the factors of production, i.e. wages, interest, rent and profits. If the government can hold down the rate of increase of these incomes, it will be successful in restricting the rate at which costs are rising. If incomes do not increase, or if they increase much more slowly than in the past, there is much less danger of excess demand causing prices to rise. Since cost-push inflation appears to be mainly due to wages rising faster than productivity, incomes policies tend to concentrate on wages.

A government may have a voluntary incomes policy. In this case, it estimates how much the Gross National Product is likely to increase in the coming year. It then appeals to trade unions and other organisations representing labour not to press for increases in wages greater than the expected rise in GNP. For example, it may estimate that GNP will increase by 5 per cent over the next twelve months. It will then announce that income over this period of time should not rise by more than 5 per cent.

If a voluntary incomes policy is not successful, the government can place a *legal* limit on the increase in incomes. Such a step would be strongly opposed by the trade unions. Legal controls have been used in the past, but only for fairly short periods of time. Unfortunately, when the controls are removed, wages tend to rise quite sharply as workers try to 'catch up' or make good the ground they feel they have lost while wages have been controlled.

Incomes policies tend to concentrate on wages, but rents and dividends are also subject to the same controls.

4 Price controls

Governments have the power to control prices, and this would seem an obvious way of controlling inflation. However, as we saw in Chapter 8, if prices are held down below the equilibrium level, shortages arise and these could lead to some form of rationing. Another problem is that if prices are held down while costs are still rising, many firms could find themselves making losses and be forced to close down. Nevertheless, it is not very likely that workers will accept controls on wages unless the government also places some kind of control on prices.

The Main Points

- Inflation means a persistent rise in the average price level.

- Most countries have experienced inflation during the post-war period, but at very different rates. An extremely high rate of inflation is described as hyperinflation.

- The rate of inflation is measured by making use of an index of prices. In the UK, the official index is the Index of Retail Prices, which is published monthly.

- Inflation affects the economy in several ways:
  - It has a tendency to accelerate.
  - It affects the distribution of income: there are 'gainers' and 'losers'.
  - It can lead to a deficit in the balance of payments.
  - Borrowers tend to benefit at the expense of lenders.

- Several theories have been put forward to explain the causes of inflation:
  - Demand-pull inflation: prices are pulled upwards by excess demand.
  - Cost-push inflation: rising costs push up prices.
  - Monetarism: prices rise when the money supply is allowed to rise faster than the output of goods and services.

- Policies to deal with inflation include
  - monetary and fiscal measures to reduce demand,
  - helping industry to become more efficient so as to increase supply, and
  - using incomes policies to keep the growth of *money income* in line with the growth of *real income*. In other words, people's money incomes should not increase faster than the supply of goods and services on which those incomes are spent.

Test Your Understanding

1. Which ONE of the following people is likely to gain from inflation?

   A someone who has borrowed money at a fixed rate of interest

   B someone living on a pension which remains unchanged

   C someone who is saving money by holding it in a cash box at home

2. The following statements all refer to the *value of money*. Which ONE of them is *incorrect?*

   A It moves in the opposite direction to the level of prices.

   B It represents the quantity of goods and services which a unit of money will buy.

   C It always increases when the supply of money increases.

   D The amount by which it changes can be measured by means of an index of prices.

3. What name is given to the type of inflation which might be caused by large increases in the prices of imported foodstuffs and raw materials?

4. A country is experiencing inflation when its (a) income is increasing faster than its (b) income. Which of the following words should be inserted at (a), and which at (b)?

   money   real

5. A simple index of prices has the following weights:

Food	30
Other goods	30
Services	40

   In one year, the prices of food and other goods both increased by 10 per cent. The prices of services remained unchanged. What was the rate of inflation in this particular year?

6. The table below shows the index of retail prices in a country. (The index is calculated at the end of each year.)

	Index of Retail Prices
1984	100
1985	110
1986	115
1987	120

   Which of the three years, 1985, 1986 and 1987, had the highest rate of inflation?

7. Why is inflation often described as a 'tax on savings'?

BOX 21
Costs of production and the rate of inflation

Retail price inflation rose to 7 per cent in mid-1985, reflecting mortgage rate increases and the weakness of sterling in the early part of the year.

However, between May 1985 and February 1986 retail prices rose by only 1.5 per cent, helped by the general easing of cost pressures. The latter is reflected in the fall by 9.8 per cent in the year to February in the prices paid by manufacturing industry for raw materials.

Overall costs in the economy are expected to be a little higher in 1986 than in 1985. Within these, import prices, which have fallen since the spring of 1985, will continue to contribute to low price increases.

Average earnings in the economy as a whole, however, grew around 7.5 per cent a year in 1985 as they have done for the past three years.

For manufacturing, the rise in unit labour costs is likely to be greater than 4 per cent in 1986, the third year in which these costs have grown substantially above the average of our competitors.

Source: Adapted from *Economic Progress Report*, HMSO, March–April 1986

Annual changes in the cost of labour per unit of output in manufacturing industry, 1979–87

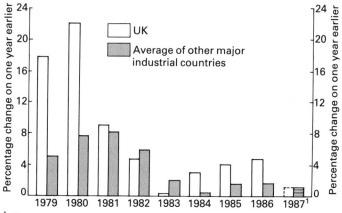

[1] Forecast

Source: *Financial Statement and Budget Report, 1987–88*, HMSO

Questions
1. What is meant by 'the weakness of sterling'?
2. Which of the changes described above tended to lower the rate of inflation, and which tended to raise the rate of inflation?
3. Assume that labour costs account for 50 per cent of the price of a manufactured good. If labour costs were to increase by 10 per cent, what would happen to the price of the good?
4. Examine the information contained in the chart for the years 1984 to 1986. On the basis of this information, describe the likely effects on (a) British exports, and (b) British imports.

CHAPTER 22

Unemployment

22.1 The costs of unemployment
22.2 Measuring unemployment
22.3 Types of unemployment
22.4 Employment policies

22.1
The costs of unemployment

Figure 22.1
Unemployed people register themselves as available for work

Unemployment represents a waste of resources. The goods and services which the unemployed might have produced are lost for ever. Producing more in the future cannot make up for the output which could have been produced if the un-employed had been working.

Unemployment has serious social effects. People who lose their jobs suffer a fall in their standard of living, and so do their dependants. Unemployment can have damaging effects on the morale of those out of work, who can be made to feel rejected and unwanted.

There is also a loss of skill: workers who are unemployed for long periods of time may find it difficult to retain their skills.

One cost of unemployment takes the form of the taxation that is necessary to provide the money to pay social security benefits to those who are out of work. If the level of unemployment could be reduced, this money might be spent on pensions, schools, hospitals, roads and so on. Alternatively, taxation might be reduced.

22.2
Measuring unemployment

1 Total unemployment

In the UK, the official unemployment figure refers to those who are both out of work *and* claiming

Table 22.1
Employment and unemployment in the UK, June 1987

	thousands
Employees in employment	
Males	11 983
Females	9 874
Self-employed	2 729
HM Forces	319
Employed labour force	24 905
Unemployed	3 002
Working population	27 907

Number unemployed as a percentage of the working population = 10.8 per cent

Source: *Department of Employment Gazette*, December 1987

benefit. This may not be a very accurate measure of the numbers seeking work. There are many unemployed married women who do not qualify for benefit, but who would take a job if one became available. There is also a large number of people who have been removed from the unemployment register by various special employment measures. Most of these people are engaged on government training schemes or have temporary jobs which are subsidised by the government. There are, however, some people claiming benefit who are not actively seeking work.

Figure 22.2
Working population and employed labour force, Great Britain, 1973–87 (seasonally adjusted)

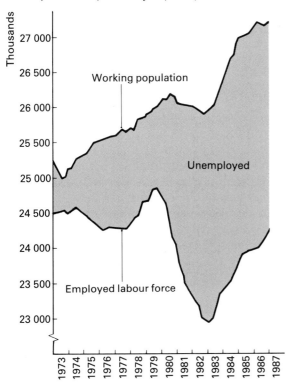

Source: *Department of Employment Gazette*, August 1987

> **Question on Figure 22.2**
> During the period 1983–86, the number of people in employment increased, but the number unemployed continued to rise. How can this be explained?

The rate of unemployment is usually expressed as a percentage of the working population. This makes it possible to compare the unemployment situations in different countries.

Figure 22.2 shows how the number of people unemployed has increased in recent years. Note that the vertical scale does *not* start at zero in this diagram.

2 The duration of unemployment

One of the most important unemployment statistics is the one which tells us how long different groups of people have been out of work. Information on the duration of unemployment is published by the Department of Employment each month.

If the average duration of unemployment is only a matter of a few weeks, then unemployment is not a very serious problem. However, this was not the case in the UK in the 1980s. Figure 22.3 shows that, in 1987, a large proportion of the unemployed had been out of work for more than one year.

Figure 22.3
Short-term and long-term unemployment in the UK, 1979–87

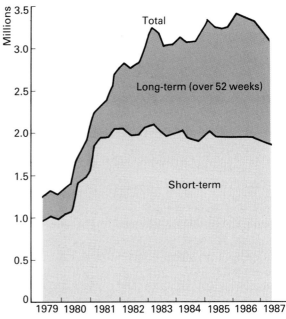

Sources: *The Economist*, 8 February 1986; *Department of Employment Gazette*, August 1987

Some features of unemployment in the UK

1. The *trend* of unemployment has been upwards since the 1950s, but it has risen at a much faster rate since 1970. Unemployment doubled in the 1970s. It doubled again between 1979 and 1982, when the total reached three million. The official figure did not fall below three million until the summer of 1987.
2. As pointed out earlier, there has been a considerable increase in the number of long-term unemployed.
3. The unemployment rate among young people is much higher than the national average. For example, in mid-1987, the average rate of unemployment for all age groups was 9.9 per cent, but for those under 19 the rate was 16 per cent.
4. Unemployment rates for semi-skilled and unskilled workers tend to be much higher than the rates for skilled workers and for people who have professional qualifications.

22.3
Types of unemployment

Frictional unemployment

Every year, for various reasons, millions of people change their jobs. Many of these people will take some time to search for another job. They may be looking for something which pays more or is more interesting then their previous job. The time they spend between jobs is described as frictional unemployment. It is a type of short-term unemployment.

Structural unemployment

This is a more serious type of unemployment, which is caused by changes in the structure of industry. It develops when a major industry is suffering a permanent decline in the demand for its product. It is particularly serious when that industry is concentrated in a particular region. In the UK, the decline in the coal, steel and ship-building industries has caused serious unemployment problems in the areas where these industries are located.

There are several possible causes of structural unemployment:

1. An industry may lose its export markets to newly-established industries in other countries. Competition from Japan, Taiwan, Korea and Hong Kong has affected several British industries in this way.
2. The loss of demand may be due to the development of a more efficient substitute. The use of oil as a source of energy led to a fall in the demand for coal. Improvements in road transport drastically reduced the demand for rail transport. The introduction of jet airliners has almost eliminated the demand for travel by ocean liners.
3. Structural unemployment can also be caused by technical progress. We are all aware of the ways in which microchips, computers, robots, etc. have revolutionised production methods in many industries. In many cases, the result has been that far fewer workers are required to produce a given output. This is sometimes described as 'technological unemployment'.

   Although jobs are created in the newer industries, workers who have lost their jobs in the declining industries may not have the skills required to take up the newly-created jobs. It may also be the case that the newer industries locate themselves in different parts of the country from those where industries are in decline.

General unemployment

This is the most serious type of unemployment. It is caused by a lack of demand. General unemployment exists when total spending in the economy is much too low to purchase all the goods and services which *could be* produced if the labour force were fully employed.

Full employment, however, does not mean that there is no unemployment. Whatever the state of demand in the economy, there will always be a large number of people changing jobs. This means that there will always be some frictional unemployment. Full employment might be defined as a situation where the number of job vacancies is equal to the number of people out of work. In this case it could be said that the demand for labour is equal to the supply of labour, even though some people are out of work.

There are a number of reasons why the demand for labour may not be high enough to prevent large-scale unemployment.

Why the demand for labour may be too low

1. If there is a slump in world trade, many British industries will be affected by a fall in the demand for exports. Many workers in these industries will lose their jobs.
2. The government may be deliberately reducing the demand for goods and services in order to reduce the rate of inflation. The 'cost' of a lower rate of inflation could well be a higher rate of unemployment.
3. It is sometimes argued that the lack of demand for goods and services is due to the fact that British industries are slower to change their methods and their products than industries in some other countries. New machines, new production methods, new materials and new designs may be introduced more easily and more quickly in other countries. If this is the case, the demands for British goods will fall relative to those for goods produced by the UK's competitors. Sometimes people oppose new techniques of production because they fear that they will cause redundancies. *Not* introducing them, however, might cause even more redundancies in the long run.
4. Some economists believe that the high rate of unemployment exists because labour has been 'pricing itself out of a job'. They maintain that, like any other commodity, labour is governed by the law of demand which says that 'less is demanded at higher prices'. If wage rates increase faster than productivity, labour costs increase, and fewer workers will be demanded. According to this view, unemployment has been caused by the fact that labour costs in the UK have risen faster than those in many other countries. The relatively higher prices of UK goods has made it more difficult to sell them, both at home and abroad.

Seasonal unemployment

In some industries there is a seasonal pattern in the demand for labour. In Europe, holiday resorts will have a high demand for labour in the summer months but a low demand in the winter – except for those which provide winter sports facilities. The demand for workers on building sites tends to fall in the winter, while farmers' demands for labour tend to be higher during the harvest period than at other times.

22.4
Employment policies

Reducing frictional and structural unemployment

Frictional unemployment cannot be eliminated. It might, however, be reduced by improving the information services and persuading people to make better use of them. Information and advice on job vacancies are available at the Job Centres which are to be found in almost all towns. The 'situations vacant' columns in the local and national newspapers are another important source of information for those seeking work.

This type of unemployment might also be reduced if young people starting work could be helped to make wiser choices when taking their first job. A high proportion of them leave their first job within a few months of starting work.

In trying to reduce *structural unemployment*, a major problem is the occupational immobility of labour. Redundant workers must be helped to move to jobs which require skills different from those they have been using in their previous jobs. The government has set up a large number of re-training centres for this purpose.

When the firms which are dismissing workers are concentrated in a particular region, it is necessary to persuade other firms to move into that area. The ways in which the government attempts to do this were explained in Chapter 13.

One way in which the government might help the situation is to slow down the rate at which an industry is declining. It could do this by granting subsidies to the firms in that industry.

Reducing general unemployment

1 Increasing the demand for goods and services

The government has the ability to increase total spending on goods and services in order to create more jobs. It can run a Budget deficit by spending more than it receives in taxation. It can also increase the money supply and lower the rate of interest to encourage more borrowing and spending.

For some 20 years after the Second World War, these policies helped governments to maintain a high level of employment. The rate of unemployment averaged 1½ per cent in the 1950s and 2 per cent in the 1960s. These low rates of unemployment were achieved without causing any serious problems of inflation. Since the late 1960s, however, the policy of creating jobs by increasing total demand has not worked very successfully.

2 Increasing total demand – recent problems

Increasing total spending in the economy can lead to either

– more goods and services being purchased at the same prices, or
– the same amount of goods and services being purchased at higher prices.

Only in the first case will increased spending lead to more jobs being created. If increased spending causes prices and wages to increase, there will be relatively little effect on the level of employment. This is what has tended to happen in recent years. Much of any increase in total demand has gone into higher prices and higher wages, rather than into an increase in output. Governments, therefore, have been reluctant to increase demand because of the danger of inflation.

A further problem arises because a fairly large proportion of consumer spending goes on imported goods and services. This means that when the government increases total demand, some part of the increased spending 'leaks out' of the economy and creates jobs abroad rather than at home.

It can now be seen why many economists think that an incomes policy is a very necessary part of any policy to reduce unemployment. Unless increases in wages and other incomes are restricted in some way, an increase in total demand will produce higher wages and higher prices, rather than more jobs.

The leakages due to higher imports might be reduced by some form of import controls or by reducing the exchange rate of the pound. These measures would make imports dearer in the UK.

Special employment measures

The very high unemployment rates experienced in the 1980s led to the government introducing a number of different schemes to provide work experience and training for the unemployed.

1 The Youth Training Scheme (YTS)

This scheme offers two years' training for 16-year-old school leavers and one year's training for 17-year-old school leavers. Trainees are paid a weekly allowance by the government. The YTS includes both training and work experience. The aim is to provide trainees with some recognised qualification at the end of the course.

2 The Community Programme

This scheme provides a year's employment for the long-term unemployed on projects of benefit to the local community. This helps those who find it difficult to obtain a job because of their lack of recent work experience.

3 The New Workers Scheme

The idea of this scheme is to encourage employers to provide more full-time permanent jobs for young people. Employers receive a subsidy of £15 per week for one year for each 18- or 19-year-old they take on at a wage of £60 per week or less, and for each 20-year-old they take on at a wage of £65 per week or less (1987 figures).

4 The Job Release Scheme

This is intended to encourage older workers to take early retirement. They qualify for an allowance until they are eligible for the state retirement pension, provided that their employer replaces them with an unemployed person.

5 The Enterprise Allowance Scheme

The purpose of this scheme is to encourage unemployed people who want to start their own businesses. Entrants, who must have at least £1000 to invest in the business, are paid an allowance of £40 per week for one year. This scheme has encouraged many people who have lost their jobs to use their redundancy payments to set themselves up in business.

6 The Jobshare Scheme

This scheme offers grants to employers who create new part-time jobs by either
– dividing an existing full-time job into two part-time jobs,
– combining the overtime hours of existing full-time jobs, or
– creating two new part-time jobs.

In 1987, it was estimated that a total of some 700 000 people were involved in the special employment measures.

The Main Points

■ There are several 'costs' of unemployment:
– The total output of goods and services is less than it might be.
– The unemployed suffer a fall in their standard of living and a loss of morale. Many of them lose some of their skills.
– The benefits paid to the unemployed must be met from taxation.

■ The official unemployment figure includes only those who are out of work *and* claiming benefit. It does not include those who are seeking work and cannot claim benefit, or those who are involved in the special employment measures.

■ The average duration of unemployment is a good indicator of the seriousness of the unemployment situation.

■ Unemployment in the UK grew rapidly in the late 1970s and early 1980s, reaching a total of three million in 1982. Much of this increase occurred in manufacturing industry. Unemployment rates are particularly high among the unskilled and semi-skilled.

■ Unemployment may be classified as
– frictional: short spells of unemployment between jobs,
– structural: longer-term unemployment, due to major changes in the structure of the economy, e.g. the decline of major industries,
– general: when the total demand for goods and services is not sufficient to purchase the output of a fully-employed labour force, or
– seasonal: in some industries, e.g. agriculture and tourism, the demand for labour varies according to the time of year.

■ Policies to deal with unemployment include
– for frictional unemployment: encouraging improvement in the quality and the use of information services;
– for structural unemployment: more and better re-training facilities, and persuading firms to move into areas where industries are declining;
– for general unemployment: increasing total demand – but this might simply mean higher wages and higher prices rather than more jobs. It could also lead to balance of payments problems. This policy might be more effective if accompanied by an incomes policy.

Test Your Understanding

1. Name two British industries which have experienced structural unemployment since the Second World War.

2. The following details refer to the labour force in a particular country:

	millions
Employees in employment	20
Self-employed	2
Members of the armed forces	1
Unemployed	2

   (a) What is the size of the *employed labour force*?
   (b) What is the size of the *working population*?
   (c) What is the *rate of unemployment*?

3. How would you explain the existence of unfilled vacancies when there is a high rate of unemployment?

4. Assuming other things do not change, which TWO of the following are likely to increase the number of people in employment in a country?

   A an increase in exports
   B an increase in imports
   C an increase in government spending
   D an increase in taxation

5. In some countries, the number of people unemployed is calculated by interviewing a sample of households to find out the numbers who are unemployed but would like to have a job. Explain why this method would give a higher unemployment figure for the UK than the method of calculation used in the UK at the present time.

6. Assuming other things do not change, which ONE of the following would tend to increase unemployment?

   A a reduction in indirect taxation
   B an increase in government spending
   C an increase in saving
   D an increase in investment

7. Why is a policy which is designed to reduce the rate of inflation likely to increase the rate of unemployment?

BOX 22
An unemployment blackspot

Unemployment in Birkenhead (population 135 000) is among the worst in the country. More than 10 000 people are registered as seeking work, and with an average of three dependants for each wage-earner this means a rate of nearly 45 per cent of the labour force.

The docks, which used to provide work for 14 000, now employ less than a tenth of that; Cammell Laird, one of the proudest names in shipbuilding, has seen its workforce shrink from 15 000 to 2000, and many former suppliers to the yard have been forced out of business.

In the town's Job Centre on one recent day, there were 33 manufacturing vacancies, compared with more than 300 in the service sector.

Hardly anyone works in Tees Street: its 150 or so residents are entirely dependent on the state.

Many residents would like to leave the street and move south. They are held back by family and regional ties and by the fact they are for the most part unqualified and have no job skills to offer. High house prices in the south and the difficulties of swapping their mouldering homes in Birkenhead for something better elsewhere is an additional barrier. Getting out is reckoned a rare privilege.

Source: Extracts from an article in *The Sunday Telegraph*, 21 December 1986

Questions
1. How does the *rate* of unemployment in Birkenhead in 1986 compare with the present national rate of unemployment?
2. What name is given to the type of unemployment described in the second paragraph?
3. Which sector of the economy offered the best prospects of employment?
4. According to the writer of the article, what were the main barriers to the geographical mobility of the unemployed workers?

CHAPTER 23

Population

23.1 Population arithmetic
23.2 World population
23.3 The population of the UK
23.4 The working population of the UK

23.1
Population arithmetic

The population of a country can increase in two ways:
- when the birth rate is higher than the death rate (this is described as the *natural rate of increase*), or
- when the number of immigrants exceeds the number of emigrants.

The *crude birth rate* is the number of live births per annum per thousand of the population. The *crude death rate* is the number of deaths per annum per thousand of the population.

The natural rate of increase of population
= Birth rate − Death rate

For example, if the birth rate is 25 per thousand, and the death rate is 10 per thousand, the annual rate of increase is 15 per thousand, or 1.5 per cent.

It is most important to realise that what appear to be very small annual growth rates can lead to very large increases in the total population in quite short periods of time. For example, if a country's population is growing at a rate of 3 per cent per annum, it will double its size in 24 years.

The *infant mortality rate* is the number of deaths of infants (children under one year old) in one year per thousand live births in that year. This figure is an important guide to the standard of living in a country.

23.2
World population

During the present century, the population of the world has grown very rapidly. Figure 23.1 shows that it has doubled in size in the last 40 years. In 1987 the world population was estimated to be about 5000 million. Its growth rate in that year was about 1.7 per cent per annum. This means that the number of people in the world was increasing by about 85 million every year – far

Figure 23.1
World population by region, 1950–2020

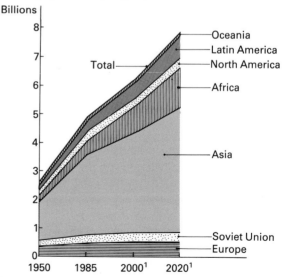

[1] Forecasts
Sources: *The Economist*, 6 September 1986; World Bank; Council of Europe

more than the total population of the United Kingdom!

The massive increase in world population has not been due to an increase in birth rates – the main cause has been a fall in death rates. Medical science has dramatically reduced the incidence of diseases such as cholera, typhoid, smallpox and malaria, which had been largely responsible for very high death rates. Improvements in sanitation, water supplies, transport, food production and education have also played an important part in lowering death rates.

Unfortunately, the high growth rates of population are taking place in the poorer regions of the world. Large areas of Asia and Africa, which have some of the world's lowest living standards, also have the highest rates of population growth.

23.3
The population of the UK

Table 23.1
The population of the UK

	millions
1801	10.5
1851	22.3
1901	38.2
1951	50.2
1985	56.6
2001	59.0 (estimate)

Sources: *Annual Abstract of Statistics*, HMSO, 1987; *Social Trends*, HMSO, 1987

The UK experienced a very large increase in its population during the nineteenth century. This growth was due to a steadily falling death rate, while the birth rate did not begin to fall until the latter part of the century.

The population has grown more slowly during the present century, and since 1971 it has remained fairly constant. It is expected that it will increase very slowly up to the end of the century. The present slow growth is due to a combination of a low birth rate and a low death rate. In the mid-1980s, the birth rate was about 13 per thousand and the death rate about 12 per thousand.

Age distribution

A long-term decline in both birth rates and death rates has led to an 'ageing' of the UK population; the average age of the population has been rising.

– In 1901, about one-third of the population was under 15 years of age. By 1987 this proportion had fallen to one-fifth.
– The proportion of the population who have reached retirement age (65 for men and 60 for women) has greatly increased. It was 6 per cent in 1901 but 20 per cent in 1987.

Changes like these have important effects on the *dependency ratio*. This is the ratio of the numbers in the working age groups to the numbers outside the working age groups.

While the whole of the population *consume* goods and services, the great majority of the *producers* of these goods and services are members of the working age groups. Hence, those *not* in the working age groups are described as dependants.

The working age groups

In the UK, these contain all the people above the school-leaving age (16 years) and below the retirement ages. (Note: the number of people in the working age groups is *not* the same as the total working population.)

The dependent age groups

These contain all those who are below the official school-leaving age plus those who have reached retirement age.

The dependency ratio

$$= \frac{\text{Number in dependent age groups}}{\text{Number in working age groups}} \times \frac{100}{1}$$

Example
A country has a total population of 56 million with 35 million in the working age groups.

$$\text{Dependency ratio} = \frac{21 \text{ million}}{35 \text{ million}} \times \frac{100}{1}$$

$$= 60 \text{ per cent}$$

This means that for every 100 people of working age, there are 60 people in the dependent age groups.

Figure 23.2

UK population: age and sex distribution

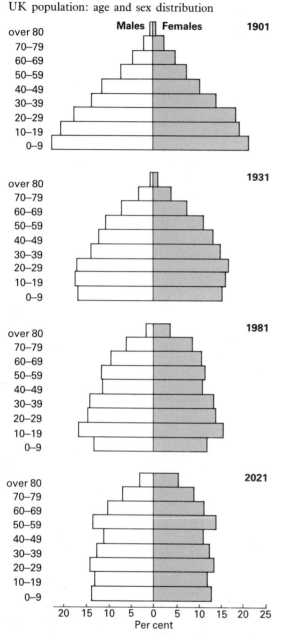

Source: *Barclays Review*, February 1985

Figure 23.2 shows how the age and sex distributions of the UK population have changed during the present century, and how they are expected to change over the next 30 years or so.

Sex distribution

The ratio of female births to male births varies little from 100 girls to every 105 boys. In spite of this, there are more females in the UK population than males – about 105 females to 100 males.

This statistic, however, is rather misleading because the excess of females is concentrated in the higher age groups. Females, on average, live longer than males. In the past, the infant mortality rates have been higher for male babies, but this situation has changed. A decrease in the male infant mortality rate has meant that now, in every age group up to 45 years, the number of males exceeds the number of females.

Regional distribution

The UK has a high population density, averaging about 600 persons per square mile. But this population is not evenly spread. England has about four-fifths of the total population and a density of about 900 persons per square mile, while Scotland has a density of only 175 persons per square mile.

Most of the people live in towns and cities – almost 80 per cent of the population live in urban areas. The seven great conurbations of Greater London, Central Clydeside, Merseyside, Teesside, South East Lancashire, West Yorkshire and the West Midlands occupy only 3 per cent of the land area but contain one-third of the total population.

In the first half of this century, there was a steady drift of population away from Scotland, Wales and Northern England to the Midlands and the South East. This was due to the decline of the traditional heavy industries – coal, iron and steel, and shipbuilding – in these older industrial areas. In more recent years, the movement of population has tended to be away from densely-populated cities to outer suburbs and to more rural areas. In the last 20 years, the areas which have had the most rapid population growth have been East Anglia and the South West. All of the great conurbations have experienced a fall in population.

Question on Figure 23.2

Over the period covered by the diagram, how has the shape of the population pyramid been changed by (a) the fall in the death rate, and (b) the fall in the birth rate?

Figure 23.3
UK population: regional distribution, 1986

Source: *Regional Trends*, HMSO, 1987

Question on Figure 23.3
What will be the likely effect of the construction of the Channel Tunnel on the regional distribution of the population?

23.4

The working population of the UK

The working population consists of those people who are employed (either as employees or self-employed persons) plus those who are registered as unemployed. In 1987 the working population was about 27 million, or approximately half of the total population. It was made up of 16 million males and 11 million females.

There was a steady increase in the size of the working population during the 1970s and 1980s. It increased by more than $1\frac{1}{2}$ million between 1971 and 1987. There were two main reasons for the increase:

1. The number of young people leaving schools and colleges to seek work exceeded the number leaving the labour force due to retirement and other reasons.
2. There was an increase in the number of people of working age who decided to join the labour force. Most of these people were women, especially married women

Occupational distribution

The most noticeable recent trends in the types of employment are set out below.

1. There has been a gradual swing from manual to non-manual occupations. This is largely due to the decline of manufacturing industry. Over the period 1966 to 1986, employment in manufacturing industry fell by 3 million.
2. The number of workers in service industries has been increasing for many years. This has been most noticeable in banking, finance, insurance, business services and the health services.
3. There has been a large increase in the number of people in part-time jobs. Many of these jobs are performed by women in the service industries, where it is easier to organise part-time employment.
4. The number of self-employed workers in the labour force has increased substantially. Many people made redundant in recent years have chosen to set up in business for themselves.

The changes in the distribution of the UK labour force over the main sectors of industry are shown in Figure 5.2 (page 31). Table 23.2 (over the page) shows recent changes in more detail.

Table 23.2
Employees in employment, by industry[1] (thousands)

	1976	1987
Agriculture, forestry, fishing	393	301
Coal, oil, gas, electricity, water supplies	721	496
Extraction of minerals other than fuels, metal manufacture, chemicals and synthetic fibres	1 157	763
Metal goods, engineering, vehicle industries	3 329	2 246
Other manufacturing industries	2 794	2 043
Construction	1 252	984
Wholesale and retail distribution, hotels, catering, repairs	3 964	4 893
Transport and communications	1 456	1 322
Banking, finance, insurance, business services	1 494	2 261
Other services	5 975	6 421
	22 535	21 730

[1] Figures do not cover all employees in local and national government. HM Forces are also excluded
Sources: *Social Trends*, HMSO, 1986; *Department of Employment Gazette*, August 1987

Question on Table 23.2
In which *service* industries was there a fall in the numbers employed? How would you account for this fall in employment?

What changes might the future bring?

The Occupations Study Group carried out a survey of some 3000 firms employing a total of 8 million workers. The firms were asked to say what changes they foresaw in their future demands for labour. The results of this survey were published in 1986. Some of the conclusions drawn from the firms' answers to the question are set out below.

1. The decline in employment in farming, manufacturing and construction is expected to continue, but more jobs will be created in the service industries.

Figure 23.4
New jobs for old: forecast changes in the UK workforce, 1985–90

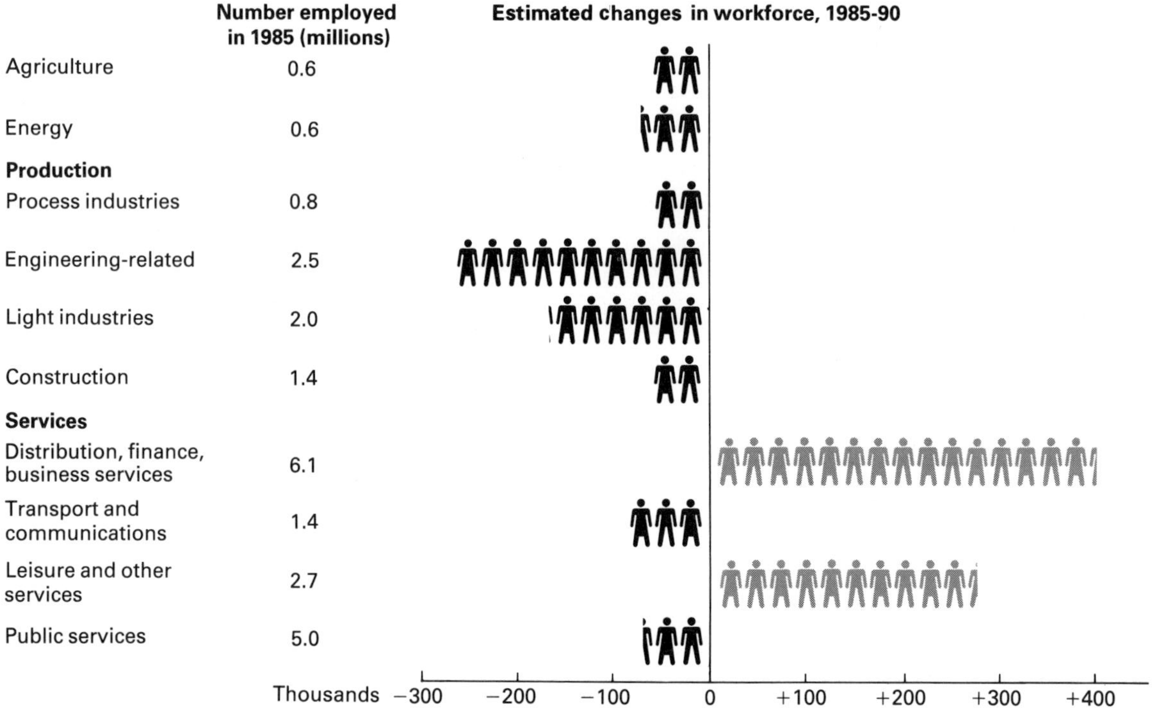

	Number employed in 1985 (millions)	Estimated changes in workforce, 1985-90
Agriculture	0.6	
Energy	0.6	
Production		
Process industries	0.8	
Engineering-related	2.5	
Light industries	2.0	
Construction	1.4	
Services		
Distribution, finance, business services	6.1	
Transport and communications	1.4	
Leisure and other services	2.7	
Public services	5.0	

Thousands −300 −200 −100 0 +100 +200 +300 +400

Sources: *The Economist*, 14 June 1986; Occupations Study Group

2. In the production industries, firms will introduce more and more new technology in order to make themselves more competitive. This means that they will require fewer workers overall, but more skilled workers.
3. Most firms expected to increase their employment of people with technical skills and professional qualifications.
4. The survey indicated that more workers will be employed by small firms – mainly because of the expected increase in the number of small firms.

The *anticipated* changes in employment are summarised in Figure 23.4. (Remember that these are only forecasts.)

The Main Points

- Birth rate = Number of live births per annum per thousand of the population

  Death rate = Number of deaths per annum per thousand of the population

  The natural rate of increase of population
  = Birth rate *minus* Death rate

- Growth rates of 2 or 3 per cent per annum will lead to large increases in the total population in comparatively short periods of time.

- World population has grown very rapidly during the present century. At its *present* rate of growth, it will double its size in about 45 years.

- After growing very rapidly during the nineteenth century, the UK population is relatively stable now. Only very slow growth is forecast for the future.

- The UK population has a large percentage of older people. Life expectancy – the average age at which death occurs – is relatively high: 75 years for men and 80 years for women.

- The dependency ratio compares the number of young and elderly people to the number in the working age groups.

- The UK has a high population density – about 600 persons per square mile. Most of the population live in urban areas, but in recent years there has been a movement of people out of the great cities.

- The occupational distribution of the working population is changing. Employment in the production industries is declining, and more people are working in the service industries.

Test Your Understanding

1. The following details refer to the population of Country X:

   At the beginning of Year 1, total population
   = 10 million
   Birth rate = 30 per thousand per annum
   Death rate = 20 per thousand per annum
   Immigration during Year 1 = 500 000
   Emigration during Year 1 = 300 000

   (a) What was the number of live births during Year 1?
   (b) What was the number of deaths during Year 1?
   (c) What was the total population at the end of Year 1?

2. This question is based on Figure 23.5.

Figure 23.5
Distribution of world population

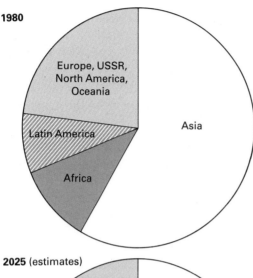

1980

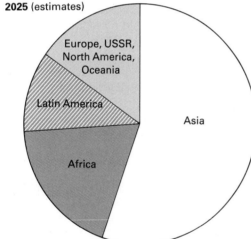

2025 (estimates)

Source: *Barclays Review*, February 1984

Say whether the following statements are true or false, and explain your answers. According to the estimates in Figure 23.5,
(a) the population of Asia will fall.
(b) the population of the world will remain the same.
(c) the percentage of the world's population living in Africa will increase.

3. The .... rate of growth of a population is obtained by subtracting the .... rate from the .... rate. What are the missing words?

4. The working population consists of
   A all those of working age
   B only those people who are in employment
   C all those in work except the self-employed
   D all employed people plus those who are registered as unemployed

Which ONE of the above statements is correct?

5. This question is based on Figure 23.6 (the figures do not apply to any particular country).

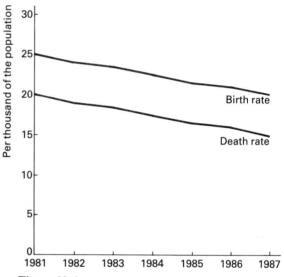

Figure 23.6

The diagram shows a steady fall in the birth rate. Does this mean that the total population is declining? Explain your answer.

6. The table below shows the numbers employed in various industries in a country.

	thousands
Agriculture	300
Insurance	200
Coal mining	350
Construction	180
Entertainment	100
Shipbuilding	190
Distribution	150
Catering	120

How many of these workers are employed in service industries?

BOX 23
Dependants and workers

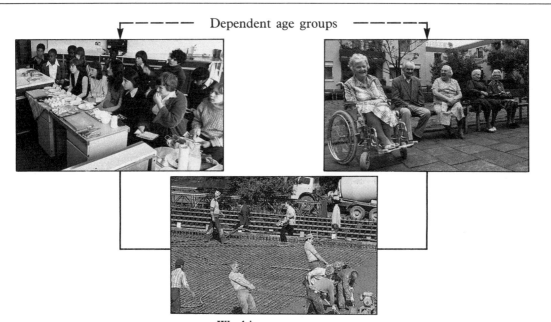

Dependent age groups

Working age groups

The main impact of low birth rates over two or three generations is an overall ageing of the population. This is happening in Europe and is raising fears about the ballooning number of elderly people to be supported by a shrinking labour force. A rising life expectancy will present governments with a much bigger pension bill.

In West Germany, there are already more than four pensioners to every ten workers; by the year 2030 their numbers will be almost equal. In 1985, Britain had 9.3 million pensioners; in 2035 the number will be 13.2 million, but the number of contributors paying for the state part of the pension will hardly change.

But the old are not the only dependants; the young are too. What is more, as societies develop, the old tend to get less dependent (because many of them stay fitter for work), while the young get more dependent (by going to school for longer).

Questions
1. What is meant by 'life expectancy'?
2. Why is it possible to forecast the future number of pensioners with reasonable accuracy?
3. Apart from an increased bill for pensions, what other items of public expenditure will be affected by an increase in the number of elderly people?
4. How would an increase in the average age at which students leave full-time education affect
   (a) the ratio of dependants to workers?
   (b) the average cost (i.e. the cost per student) of state education?

CHAPTER 24
Economic growth

24.1 The meaning and measurement of economic growth
24.2 The benefits of economic growth
24.3 The causes of economic growth
24.4 The costs of economic growth
24.5 The trade cycle
24.6 Economic growth in the UK

24.1
The meaning and measurement of economic growth

The average income of the 121 million Japanese is now higher than that of the 242 million Americans: $17 000 a year compared with $16 000. As recently as 1965, Japan's average was only a quarter of America's.
Source: *The Economist*, 25 October 1986

Economic growth refers to an increase in a country's annual output of goods and services. The measurement of output which is used to measure economic growth is normally the Gross National Product (GNP). However, the Gross Domestic Product (GDP) is also used for this purpose. Both these measures were explained on page 204.

The rate of economic growth is often used as a measurement of changes in the standard of living. This means that it is changes in *real* GNP which are important. Increases in GNP which are simply due to price increases cannot be treated as economic growth.

If changes in GNP are to be used to measure how the standard of living is changing, we must also take account of population changes. For example, if real GNP increases by 3 per cent in one year, but total population also increases by 3 per cent in the same year, there would be no change in the average standard of living. It is growth in output per person which makes higher living standards possible.

Economic growth can come about in two ways:

1. A country may have many people out of work and much capital and land lying idle. If these resources are put to work, GNP will increase. This is described as *short-run growth* because, if other things do not change, there will be no further growth once full employment has been achieved.

2. Even when all resources are fully employed, however, economic growth is still possible. Increases in the supplies of labour and capital, and increases in the efficiency with which economic resources are being used, will lead to increases in total output. This is described as *long-run growth*.

Effects of different rates of growth

Chapter 23 described how quite small annual rates of increase can lead to large increases in the total population in relatively short periods of time. This also applies to economic growth. For example, if real GNP per head increases steadily at an annual rate of 2.5 per cent, it would double in about 30 years. If this rate could be maintained, the average standard of living would quadruple in a person's lifetime. This simple example helps us to understand the remarkable transformation of the Japanese economy. Between 1964 and 1973, this economy grew at about 10 per cent per annum.

If a rich country and a poor country have the *same* rates of economic growth, the difference in their living standards will not stay the same, it will be getting larger and larger. This is made clear in the following example:

Two countries, A and B, are both growing at a rate of 5 per cent per annum.

Country A's GNP per head = £5000

Country B's GNP per head = £300

Annual growth of Country A's GNP per head = £250

Annual growth of Country B's GNP per head = £15

24.2
The benefits of economic growth

1 Improvements in living standards

The main reason for desiring economic growth is to raise the living standards of the population. During the course of the present century, economic growth has enabled millions of people to escape from destitution and poverty.

In 1980, the real income per head in the UK was four times greater than in 1870. In Japan, it was 18 times greater.

More than half of the world's population now live in great poverty. For most of these people, the economic problem is getting enough to eat. Economic growth – more output per person – offers the only real hope of raising their living standards above a bare subsistence level.

The benefits of economic growth need not be taken solely in the form of more goods and services – they can take the form of more leisure. People in the UK not only have far more goods and services available to them than their great-grandparents enjoyed, they also have a much shorter working week.

2 Better social services

When real income per head is increasing, the government will be able to raise more revenue without increasing the *rates* of taxation. People will be paying more in taxation but still be better off. This means that the government will be able to spend more on education, health and other social services without anyone being worse off.

If there is no economic growth, the government can only improve the social services by increasing taxation. Some people will be worse off, because their disposable real income will have to be reduced to pay for the increased government spending.

3 National prestige

'League tables' showing the rates of economic growth in different countries are now given a great deal of publicity in newspapers and on television. West Germany, for example, gained a great deal of prestige from the high growth rates it achieved in the 1950s and 1960s. In the modern world, a government is often judged to be successful or unsuccessful according to the country's rate of economic growth.

24.3
The causes of economic growth

A country can increase its total output of goods and services by
– using more land, labour and capital, and
– using its land, labour and capital more efficiently.

1 Capital

In all the countries which have achieved high growth rates, the stock of capital has increased faster than the number of workers. For example, in the USA, during the course of this century, the supply of labour has tripled, but the stock of capital has increased eight-fold. Providing workers with more machinery, more equipment and more power is one of the main causes of the great increases in productivity achieved by many countries in recent years.

Increasing the stock of capital is described as *net investment* – it is one of the most important causes of economic growth.

2 Labour

An increase in the number of workers makes it possible to increase a country's output. Output per head, however, is not likely to increase very much unless there are adequate supplies of land and capital to keep the additional workers fully employed.

In the richer industrialised countries, population and the labour supply are increasing very slowly. In these countries, increases in output per head depend upon improvements in the *quality* of labour, i.e. on raising its productivity.

3 Land

In agricultural countries, land is obviously a most important resource. In these countries, investments in drainage, irrigation and fertilisers, the use of more efficient farm implements, and improvements in transport can increase both the area of cultivated land and its quality.

In industrialised countries, the supply of land is a less important source of economic growth.

4 Mobility

In a changing world, a country's rate of economic growth depends very much on its willingness and ability to shift its economic resources from declining and low-growth industries to industries which have better prospects of growth. Countries which have achieved high rates of growth have been able to introduce new products, new designs and new production methods much more quickly than other countries.

5 Technical knowledge

A most important cause of economic growth is the increase in technical knowledge. This takes many forms, such as inventions, improvements in the design and performance of machinery, the development of new materials, and changes in the organisation and methods of production. For example, suppose a machine is replaced by one which is much more advanced in design and much more productive. In this case, the increase in output is not due to any change in the capital stock but to an increase in technical knowledge.

24.4
The costs of economic growth

1 Social costs

The technical efficiency which makes possible high rates of economic growth can impose some heavy social costs on the community:
– Large industrial installations such as steel works, chemical plants, power stations and major airports often destroy rural amenities and create problems with pollution and noise.
– The concentration of industry leads to the growth of large sprawling urban areas. Con-

gestion and overcrowding in these areas creates a variety of social problems.
– High rates of economic growth mean a speeding-up in the rate of technical change. Workers have to be far more mobile. More and more of them will have to change their jobs, their place of work, and the way in which they do their work. Frequent changes of this kind can be unpleasant and unsettling experiences.

2 Opportunity cost

Economic growth requires more investment – the production of more capital goods. This means that fewer resources can be used to produce consumer goods. The opportunity cost of increasing the rate of economic growth is a reduced output of consumer goods while more capital goods are being produced.

3 Non-replaceable resources

Many people are worried by the fact that our present standard of living depends very much on the use of resources which cannot be replaced. There are fixed amounts of coal, oil, iron ore and other valuable minerals in the earth's surface. The faster these resources are used up, the sooner the supplies will be exhausted.

Figure 24.1
Does this photograph show benefits or costs of economic growth?

24.5
The trade cycle

Economic growth does not proceed along a smooth upward path. It takes the form of a series of booms and slumps. In some years, total output rises very quickly; in others, it grows very slowly or might actually fall. On average, it takes very roughly five years to move from one slump to the next or from one boom to the next.

These fluctuations are described as the trade cycle. Figure 24.2 illustrates the general shape of the trade cycle, showing how an economy moves from boom to slump, and from slump to boom.

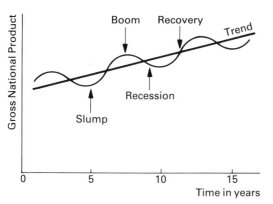

Figure 24.2
The trade cycle

24.6
Economic growth in the UK

Since the Second World War, the UK economy has grown, on average, by about $2\frac{1}{2}$ per cent per annum. This compares unfavourably with some other industrialised countries. Even so, it still compares favourably with the average growth rates achieved by the UK in earlier periods. Remember that the $2\frac{1}{2}$ per cent is an average figure. In some years the growth was as high as 8 per cent; in others it was negative.

During the present century, its relatively slow rate of growth has caused the UK to slip down the 'league table' which ranks countries according to their real GNP per head. When the Second World War ended, the UK's GNP per head was second

Figure 24.3
Average annual growth rates of real Gross Domestic Product, 1960–85

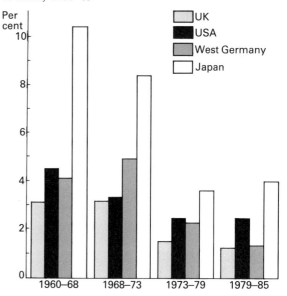

Source: *Historical Statistics, 1960–85*, OECD, Paris

only to that of America, and was well ahead of the GNPs per head of Germany, France and Japan. By the 1980s, however, Britain had dropped to eighteenth in the world rankings. Figure 24.3 shows the average annual growth rates, since 1960, for the UK and some other major industrialised countries.

In the 1980s Britain's growth rate compared quite favourably with rates achieved by other industrialised countries. Some reasons why it tended to lag behind several other countries for much of the post-war period are set out below.

1 Investment

Britain's rate of investment in new capital equipment has tended to be less than that of several other industrialised countries. Just as important, however, is the fact that much of this investment has been devoted to propping up declining industries. Several of Britain's competitors have put more investment into high technology industries producing advanced products of high quality.

2 Productivity and labour costs

Until the 1980s, wages in the UK tended to rise faster than in similar countries, but its productivity rose more slowly. The result was that Britain's labour costs tended to rise more rapidly than those of countries with which it had to compete. For example, between 1974 and 1984 wage costs per unit of output in British manufacturing industry rose by about 200 per cent, compared with 25 per cent in Germany and 50 per cent in the USA.

3 Inflation and the balance of payments

There have been several periods since the Second World War when the government has had to reduce the total demand for goods and services. These actions were necessary to deal with increasing rates of inflation and serious balance of payments deficits. Restricting the demand for goods and services obviously puts a brake on the rate of economic growth.

The Main Points

- Economic growth refers to an increase in a country's total output of goods and services, i.e. an increase in real GNP.

- Short-run growth occurs when unemployed resources are put to work. Long-run growth is possible when there is an increase in the supplies of the factors of production, and/or economic resources are used more efficiently.

- Quite small annual rates of economic growth, if maintained, can lead to great improvements in the standard of living in a person's lifetime.

- The causes of economic growth are complex. There is little doubt, however, that increases in the stock of capital, improvements in the productivity of labour, increases in technical knowledge, and a greater mobility of labour and capital all play important parts in determining the rate of economic growth.

- Economic growth has its costs as well as its benefits. There are social costs in the forms of pollution, noise and congestion, and the unsettling effects of frequent changes in the organisation and methods of production. Technical progress may make workers redundant as well as machines.

- In the post-war years the British economy grew more rapidly than it had in the past. However, its rate of growth was less than that achieved by several other industrialised countries.

Test Your Understanding

Use the following terms to complete the sentences in questions 1–5:

per head   *net investment*
leisure   *non-replaceable*
mobility

1. A country experiencing a high rate of economic growth may take some of the benefits in the form of increased ....

2. We can obtain some idea of what is happening to the average standard of living by looking at what is happening to real GNP ....

3. An increase in the stock of capital (a major cause of economic growth) is described as ....

4. An increase in the rate of economic growth requires an increase in the .... of the factors of production.

5. When economic growth is taking place, more and more oil and other valuable minerals are being used up. This worries some people because these resources are ....

6. In one year, the GNP of a country was £1000 million and its population was 500 000. A few years later, its GNP was £1500 million and its population had risen to 600 000. There was no change in the average price level during this period.
   (a) What change had taken place in the country's real GNP?
   (b) What had happened to the average standard of living – had it risen or fallen?

7. Give three or four examples of *replaceable* resources.

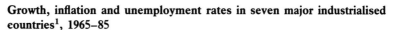

Growth, inflation and unemployment

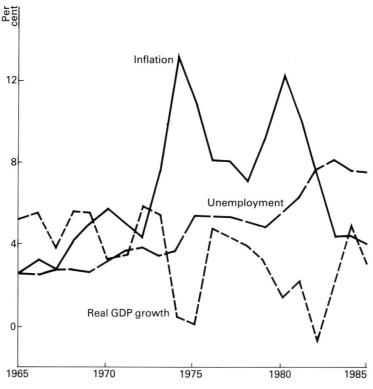

Growth, inflation and unemployment rates in seven major industrialised countries[1], 1965–85

[1] Data are for Canada, France, Germany, Italy, Japan, the UK and the USA

Source: World Bank Development Report, 1986; OECD, Paris

Questions
1. What name is given to the fluctuations in the growth of real GDP?
2. What, approximately, was the average rate of growth experienced by these countries over the period 1965–85?
3. Can you think of any reasons why high rates of inflation should be associated with serious falls in the rates of economic growth?
4. Between 1965 and 1985, despite the fact that there was some economic growth in almost every year, unemployment increased steadily. Suggest one reason why this happened.

CHAPTER 25
Economic development

25.1 Developed and developing countries
25.2 Major problems facing developing countries
25.3 Aid to developing countries
25.4 Foreign trade and developing countries
25.5 The World Bank

25.1
Developed and developing countries

There are some five billion people in the world, and the majority of them live in what are described as *less developed countries* or *developing countries*. A developing country is one in which the average standard of living is very low compared with living standards in North America and Western Europe. The low-income developing countries are often described as *Third World* countries. Countries which have high standards of living – mainly industrialised countries – are described as *developed countries*.

Probably the most striking feature of the world economy is the very great difference between the average incomes of people in the developed countries and those in developing countries. For

Figure 25.1
Shares of the world's population living in countries with different levels of GNP per head

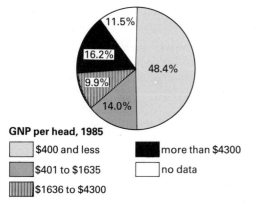

GNP per head, 1985

☐ $400 and less	■ more than $4300	
▨ $401 to $1635	☐ no data	
⦀ $1636 to $4300		

Source: *World Bank Atlas*, 1987

example, in 1985, GNP per head in the USA was $16 690, but GNP per head in Pakistan was $380. The average US citizen, therefore, enjoyed an

Table 25.1
The developed and developing worlds, 1985

Developing countries

Low-income countries
GNP per head is less than $400.
The total population in these countries was about 2.5 billion in 1985.

Examples:	Country	GNP per head
	Bangladesh	$150
	India	$270
	China	$310
	Pakistan	$380

Middle-income countries
GNP per head is between $400 and $5000.
The total population in these countries was about 1.2 billion in 1985.

Examples:	Country	GNP per head
	Egypt	$610
	Turkey	$1080
	Mexico	$2080
	Greece	$3550

Developed countries
GNP per head is more than $5000.
The total population in these countries was about 800 million in 1985.

Examples:	Country	GNP per head
	UK	$8 460
	Japan	$11 300
	Sweden	$11 890
	USA	$16 690

Source: *World Bank Development Report*, 1987

Figure 25.2
Distribution of GNP per head, 1985

GNP per head, 1985
- $400 and less
- $401 to $1635
- $1636 to $4300
- more than $4300
- no data

Source: *World Bank Atlas*, 1987

income 40 times greater than the average citizen of Pakistan.

Figure 25.1 shows how very unequally world income is distributed. Nearly half of the world's population lives in countries where the average annual income per head is $400 or less. The richer countries contain about 25 per cent of the world's population but they produce about 75 per cent (by value) of the world's output.

The geographical distribution of developed and developing countries

Figure 25.2 shows how the richer developed countries are heavily concentrated in the northern hemisphere – in North America, Europe and Japan. Although it is not included in Figure 25.2, the USSR should also be included in this group of countries. The low-income developing countries are very much concentrated in Asia, Africa and South America.

Table 25.1 gives more details of the way in which GNP per head varies between countries. It also tells us the approximate numbers of people living in the developed and less developed regions of the world. (Differences in GNP per head are often taken as rough indications of differences in living standards.)

Question on Figure 25.2
Can you suggest one reason why most of the low-income countries tend to be concentrated in the tropics?

Question on Table 25.1
Money values in international statistics are expressed in terms of the US dollar. In 1985, the average exchange rate was about £1 = $1.3. Use this rate of exchange to convert the GNPs per head of (a) India, (b) Mexico, (c) the UK and (d) the USA into pounds sterling.

Other measures of the standard of living

GNP per head is an average figure, and for many countries it is only a very rough estimate. GNP only measures output which goes through the market, i.e. what is bought and sold. In many developing countries, people grow their own food, make their own clothes and provide their own shelters. GNP per head may, therefore, underestimate their real incomes. Nevertheless, the differences between developed and developing countries are very great indeed.

Table 25.2 (over the page) gives details of some other measurements which can be used to obtain an idea of a country's standard of living.

Table 25.2
Some other indicators of living standards

Country	Life expectancy at birth (1985)	Infant mortality rate (1985)	Population per doctor (1981)	Number enrolled in secondary schools, as a percentage of the age group (1984)
Ethiopia	45	168	88 000	12
Kenya	54	91	10 000	19
Brazil	65	67	1 300	35
Mexico	67	50	1 200	55
Australia	78	9	500	94

Source: *World Bank Development Report*, 1987

The gap has been getting wider

The large gap in living standards between rich and poor countries can only be reduced if GNP *per head* in the poorer countries grows faster than GNP per head in the richer countries. This has not been happening.

The large increases in population which have been taking place in the low-income countries have meant that output *per person* has been rising much more slowly than total output. The example on page 241 clearly shows that even if rich and poor countries grow at the same rate, the gap in living standards will continue to widen.

Developing countries – some differences

Poverty is a feature of all developing countries, but there are many differences between them:

1. Some are very primitive, but others such as China and India have civilisations which are much older than those in Western countries.
2. Some developing countries have good supplies of natural resources, but many others have unfavourable climates, little fertile land and few valuable mineral deposits.
3. Some of these countries are densely populated but others have vast open spaces.
4. A number of developing countries are making good economic progress; in others, the rate of growth of GNP is extremely slow.

25.2

Major problems facing developing countries

1 Low-productivity agriculture

In low-income countries, 70 per cent or more of the labour force works on the land. Tractors and other types of mechanical farm equipment are very scarce. The output per worker in agriculture is extremely low compared with that in Europe and North America.

Figure 25.3
Agricultural land severely affected by drought

2 Poor natural resources

Many developing countries have very poor supplies of natural resources. Features common to many of them are soil lacking in fertility, large desert areas and climates which are not favourable to high productivity because they are too dry or too hot. Some of the developing countries which have grown at an encouraging rate have been fortunate enough to possess valuable mineral deposits such as oil.

3 A shortage of capital

Developing countries are severely handicapped by their lack of electricity supplies, water supplies, transport and farming equipment, good roads and railways, port facilities, and other capital goods. They have very little modern technology – human beings and animals do virtually all the work in agriculture, and handicraft methods dominate small-scale industry.

4 Large-scale unemployment and underemployment

In developing countries, the rapid growth of population has been accompanied by a large-scale movement of people from the rural areas to the towns and cities. This has created serious unemployment problems in these urban areas, especially among the younger age groups.

Figure 25.4
Capital is scarce in developing countries

Underemployment, or disguised unemployment, is also a serious problem. For example, ten people may be employed in a job for which only six are needed. This situation applies especially in agriculture where peasant holdings are very small but all the members of the peasant's family work on the family plot.

5 A low-productivity labour force

Workers are lacking in education and especially in technical training. This, together with relatively low standards of health (especially in tropical regions), often means a low level of physical performance.

6 Population growth

In the great majority of developing countries, the rate of population growth is very much higher than it is in developed countries. This means that it is difficult for them to achieve increases in GNP *per head*.

Figure 25.5
Birth and death rates, 1950–80: the graphs show why population growth rates are high in developing countries and low in developed countries

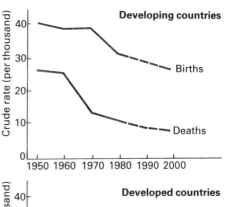

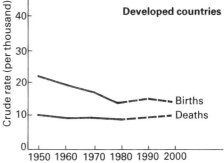

Source: *Finance and Development*, IMF and the World Bank, September 1984

If a country's population is growing at 3 per cent per annum, then total output will have to grow at 3 per cent per annum in order for the country to 'stand still', i.e. just to maintain the existing standard of living.

7 Social barriers

In societies where most people lack education and where the way of life has been unchanged for centuries, social customs, religious beliefs and superstitions may be barriers to economic growth. It will be difficult to persuade people in such societies to accept the kinds of changes in their way of life which might be necessary if they are to achieve a good rate of economic growth.

Progress is being made

In spite of all the difficulties facing them, developing countries are managing to achieve increases in GNP per head. New technologies applied to agriculture have helped to increase food production faster than population has been growing.

A further encouraging sign is that population growth rates have begun to fall in many of the less developed regions of the world. In spite of this, world population will continue to grow for many years to come.

25.3
Aid to developing countries

The developing countries will need a great deal of help from the richer countries if they are to make satisfactory economic progress. There are two main arguments for helping the poorer countries:

Humanitarian motives

The fortunate minority of the world's population who live in the developed countries should and do feel moved to help those who are so much worse off.

Economic motives

If the developing countries become more efficient and more prosperous, the people in the developed countries will benefit as well as those in developing countries. As incomes rise in the poorer countries, they will be able to buy more goods and services from the developed countries.

Economic aid can take many forms.

1 Gifts of food

Food surpluses from North America, Western Europe and other regions are distributed to poorer countries, especially when these countries have been badly affected by drought or floods.

2 Loans and grants

Developing countries are very dependent on imports of materials, machinery, oil and, in many cases, foodstuffs. These imports must be paid for in foreign currency. In most cases, the exports of the developing countries do not earn sufficient foreign currency to pay for the imports they need in order to make economic progress. They depend very much on loans and grants from the wealthier countries. Some loans may be arranged on commercial terms, i.e. at market rates of interest. Other loans, known as 'soft loans', are arranged on concessionary terms, i.e. at well below the market rate of interest.

Grants (i.e. gifts) and concessionary loans are usually provided by governments or by international agencies such as the World Bank, the IMF, the United Nations, the EEC and OPEC (the Organisation of Petroleum Exporting Countries).

Commercial loans are supplied by various banking organisations in the developed countries. Several developing countries have borrowed very heavily from the commercial banks and are now finding it very difficult to meet their annual interest payments and to make repayments of these loans.

3 Technical assistance

The industrialised nations send technical experts to advise and assist developing countries. In some cases, developed countries undertake to build such things as steelworks, chemical plants, power stations, roads, railways and port facilities in the poorer countries as a form of economic aid.

4 Education and training

Teachers and instructors are supplied to developing countries to help raise their standards of education and training. Students from these countries are also granted scholarships so that they can study in developed countries.

5 Direct foreign investment

One way in which the stock of capital in poor countries can be increased is by foreign firms setting up factories, mines, quarries, etc. in these countries.

25.4
Foreign trade and developing countries

If developing countries are to make progress and become less dependent on foreign aid, they must increase their exports. This is the only way they can earn the foreign currency they need to buy all the things they must import from the developed countries.

They face problems, however, because many of them export primary products for which the demands are inelastic. For example, large increases in the world supplies of products such as coffee, cocoa, tea and sugar would almost certainly lead to a substantial fall in their prices. Producers of these commodities would gain little, if anything, from large increases in production.

There is also a problem when developing countries begin to export manufactured products. Workers in developed countries often regard manufactured goods from low-income countries as 'unfair' competition, because they are produced by workers who receive very low wages. There are usually demands for such imports to be restricted by tariffs and quotas. Nevertheless, some developing countries have proved to be extremely efficient producers of manufactured goods and have become major exporters. South Korea, Taiwan, Singapore, Hong Kong and Brazil are well-known examples.

25.5
The World Bank

This is a sister institution to the IMF and was set up at the same time. It now has some 150 member countries.

While the IMF exists to provide short-term loans to nations with balance of payments difficulties, the purpose of the World Bank is to provide long-term loans to assist economic development. In its early years, it was engaged in helping to finance the reconstruction of war-damaged Europe. Nowadays its main role is to channel flows of capital from the rich countries of Western Europe, North America, Japan and the rich oil producers to the poor and mainly agricultural countries of Africa, Asia and South America.

It finances projects such as roads, railways, communications, power stations, water supplies, irrigation and rural development. Its financial assistance takes the form of long-term loans. It obtains some of its funds in the form of subscriptions from member countries. Most of the money it lends, however, is obtained by borrowing on the world's capital markets.

An affiliate of the World Bank – the International Development Association (IDA) – offers *soft* loans to the extremely poor countries. These loans are interest-free in many cases.

In addition to financial help, the World Bank can supply a variety of financial and technical services to developing countries. Its engineers, surveyors, accountants, economists and other experts are prepared to help countries plan and carry out their development projects.

The Main Points

- Most of the world's population lives in developing countries, sometimes known as Third World countries. These countries are found mainly in Asia, Africa and South America.

- There are enormous differences between the standards of living in developing countries and those in high-income industrialised countries.

- Features common to many developing countries are
  - a high rate of population growth,
  - climates unfavourable to high productivity in agriculture,
  - a serious shortage of capital, and
  - a poorly educated and largely untrained labour force.

- In spite of great difficulties, many less developed countries are managing to increase their output per head, but the gap between rich and poor countries tends to grow wider.

- There are also signs that the rates of population growth in Third World countries are beginning to decline.

- Developed countries and international agencies provide aid to developing countries in the forms of loans, grants, technical assistance, education and training, and gifts of food in emergencies.

- Developing countries experience difficulties in trying to increase their exports. Manufactured goods from developing countries may face restrictions in developed countries because workers in these countries tend to regard these goods as 'unfair competition'. Furthermore, many primary products exported from developing countries have inelastic demands.

Test Your Understanding

1. Why is the rate of increase of output per head much less than the rate of increase of total output in many developing countries?

2. Which of the following countries are (a) developed countries, and which are (b) developing countries?

Denmark	Austria	Jamaica
Burma	New Zealand	Norway
Ghana	Morocco	

3. Most farmers in developing countries have had no form of technical training, and their farms tend to be very small. What kind of capital equipment might be most useful in helping them to raise their productivity?

4. What is meant by the *social barriers* to economic growth?

5. Why would a rise in the world prices of manufactured goods and a fall in the world prices of primary products prove to be serious handicaps to many developing countries?

BOX 25
The World Bank and economic development

Tea being sifted in Sri Lanka

The Bank has historically developed as a lender for investment. I intend to see that we go on to do it even better.

We have seen in Asia and Africa, in Latin America and in parts of Europe, how the foundation for growth is laid in the concrete of dams, in the asphalt of roads, in power and communications lines, and in the fertile soil of educated minds.

High population growth rates strain both natural and financial resources. Environmental neglect destroys assets vital not just to the quality of life but to life itself.

Women do two-thirds of the world's work. They produce 60 to 80 per cent of Africa's and Asia's food, 40 per cent of Latin America's. Yet they earn only one-tenth of the world's income and own less than one per cent of the world's property. They are among the poorest of the world's poor.

We cannot provide leadership for sustained development without providing leadership, as well, to restrain overpopulation, to balance growth with environmental protection, and to match the contributions women make with contributions to their welfare.

Source: Extracts from a speech given by the President of the World Bank, 1986

Questions
1. How does a high rate of population growth put a strain on natural resources?
2. Give some examples of what is meant by 'environmental neglect'.
3. Which statement indicates that investment in people is just as important as investment in capital goods?
4. In addition to their work on the land, what other aspects of life in developing countries place a heavy burden on women?

CHAPTER 26

Coursework

26.1 Some general guidelines
26.2 An example – the pricing of electricity

The aim of this chapter is to provide some information and helpful advice on the various tasks which you will need to undertake in order to produce a piece of coursework. The chapter is divided into two sections:

– Section 26.1 contains some general guidelines on what is expected of you, and on the methods of obtaining, presenting and analysing information on your chosen topic.
– Section 26.2 consists of an example of a piece of coursework on the pricing of electricity. The purpose here is to show how the procedures outlined in Section 26.1 may be applied to a particular topic.

26.1
Some general guidelines

Using your knowledge of economics

Coursework is an important part of the GCSE examination in economics. It should, therefore, bring out some of the *economic* aspects of the subject you are investigating. You should be looking for opportunities to use your knowledge of such matters as supply and demand, markets, specialisation, economies of scale, different types of cost, influences on the location of firms, and so on.

Deciding what information you need

This needs careful thought. You will need to draw up a plan which shows how you propose to deal with the topic.

It is advisable to think of the main features of the subject you intend to study. Make each of these features a heading of a particular section of the work, and then arrange these headings in a sensible and logical sequence. For example, if you are writing about the car industry, the production of cars would come before the marketing of cars.

When you have decided on the headings and arranged them in a sensible order, you can then fill in, under each heading, the kind of information you need on each of these separate features of the topic.

The sources of information

There are two main ways of getting the information you need.

1 Fieldwork

This method provides first-hand information. It requires you to go out and meet and question the people who are carrying out the activities you intend to study. It also requires you to observe carefully what is taking place in the factory, office, shop, market, farm or whatever type of organisation it is that is the subject of your coursework.

You will need to make careful notes of what you hear and see. You will need prior permission to interview people, and you must make sure that you go with well-prepared and carefully thought-out questions. Whatever topic you select, it is necessary to begin by doing some background reading. You must have some knowledge of the subject before you can prepare sensible questions for your fieldwork.

2 Published material

For some topics, there will be little opportunity for fieldwork. Where this is the case, you will need to obtain most of the information you need from various publications – books, journals, magazines, newspapers, government publications and so on.

The public lending and reference libraries are excellent sources of information because they hold large stocks of books covering a wide range of subjects. Of particular importance is the fact that the public reference libraries carry a wide range of current periodicals. Trade journals, for example, could be of particular interest. Whether you are studying a firm in a primary industry, a manufacturing industry or a service industry, you are very likely to find a trade journal, published weekly or monthly, which describes recent developments in that industry.

The reference libraries also carry a range of government publications which give up-to-date information on all aspects of the economy. A short list of such publications is given at the end of this section.

A polite letter of enquiry to a firm, government department or local authority may also provide you with some of the information you are seeking. It is, however, advisable to seek the advise of your teacher on this particular source of information.

It is most important that you make careful notes on the sources of information which you intend to use, because you will be required to say how and where you obtained the facts and figures which your coursework contains.

Presenting the information

There are various ways of presenting the information you have gathered. Much of your work will probably be presented in written form. It is, of course, very necessary to present the results of your study in a sensible sequence. If you have planned your work under a series of headings, as suggested earlier, you can use this plan to present the finished work.

Within this planned layout you should use a variety of ways of presenting your information. To support the written work, you could use graphs (line graphs, bar graphs and pie charts), tables, maps, other types of diagram and photographs. All of these ways of presenting information have been used in this book.

Your work will have a much more interesting appearance if you use several different methods of presenting your information.

Analysing and explaining the results of your survey

This is an important part of the coursework. You will be expected to summarise the results of your study and to identify the more important economic features you have discovered. In giving your overall impressions, you should try to use your knowledge of economics to analyse the facts and figures you have accumulated.

In the earlier sections of the coursework you will have been *describing* the things you have heard, seen and read about. In this section of the work, you are being asked to say something about the *causes* and *effects* of the situations you have described.

Some examples may help to make this a little clearer.

Example 1

You have been collecting information on, and describing the changes in, the price of some particular commodity, such as coffee, sugar or fresh vegetables.

A knowledge of economics tells you that these price changes come about because of *changes in demand, changes in supply* or *changes in both*. It will be necessary therefore, to look for *evidence* of changes in demand and/or supply. Having obtained this evidence, you should then try to find out what *caused* these changes in demand and/or supply.

You can then say something about the likely *effects* of these price changes.

Example 2

The topic requires you to describe and account for the recent changes in the structure of retailing in your neighbourhood. After collecting and presenting information on these changes, you will need to discuss the causes and effects of these changes.

A knowledge of economics can help you to explain some of them by using the following ideas:

1. *Economies of scale* – this idea should help to explain the increasing importance of super-stores, supermarkets and the large multiple stores.
2. *Location* – why have so many retail outlets moved to sites on the outskirts of cities?
3. *Rising real incomes* – how has the growth in the ownership of motor cars and freezers affected the structure of retailing?
4. *Demand for variety* – are consumers demanding more choice? If so, how has it affected the retail trade?
5. *Convenience and personal attention* – do these features explain the survival of the small independent retailer?

Example 3

This topic concerns the costs of owning and running a motor car. You will have obtained information on the various costs of owning and running, say, an expensive car, a medium-priced car and a low-priced car. You will need to classify and analyse these costs, using the following ideas:

1. *Opportunity cost*, e.g. the loss of interest when money is withdrawn from savings in order to purchase the car.
2. *Fixed costs*, e.g. taxation, insurance and, most important, depreciation.
3. *Variable costs*, i.e. those costs which tend to vary directly with the mileage.
4. *Average cost*, i.e. the cost per mile – the total cost divided by the mileage.

Further analysis might lead to explanations of why

- the cost per mile tends to fall as the mileage increases,
- the fixed costs are a much greater proportion of total costs for an expensive car than for a low-priced car, and
- running costs are much higher for urban journeys than for rural journeys.

In giving your summary and expressing your opinions, you must be careful to provide some good evidence and sound reasons for the particular views you express.

Useful official publications

Social Trends (published annually)

For the purposes of the GCSE examination, this is probably the best source of information about the economic and social conditions in the UK. The information is easy to find and easy to understand, and is presented in a most interesting manner.

Department of Employment Gazette (published monthly)

This contains information and statistics on such matters as employment, unemployment, wages, earnings, labour costs and many other aspects of the labour market. It also includes information on the changes in retail prices.

Economic Progress Report (published every two months)

This publication gives summaries of the main changes in the economy, together with a more detailed article on some particular topic.

The Annual Abstract of Statistics

This book contains a most comprehensive collection of statistics on all aspects of life and work in the UK.

The Monthly Digest of Statistics

This is an excellent source of up-to-date information about the economy.

Useful local sources

A very wide range of booklets and leaflets which would be useful to GCSE candidates are available from various local offices. Some examples are given below.

1. *The local tax office* will have leaflets explaining the various types of personal taxation and other forms of taxation.
2. *The city or county council offices* can provide leaflets which explain
   - the rating system,
   - other forms of local authority income, and
   - how the authority spends its income.

3. *The local Job Centre* has various publications which explain the many different government training schemes.
4. *Consumer Advice Centres* will supply booklets and pamplets which offer advice on the buying of goods and services. The information provided helps consumers in many ways. For example, there are booklets and pamphlets which
    – explain the ways in which the law protects consumers against unfair trading practices which may be used by the sellers of goods and services,
    – describe the procedures for buying a house and obtaining a mortgage,
    – give useful information on the various kinds of insurance,
    – describe the various ways in which goods and services can be bought on credit (e.g. hire purchase), and offer sensible advice on how to use this method of buying things.

26.2
An example – the pricing of electricity

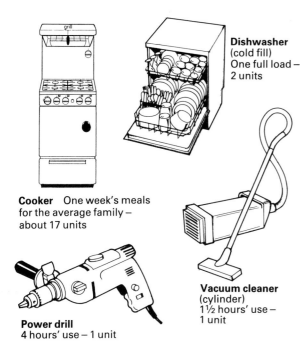

Cooker One week's meals for the average family – about 17 units

Dishwasher (cold fill) One full load – 2 units

Vacuum cleaner (cylinder) 1½ hours' use – 1 unit

Power drill 4 hours' use – 1 unit

Figure 1

Introduction

The consumption of electricity is measured in *units*. Each unit of electricity provides a certain amount of lighting, or heating, or power. Figure 1 gives some examples of the rates at which different appliances use up units of electricity.

Although all units of electricity are identical, they are not all sold at the same price. The different systems of pricing electricity are described as *tariffs*. The purpose of this study is to examine the different tariffs and to discuss the economic reasons for charging different prices for the same product (i.e. a unit of electricity).

Electricity in the home

The Domestic tariff

This tariff has two parts:

1. A quarterly standing charge. This is a fixed payment which must be made however much electricity is used.
2. A price for each unit of electricity consumed.

These two features of the Domestic tariff are listed separately in the bill shown in Figure 2 (overleaf).

Under this system, the *average cost* of electricity falls as more of it is consumed. The following examples make this clear. In both of them, assume that the standing charge is £7.50 per quarter and the price per unit is 6p.

Example 1

In one quarter, 1000 units are consumed.

Standing charge	= £7.50
Cost of 1000 units	= £60.00
Total quarterly payment	= £67.50

Average cost per unit = £67.50 ÷ 1000 = 6.75p

Example 2

In one quarter, 3000 units are consumed.

Standing charge	= £7.50
Cost of 3000 units	= £180.00
Total quarterly payment	= £187.50

Average cost per unit = £187.50 ÷ 3000 = 6.25p

Figure 2

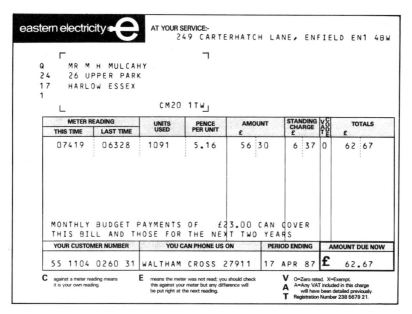

Q   MR M H MULCAHY
24   26 UPPER PARK
17   HARLOW ESSEX
1
                    CM20 1TW

METER READING		UNITS USED	PENCE PER UNIT	AMOUNT £	STANDING CHARGE £	VAT	TOTALS £
THIS TIME	LAST TIME						
07419	06328	1091	5.16	56 30	6 37	0	62 67

MONTHLY BUDGET PAYMENTS OF £23.00 CAN COVER
THIS BILL AND THOSE FOR THE NEXT TWO YEARS

YOUR CUSTOMER NUMBER	YOU CAN PHONE US ON	PERIOD ENDING	AMOUNT DUE NOW
55 1104 0260 31	WALTHAM CROSS 27911	17 APR 87	£ 62.67

C against a meter reading means it is your own reading.

E means the meter was not read; you should check this against your meter but any difference will be put right at the next reading.

V A T O=Zero rated. X=Exempt.
A=Any VAT included in this charge will have been detailed previously.
Registration Number 238 5679 21.

The Domestic Economy 7 tariff

This tariff provides electricity for seven hours at night-time at a much cheaper rate than normal daytime electricity. For example, in 1987 a typical Economy 7 tariff was supplying night-time electricity at 1.9p per unit compared with 5.45p for units consumed during the day.

The tariff requires the installation of a special two-rate meter, which records consumption at the cheaper rate and consumption at the dearer rate.

The Economy 7 tariff gives you 7 hours of less than half-price electricity every night.
On Economy 7 all the electricity you use during the overnight period is charged at the special cheap rate. So the more electricity you use during the night period the more you can save on your electricity bills!

Figure 3

Electricity for industry, commerce, farms, etc.

The electricity tariffs for industry are more complicated than those for households. They take into account

- the type of electricity used – whether it is high-voltage or low-voltage,
- the maximum demand and when it occurs, and
- any special metering or equipment which the electricity board may have to install.

Nevertheless, these tariffs contain similar features to the Domestic tariff. There is some form of standing charge, and electricity consumed at night is supplied at lower prices.

For smaller firms, there are tariffs which offer cheaper electricity during the evenings and at week-ends. An Economy 7 tariff is also available for smaller businesses. This tariff has four parts. A typical example is given below.

1. A standing charge of £11.73 per quarter.
2. A price of 7.46p per unit for the first 750 units.
3. A price of 5.45p per unit for each additional unit.
4. A price of 1.9p per unit for each unit supplied during the night.

This tariff is illustrated in Figure 4.

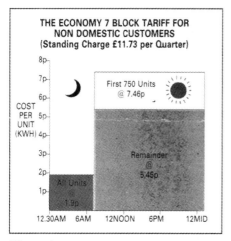

Figure 4

Economic features of the different tariffs

1 Reasons for the standing charge

The reason for the standing charge is the fact that, in order to supply households and firms with electricity,
– mains have to be laid,
– premises have to be connected to the mains,
– meters have to be installed, and
– meters have to be read at regular intervals.

To the electricity boards, all these items are *fixed costs*. They remain the same whether the household or firm consumes a great deal of electricity or very little.

The purpose of the standing charge, therefore, is to cover all or some of these fixed costs.

2 Reasons for having different prices at different times

The total demand for electricity varies greatly according to the time of day, the day of the week and the time of year.

Daytime and night-time

During the day, when people are at work in factories, offices, shops and other types of business, there will be a high demand for electricity. This high demand occurs between 7.30 am and

7.30 pm. A large percentage of the population finishes work between 5 pm and 7 pm, so in the evening, the demand for electricity will drop quite sharply. During the night, say from midnight until 6.30 am, the demand for electricity will be very low.

Week-ends

Since a large percentage of firms work a five-day week, the demand for electricity at week-ends will be much less than the demand from Monday to Friday.

Summer and winter

The colder weather and longer nights cause the total demand for electricity to be very much higher in the winter than in the summer.

3 Large changes in demand increase the costs of producing electricity

The power stations must have generators which are capable of meeting the peak demands which occur during the day from Monday to Friday. In the off-peak periods – evenings, night-time and week-ends – the power stations will have some of their generators lying idle or working well below their full capacity.

The problem is that the heavy *fixed costs* of boilers, generators and other equipment must be met whether they are producing electricity or not. These fixed costs consist of such items as depreciation, interest on loans, rent, insurance and some labour costs (since the power stations must be manned all the time).

If the total demand for electricity could be spread out evenly throughout the day, throughout the week and throughout the year, the electricity authorities would not need so much plant and equipment. They could have a smaller capacity to produce electricity which could be fully utilised at all times instead of a much larger capacity which is grossly underutilised for long periods.

In other words, if demand did not vary so widely, the fixed costs of producing electricity would be much lower.

Figure 5 shows quite clearly how the demand for electricity varies
- throughout a period of 24 hours,
- according to the day of the week (demand is much lower on Sundays), and
- between winter and summer.

Figure 5

Summer and winter demands on the CEGB system in 1985–86, including days of maximum and minimum demand

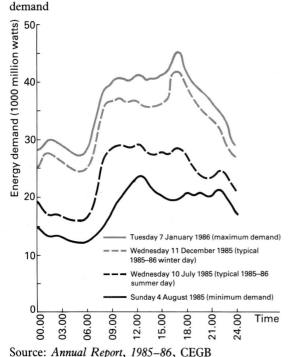

Source: *Annual Report, 1985–86*, CEGB

4 Using different prices to change the pattern of demand

Several of the electricity tariffs are designed to spread out the load on the power stations. Different prices are charged so as to persuade people to use more electricity during off-peak periods and less during the peak periods.

For example, the Economy 7 tariffs explained earlier offer much cheaper electricity to households and firms during the night hours. Another Economy 7 tariff for small businesses offers cheaper electricity during the evening, at night-time *and* at week-ends. This tariff is illustrated in Figure 6.

5 Why electricity can be sold at different prices

Why are the electricity boards able to charge different prices for the same product, i.e. a unit of electricity?

The main reason is the fact that, unlike most other commodities, electricity cannot be stored; it is used up the instant it is produced. This means that consumers cannot buy electricity at the cheaper rates (during the night), and then use it later, when electricity prices are higher (during the day).

The electricity boards are able to use meters which record the consumption of electricity which takes place at different times. They can, therefore, charge different prices.

Summary

Most consumers of electricity pay some kind of standing charge. The purpose of this standing charge is to help cover the fixed costs of the mains, cables, meters, etc. which are necessary to bring electricity into the premises occupied by households and firms.

Electricity boards have to deal with the difficult problems caused by the great variations in the demand for electricity. The demand varies according to the time of day, the day of the week and the time of year.

Many other industries suffer from variations in demand, but they can overcome the problem because the goods they produce can be stored. The firms can produce at a fairly constant daily rate. In times of low demand, some of the output can be placed in stocks. In times of high demand, the firms can increase supply by taking goods out of stock.

This is not possible with electricity. Power stations have to be big enough to meet the peak demands. During off-peak periods, therefore, some plant and equipment will be lying idle or grossly underutilised. But when this expensive equipment is either not producing electricity or not being fully used, the fixed costs still have to be covered. These costs do not change whether the generators are working or not.

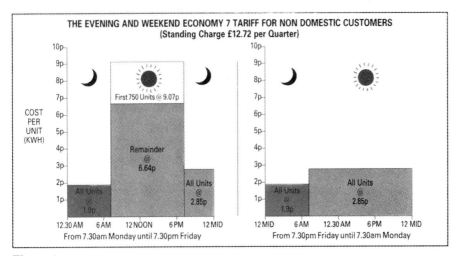

Figure 6

If the demand for electricity could be evenly spread over each 24 hours, less generating equipment would be required, and fixed costs would be much lower. The electricity boards cannot eliminate the problem of peak demand, but they do try to reduce it. They encourage households and firms to use more electricity during off-peak periods and less during the peak periods. They do this by offering to supply electricity at lower prices in the evening, at night and at week-ends.

This particular problem is not peculiar to the electricity industry. The industries supplying telephone services and railway passenger transport have to deal with the same kind of problem. These industries also try to deal with the problem in a similar manner – they charge lower prices for services supplied during off-peak periods.

Sources

1. The local Electricity Board – pamphlets and leaflets.
2. The Central Electricity Generating Board – annual reports.
3. The family's quarterly electricity bills.

Index

Answers to selected questions

Chapter 2
3. A, B and C   7. (b) £0.5 million

Chapter 3
1. C, D and E   2. A and D   3. C

Chapter 4
1. (a) C (b) A (c) A (d) B (e) C
2. (a) Family B (b) Family A   3. C
4. (a) £227 (b) £207

Chapter 5
2. B and D   3. D

Chapter 6
1. B and D
2. TP = 220, AP = 110, MP = 140
4. 3   5. C   6. £5

Chapter 7
5. A   6. A and C   7. B and C

Chapter 8
5. C   6. D
8. (c) £240 (e) £8 (f) 60 units

Chapter 9
1. B and C   2. 2   4. A and C
5. A and C

Chapter 10
4. (a) D (b) A (c) C

Chapter 11
5. (a) A and B (b) B (c) C   6. C
7. (a) B (b) A (c) E (d) C

Chapter 13
4. (a) B and D (b) A and C

Chapter 14
9. B and D   10. A and C
11. (a) B (b) A (c) C
13. £2000 million

Chapter 15
10. (a) £100 (b) 10 per cent
Box 15: 2. £15 000   3. 10 per cent

Chapter 16
9. 1984, 1985 and 1986   11. C   12. D

Chapter 17
1. C   2. B   5. (a) C (b) A (c) B
8. 80p   9. (a) £75 million (b) £120 million
Box 17: 1. (a) £12 575 (b) 27 per cent
2. (a) £21 205 (b) 27 per cent on £17 900 and
40 per cent on £3305   3. £3395.25

Chapter 18
2. (a) B (b) C (c) A
5. (a) Country B (b) Country A
6. (a) 4 (b) 2   7. Country B

Chapter 19
4. D   5. B
Box 19: 1. £6 billion   2. −£877 million

Chapter 20
1. (a) £52 billion (b) £47 billion
2. A, C and E   5. (a) 1 and 4 (b) 6
(c) 5 and 9 (d) 5 and 7 (e) 3
Box 20: 1. £22 000   2. £9000   3. £900

Chapter 21
1. A   2. C   5. 6 per cent   6. 1985
Box 21:   3. It would increase by 5 per cent

Chapter 22
2. (a) 23 million (b) 25 million (c) 8 per cent
4. A and C   6. C

Chapter 23
1. (a) 300 000 (b) 200 000 (c) 10.3 million
4. D   6. 570 000

Chapter 24
6. (a) increased by 50 per cent